MAST

JAPA...

M000234503

HIPPOCRENE MASTER SERIES

These imaginative courses, designed for both individual and classroom use, assume no previous knowledge of the language. The unique combination of practical exercises and step-by-step grammar emphasizes a functional approach to new scripts and their vocabulary. Everyday situations and local customs are explored through dialogue, newspaper extracts, drawings and photos.

MASTERING ARABIC
ISBN 0-87052-922-6, $14.95

MASTERING FRENCH
ISBN 0-87052-055-5, $11.95

MASTERING GERMAN
ISBN 0-87052-056-3, $11.95

MASTERING ITALIAN
ISBN 0-87052-057-1, $11.95

MASTERING JAPANESE
ISBN 0-87052-923-4, $14.95

MASTERING SPANISH
ISBN 0-87052-059-8, $11.95

Cassettes for learning (2 for each language) are also available. Each cassette set costs just $12.95.

Books and cassettes may be ordered directly from the publisher.
Send the total amount plus $3.50 for shipping and handling to:
Hippocrene Books, Inc.
171 Madison Avenue
New York, NY 10016.

HIPPOCRENE MASTER SERIES

MASTERING
JAPANESE

HARRY GUEST

EDITORIAL CONSULTANT
BETTY PARR

HIPPOCRENE BOOKS
New York

First published in the United States of America in 1991 by
HIPPOCRENE BOOKS, INC., New York,
by arrangement with Macmillan Education, Ltd., London.

For information, address:
HIPPOCRENE BOOKS, INC.
171 Madison Ave.
New York, N.Y. 10016

First published in 1989 and reprinted with corrections in 1990 by
Macmillan Education, Ltd., London.

ISBN 0-87052-923-4

DEDICATION

This book is dedicated to **Gôshi Makoto** for all his help and advice during each stage of its construction.
to the staff of the Tôkyô Nihongo Gakkô for their assistance and encouragement when I was a pupil there in the 1960s.
to my colleagues at Yokohama National University, especially Professor Sawasaki Kunizo, Professor Gôshi Keigo, Professor Kajima Shôzô.
to the Mugishima family for their kindness as landlords.
to all those many friends who made our stay in Japan such a happy one – and to the land itself which will always have a special place in our hearts as the place where our daughter grew up and our son was born.

CONTENTS

I. TEACHING UNITS

CONTENTS

Grammar – Making an enquiry; aku; the plain form
of the negative; past negative plain forms;
expressions of time; to after the infinitive

II. REFERENCE MATERIAL

ACKNOWLEDGEMENTS

The author and publishers wish to acknowledge, with thanks, the following photographic sources: Japan Information Centre (Embassy of Japan); Japan National Tourist Organisation. The publishers have made every effort to trace all the copyright-holders, but if any have been inadvertently overlooked, they will be pleased to make the necessary arrangements at the first opportunity.

SERIES EDITOR'S PREFACE

The first six foreign language courses in this series were concerned with West European languages, with relatively familiar cultural and linguistic systems from neighbouring countries. Our seventh course involves a journey to the East, to a country with a long and rich tradition unfamiliar to most of us and a language of new sounds, symbols and concepts to which we have no easy access, even on our radio network.

Our course in Japanese, which is designed for adult beginners with or without a teacher, seeks to provide a realistic approach to the spoken language in the context of present-day Japan and the life and thoughts of the people who live there. Our other courses have introduced all the language skills of understanding, speaking, reading and writing, but in Japanese the main objective is the spoken language, and the student wishing to acquire an accurate grasp of the sounds of the language will need the accompanying cassette, on which native speakers have recorded all the relevant material contained in the book.

As in our other books, each chapter begins with a series of dialogues on everyday topics; all the subsequent teaching – explanation of words and structures, background information, and exercises – is based on the content of these dialogues, so that the language is studied in a real context, and practice always precedes theory. Exercises are pitched at two levels, **A** easier than **B**, to enable the student to devise a suitable learning strategy. A key to the exercises and to the self-assessment tests provided after every five chapters will help the learner to take stock of progress achieved. An attractive feature of the book is the background information about Japan and the Japanese, which reveals the author's own knowledge of the country and his sympathetic understanding of the language and those who speak it.

Throughout the book, Japanese words are printed in rômaji, the system of representing sounds in terms of our own alphabet. Some elements of written Japanese are introduced towards the end of the book, which will offer help in identifying certain useful words and give a basis for further study of the language.

The author's preface contains more information about the course and guidance in ways of using it effectively. It is to be hoped that the student will capture some of the author's own enthusiasm and will find enjoyment and satisfaction in mastering spoken Japanese.

BETTY PARR
Editorial Consultant

AUTHOR'S PREFACE:
HOW TO USE THIS BOOK

LEARNING AIMS

This book is intended for complete beginners who are interested in mastering spoken Japanese. For anyone planning to go to Japan as a tourist or on a business trip, an ability to communicate in Japanese will not only be useful but will add immeasurably to the pleasure of the visit. Although English is compulsory in all Japanese schools from the age of eleven, a visitor to Japan must be prepared to find very few people who have more than the merest smattering of English.

This course, which can be used *without* a teacher, sets out to provide visitors or temporary residents with an everyday 'survival-kit' of language, so that they can cope with the normal situations of travel, shopping, going to restaurants, banks and the post-office, as well as the – we hope – unusual problems of sickness and visits to the doctor. It also introduces the reader to Japanese society – so very different from any other – and gives a background of information about day-to-day life in that endlessly fascinating country.

Each chapter begins with a 'real-life' dialogue. There is a cassette accompanying this book. Sections of the book included on the cassette are indicated by the symbol ▣ . All the dialogues and many of the exercises are recorded by native speakers to enable students to hear the language spoken first-hand so that, right from the start, they can imitate the correct sounds. In fact, as they will soon discover, speaking Japanese presents fewer problems for the native English speaker than many other languages.

In the second section of each chapter, the vocabulary used for the first time is listed. In the third section, the grammar that has been introduced in the dialogues is explained, and any relevant background information given. The final section consists of exercises – more straightforward exercises grouped under **A**, and somewhat more complicated ones under **B**; these should not be tackled until the student feels entirely confident. It is recommended that each chapter should be thoroughly mastered before the next is attempted, as every one builds on what has gone before. After every five chapters, there is a self-assessment test, which gives useful revision and helps the student to gauge progress achieved.

DIALOGUES

These should be studied with the cassette. Each phrase should be repeated and the pronunciation and intonation checked against the native speaker's. When the exercises in each chapter have been completed, the dialogues should be played again and what may have seemed baffling at first will become surprisingly clear.

VOCABULARY

There is no vocabulary-list at the end of this book. Students should make their *own* list, because the act of writing a word down helps to commit it to memory. What is more, the words may be grouped under various headings – food, leisure, etc. – bringing together the necessary words for every situation. The best way to experiment is to conceal the Japanese column. When a mistake is made, it is important to unlearn it by seeing *why* it happened – was it the 'shape' of the word? was it confused with a very similar word? did it seem to resemble a word in English or some other familiar language?

EXPLANATIONS

After the introductory chapters, the third section of most chapters begins with some information about life in Japan which is intended to fill out the situation given in the dialogues. Then grammatical explanations are provided, which should assist the student with the exercises that follow. Japanese grammar is utterly different from English – in some ways simpler, in others rather more complicated – and very often reflects the *way* that the Japanese look at life.

At the end of the book is a complete Grammar Summary containing all the material introduced in the book.

As far as possible, important lists – days of the week, verb-forms, etc. – are given in the explanations as they crop up in the dialogues, but there are several sections of reference material at the end of the book where checking can easily be made.

EXERCISES

Some of these are on the cassette, so that listening and speaking may be associated with the printed word. Past exercises – even the easy ones! – should be repeated again and again until the response is automatic. In one's own language, this tends to be instinctive; in a foreign language, the mind must realise that there is a new sound or set of sounds expressing familiar ideas or objects until, when a question is asked, 'translation' is unnecessary and the right reply comes at once.

Instructions about each exercise are usually given in English but, occasionally, in order the help the reader feel that he or she is involved in a conversation with a native speaker, the opening question is given in Japanese.

The translations of each exercise in the Reference Material section (p. 229) are meant to be equivalents (in so far as that is possible) rather than exact versions. In the explanations for each chapter, literal renderings will be given of thorny problems, but the translated dialogues try to be as believably colloquial as are their Japanese originals.

REFERENCE MATERIAL

This section contains a Note on Written Japanese (p. 227), the translation of all the dialogues (pp. 229–51), a key to all the exercises (except the very few that deal with facts only the student can know, such as birthdays!) (pp. 252–88) answers to the four self-assessment tests (pp. 289–96), the grammatical appendices and the Grammar Summary and a list of books and addresses that may be useful in further studies of Japanese.

TYPOGRAPHY

In this book words in Japanese are set in a different type-face so that they can be easily distinguished from the English text. Thus: Ogenki desu ka? but, How are you?

GUIDE TO PRONUNCIATION

VOWEL SOUNDS

There are *five basic vowel-sounds* in Japanese: a, i, u, e, and o. These correspond, roughly, to:

car   key   cool   cage   coat

though it must be stressed that the Japanese sounds are much 'purer' than English ones.

   Pronounce the following words which are made up entirely of vowels, and ensure that *each separate vowel* is clearly pronounced – and does not 'run in' to its neighbour:

aoi   ie   ue

(**Say**: a–o–i; i–e; u–e).

ONE CONSONANT

There is *one single consonant*, final -n or -m. When saying it as n, try not to let your tongue touch the roof of your mouth:

san   hon   pan

It is pronounced as m before b, p and m:

sembei   sampo   nammai

CONSONANT AND VOWEL

All other Japanese sounds consist of a *consonant and a vowel*:

ka	ki	ku	ke	ko	k as in *khaki*
sa	shi	su	se	so	s as in *sow*
					shi as in *sheet*
ta	chi	tsu	te	to	t as in *tea*
					chi as in *cheese*
					tsu as in the
					middle of *catsup*
na	ni	nu	ne	no	n as in *nice*
ha	hi	fu	he	ho	h as in *high*

To say fu get your mouth ready to pronounce *fool*, but do not let your lower lip actually touch your top teeth.

ma	mi	mu	me	mo	m as in *meet*
ya		yu		yo	y as in *yes*
ra	ri	ru	re	ro	

The Japanese r is more 'liquid' than the English. If you put your tongue halfway between where you place it for the English 'r' and the English 'l', you will make the Japanese r sound. There is no 'l' sound in Japanese, though, as you can now tell, their r has a bit of an 'l' in it.

wa					w as in *watch*
ga	gi	gu	ge	go	g as in *give*
za	ji	zu	ze	zo	z as in *zoo*
					ji as in *jeans*

(sometimes the '3'-sound is nearer d₃)

da			de	do	d as in *done*
ba	bi	bu	be	bo	b as in *big*
pa	pi	pu	pe	po	p as in *pot*

As you have seen you cannot say *see, tea, too, who, ye, yea, wee, woo, way* or *whoa*. There is no v, l, or f sound (with the exception of fu above).

PRONUNCIATION

DOUBLE VOWELS

There are a number of *double vowel-sounds*:

kya	kyu	kyo
sha	shu	sho
cha	chu	cho
nya	nyu	nyo
hya	hyu	hyo
mya	myu	myo
rya	ryu	ryo
gya	gyu	gyo
ja	ju	jo
bya	byu	byo
pya	pyu	pyo

These are two sounds said so quickly that they *become one*: kya is only ki and ya run together; ju is ji and yu run together, and so on.

When a final -n is involved, a *break between the two components of a word* is shown thus:

hon'ya bookshop (from hon, a book and ya, a shop) as opposed to gyûniku, beef (from gyû, a cow and niku, meat)

Japanese is therefore made up of *five vowels, one separate consonant* and various *combinations of a consonant followed by vowel-sounds*:

Yokohama	Yo/ko/ha/ma
Nihongo	Ni/ho/n/go
sambyaku	sa/m/bya/ku
ikitai	i/ki/ta/i

SYLLABLE STRESS

Unlike English, each syllable carries an *even stress*. Not Yókoháma but Yo–ko–ha–ma.

LONG VOWELS

Sometimes vowels are *long*. When this happens, they carry a *circumflex* accent: ô, â or û, or are *written twice*, eeto, iie. All this means is that the syllable takes exactly *twice as long to pronounce*:

Tôkyô	To/o/kyo/o
yûbin	yu/u/bi/n
ôkii	o/o/ki/i
eeto	e/e/to
iie	i/i/e

DOUBLE CONSONANTS

There are *doubled consonants*, too. It is very important to distinguish between kite and kitte, for example. When these occur, merely 'hold up' the succeeding vowel for a beat, as if you were saying in English:

He'll ba*t t*enth
Si*p P*ernod
As*k K*eith
Thi*s sh*oe

Practise these sounds:

gakkô	ga/ /kk/ô
kippu	ki/ /pu
issho	i/ /sho
atte	a/ /te

shi **and** su

The sounds shi and su are exceptions. Especially in verbs, the vowel sound is *hardly pronounced at all*:

desu	de/s(u)
arimasu	a/ri/ma/s(u)
mimashita	mi/ma/sh(i)/ta

This is why the famous Japanese musician Yamashita Tsutomu prefers to write his name in rômaji, or Western script, as Yamash'ta S'tomu or (since he puts his name European-style with the surname *last*) S'tomu Yamash'ta.

When the syllables -su and -shi are structurally important they are *fully pronounced*:

PRONUNCIATION

suru	su/ru
sumimasen	su/mi/ma/se/n
suzushii	su/zu/shi/i
shimasen	shi/ma/se/n

Some of this may seem a little complicated at the moment. Listen to your cassette and, after the first few exercises, return to this section. All should then (ideally) become clear.

PITCH

Japanese words and phrases are pronounced very evenly, and stress is used only to *emphasise meaning*. However, the spoken language tends to vary in pitch. A normal sentence will begin on a 'high' note and finish on a 'low' one:

Kore wa /
       kanai desu

Questions usually have an interrogative 'lift' towards the end, much like English:

               ka?
Kaban wa /
       ôkii desu /

As in any language, the best way to acquire the correct intonation is to imitate native speakers. It is easier to theorise *after* practice than *before*!

AN INTRODUCTION TO THE
JAPANESE LANGUAGE

VERBS

Every Japanese sentence ends with a verb which, most of the time, has a sound after it to give *emphasis* or *doubt* or *agreement*, because the Japanese are not very keen on making a definite statement! Japanese communication is really a series of *hints* and *shades of meaning* – which may well be why Japanese poetry is so beautifully enigmatic and why it seems so difficult for Western businessmen in Japan to reach hard and fast agreements!

'POSTPOSITIONS'

Japanese has been called the 'mirror-language' to English and, certainly, where we have *pre*positions – 'to' Yokohama – the Japanese have *post*positions: Yokohama e.

PRONOUNS

There are pronouns in Japanese, but in practice they are very rarely used. Once it is established who it is one is talking about, pronouns are dispensed with. The sentence Tôkyô e ikimashita means 'I, you, he, she, we or they went to Tokyo', and we would know who in fact went to Tokyo because of the *preceding sentence or sentences*. In the exercises after the following chapters, the assumption most of the time is that it is *you* who are being questioned, so the pronouns are mostly *omitted*. Similarly, in your responses, you can usually leave out the 'I'. In other words, use pronouns only to *avoid confusion*.

INTRODUCTION

LOOKING AT THE WORLD

Each language is a different way of looking at the world. Accept –
and relish – the differences that abound in Japanese, and treat the
language on its own terms without comparing it with English or any
other language.

It is hoped that *Mastering Japanese* will represent a 'first stage', and
that the reader will wish to go on experimenting with the language –
especially to go on to read and write. On pp. 227–8 there is an
introduction to the written language which is intended to whet the
student's appetite for further study.

I TEACHING UNITS

GREETINGS

AND

INTRODUCTIONS

1.1 DIALOGUES

Dialogue 1

Mr and Mrs Foster arrive at the airport. They meet Mr Itô. He asks about their luggage.

Mr Foster: Itô-san desu ka?

Mr Itô: Sô desu. Watakushi wa Itô desu.

Mr Foster: Watakushi wa Foster desu.

Mr Itô: Sô desu ka? Foster-san desu ka? Hajimemashite.

Mr Foster: Hajimemashite. Kore wa kanai desu. Mary desu.

Mr Itô: Okusama desu ka? Mary-san desu ka?

4

Mrs Foster: Sô desu. Watakushi wa Mary desu. Hajimema-
shite.
Mr Itô: Ogenki desu ka?
Mrs Foster: Hai, arigatô gozaimasu. Genki desu. Anata mo
ogenki desu ka?
Mr Itô: Hai, genki desu. Arigatô gozaimasu. Ano . . .
Anatagata no keisu wa doko desu ka?
Mr Foster: Koko desu. Kore wa watakushitachi no keisu desu.
Sore wa watakushi no keisu ja arimasen.

Dialogue 2

Mr and Mrs Foster describe their luggage.

Mrs Foster: Watakushi no keisu wa akai desu.
Mr Itô: Ôkii desu ka? Chiisai desu ka?
Mrs Foster: Ôkii desu. Shujin no keisu mo ôkii desu.
Mr Foster: Watakushi no keisu wa ôkii desu. Akaku wa arima-
sen. Kuroi desu.
Mr Itô: Kore desu ka?
Mr Foster: Sô desu. Sore wa watakushi no keisu desu.
Mrs Foster: Akai keisu wa watakushi no desu. Arigatô gozai-
masu.
Mr Foster: Watakushi no kaban wa doko desu ka?
Mrs Foster: Itô-san! Shujin no kaban wa doko desu ka?
Mr Itô: Goshujin no kaban wa ôkii desu ka?
Mrs Foster: Iie, ôkiku wa arimasen. Chiisai desu.
Mr Itô: Akai desu ka? Kuroi desu ka?
Mrs Foster: Kuroi desu.
Mr Itô: Kore wa goshujin no kaban desu ka?
Mrs Foster: Sô desu.
Mr Foster: Sô desu. Sore wa watakushi no kaban desu. Arigatô
gozaimasu.

1.2 VOCABULARY

-san	Mr, Mrs, Miss
desu	am, is, are
ka	an audible question mark
sô desu	that is so
watakushi	I, me
wa	particle calling attention to the word preceding it
hajimemashite	how do you do?
kore	this (pronoun)

kanai	(my) wife
okusama	(your) wife
(o)genki	well, healthy
hai	yes
arigatô gozaimasu	thank you very much
anata	you (singular)
mo	as well, too
ano	Now! Well!
anatagata	you (plural)
no	a possessive particle; watakushi no = my; anata no = your
keisu	suitcase
doko	where
koko	here
sore	that (pronoun)
ja arimasen	negative of **desu** = is not
akai	red
ôkii	large
chiisai	small
shujin	(my) husband
akaku wa arimasen	is not red
iie	no
ôkiku wa arimasen	is not large
kaban	briefcase
goshujin	(your) husband
kuroi	black

1.3 EXPLANATIONS

(a) desu
desu, the verb used in this exercise, is the entire present tense of the verb 'to be', equalling 'am', 'is', 'are'.
The negative form is **ja arimasen**:

Kore wa keisu desu.	This is a case.
Sore wa watakushi no kaban ja arimasen	That is not my briefcase.
Watakushi wa Itô desu.	I'm Itô.
Foster-san desu ka?	Are you Mr Foster?

The *subject of a sentence* is frequently *omitted if the sense is clear*:

Keisu desu.	(It/That/This) is a suitcase.

(b) True adjectives
All *true adjectives* end in -i (remember the remarks concerning the Japanese syllabary in the Guide to Pronunciation). a–ka–i is a true adjective; ge–n–ki is not, and the *negative* is formed by substituting -ku wa arimasen for -i desu:

Kore wa kuroi desu.	This is black.
Sore wa kuroku wa arimasen.	That isn't black.

(c) -san
The use of the honorific often 'short-cuts' the need for a *pronoun*. -san is the suffix used after a person's name and equals Mr, Mrs, or Miss. It is *never* used when referring to *oneself*:

Itô-san desu ka?	Are you Mr. Itô?
Hai, Itô desu.	Yes. I'm Itô.

In practice, Western men tend to be referred to by the surname, Foster-san; Western women by the Christian name, Mary-san.

(d) o-
Similarly, the honorific prefix o- means you are addressing *someone else*:

Ogenki desu ka?	Are you well?
Genki desu.	I am well.

(e) Plural and singular
There is a plural form for watakushi, I–watakushitachi, we; and for anata, you (singular)–anatagata, you (plural). With other nouns or pronouns *no distinction* is made between plural and singular: kaban means briefcase or briefcases.

(f) Kore
kore, the pronoun 'this', refers to an object or to objects *near the speaker*.
sore, the pronoun 'that', refers to an object or to objects *near the one addressed*.

(g) Particles
wa is an *attention-calling particle*:

Kore wa kaban desu.	*As for* this, it is a briefcase.

wa usually calls attention to the *subject of the sentence*:

Keisu wa akai desu.   *As for* the case, it's red.

mo means 'as well', 'also', 'too':

Kore mo kuroi desu.   This one's black, too.

no is best thought of as equivalent to 's:

Yamada-san no kaban desu.   It's Mr Yamada's briefcase.

hence:

watakushi no kaban   my briefcase ('I's' briefcase)
anata no keisu   your case ('you's' suitcase)

ka is a *verbal question mark*:

Kore wa keisu desu.   This is a case.
Kore wa keisu desu ka?   Is this a case?

(h) sô desu
sô desu, meaning 'that is so', 'that is correct', is frequently used instead of hai, yes. When ka is added, the useful social question 'Is that so?' is created.

(i) The Japanese sentence
The simplest Japanese sentence is ———— wa ———— desu (ka):

Kore wa keisu desu.   This is a suitcase.
Watakushi wa Itô desu.   I am Itô.
Sore wa anata no kaban desu ka?   Is that your briefcase?
Anata wa Foster-san desu ka?   Are you Mr Foster?

(j) Conversational omissions
As in English, there are *conversational omissions*:

> Kore wa Itô-san no keisu This is Mr. Itô's case.
> desu.
> Kore wa Satô-san no This is Mr Satô's.
> desu.

(k) Wife and husband
Referring to *one's own* spouse, one uses kanai (my wife), shujin (my husband). Referring to *someone else's*, one uses the honorific form: okusan, or – even more polite – okusama (your or his wife), goshujin (your or her husband)

1.4 EXERCISES

Section A
Exercise 1
Put in the appropriate particles (wa, ka, ja, mo):
1. Watakushi —— Foster desu.
2. Anata —— Itô-san desu ——?
3. Keisu —— arimasen.
4. Kaban —— arimasen.
5. Kore ——keisu desu. Sore —— keisu desu ——?

Exercise 2
Put in the appropriate particles (no, wa, ka).
1. Watakushi —— keisu desu.
2. Kore —— watakushi —— keisu desu.
3. Anata —— kaban —— ôkii desu ——?
4. Sore —— anata —— keisu desu ——?
5. Shujin —— keisu —— akai desu.
6. Anata —— keisu —— chiisai desu ——?
7. Goshujin —— kaban —— akaku —— arimasen.
8. Kanai —— keisu —— kuroi desu. Chiisaku —— arimasen.
9. Watakushi —— kaban —— ôkii desu. Kuroku —— arimasen.

Exercise 3
Put into the negative:
1. Kore wa kaban desu.
2. Kore wa keisu desu.

3. Kore wa chiisai desu.
4. Kore wa akai desu.
5. Kaban wa ôkii desu.
6. Keisu wa ôkii desu.
7. Watakushi wa Itô desu.
8. Watakushi wa Yamamoto desu.

Section B
Exercise 4

1. Ask if someone's suitcase is: (a) large?
        (b) black?
        (c) red?
2. Ask if someone's husband's briefcase is: (a) small?
        (b) red?
        (c) black?
3. Ask if this is someone's suitcase.
4. Ask if this is someone's briefcase.
5. Ask if this is someone's husband's suitcase.
6. Ask if this is someone's wife's briefcase.
7. Ask if that is someone's suitcase.
8. Ask if that is someone's briefcase.
9. Ask if that is someone's husband's briefcase.
10. Ask if that is someone's wife's suitcase.

Exercise 5
Translate into Japanese.
  1. How do you do?
  2. Thank you very much.
  3. Are you Mr. Itô? Yes, I am.
  4. How are you? I'm fine.
  5. Is that your suitcase? Yes, it is.

Exercise 6
Play the part of Mr Jones in the following dialogues:

Dialogue 1 📼
Jones-san desu ka?
.... (Yes. I'm Jones.)
Watakushi wa Yamamoto
desu.
.... (Is that so? Are you Mr
Yamamoto? How do you
do?)

Hajimemashite. Ogenki
desu ka?

.... (Yes, I'm fine. How are
you?)

Hai, arigatô gozaimasu.
Genki desu.

Dialogue 2 📼

Anata no keisu wa doko
desu ka?

.... (It's here, by me.)

Kore wa anata no keisu
desu ka?

Iie, ... (......... that isn't my case.)

Ah sô desu ka. Ano . . . Kore desu ka?

Hai,................................... (.... that is my case. Thank
you.)

Dialogue 3 📼

Okusama no kaban wa
ôkii desu ka?

Iie, ... (.... it's not big. It's small.)

Akai desu ka?

Hai,................................. (....... it's red. Thank you.)

THE FAMILY CAR

2.1 DIALOGUES

Dialogue 1

Mr Itô and the Fosters discuss their cars.

Mr Foster: Anata no kuruma wa doko desu ka?

Mr Itô: Asoko desu. Ano akai kuruma desu.

Mr Foster: Igirisu no kuruma desu ka?

Mr Itô: Iie! Igirisu no kuruma ja arimasen. Nihon no kuruma desu.

Mr Foster:　Sô desu ka. Nihon no kuruma desu ka? Honda desu ka?

Mr Itô:　Iie. Honda ja arimasen. Mitsubishi desu.

Mr Foster:　Watakushi no kuruma wa Honda desu. Igirisu no kuruma ja arimasen!

Mrs Foster:　Shujin no kuruma wa Honda desu ga watakushi no chiisai kuruma wa Igirisu no kuruma desu.

Mr Foster:　Sô desu ne. Kanai no kuruma wa Austin desu.

Dialogue 2 📼

Mr Itô and the Fosters discuss Japanese names.

Mr Itô:　Ah! Kore wa Igirisu no kuruma desu ne.

Mr Foster:　Sô desu ne. Kono kuruma wa Hillman desu.

Mr Itô:　'Hi-ru-man'! Igirisu no namae wa muzukashii desu nê!

Mr Foster:　Muzukashii desu ka?

Mr Itô:　Sô desu. Taihen muzukashii desu.

Mrs Foster:　Nihon no namae mo muzukashii desu. 'Yokohama'. 'Yamashita'. 'Kawasaki'. Hatsuon wa muzukashii desu.

Mr Itô:　Sô desu ka? 'Itô' wa muzukashiku wa arimasen! Yasashii desu ne.

Mrs Foster:　Yasashii desu keredomo Igirisujin to Amerikajin niwa muzukashii desu.

Mr Itô:　Sô desu ne. Nihon no namae wa Nihonjin niwa yasashii desu keredomo gaikokujin niwa muzukashii desu.

Mr Foster:　Igirisu no namae wa watakushitachi niwa yasashii desu.

Mr Itô:　Sô desu nê! Anatagata niwa yasashii desu. Ano. . . Koko desu. Kore wa watakushi no kuruma desu. Chiisai desu nê!

Mrs Foster:　Iie, chiisaku wa arimasen. Ôkii desu.

Mr Itô:　Ôkiku wa arimasen.

2.2　VOCABULARY

kuruma	car
asoko	over there
ano	that (adjective)
Igirisu	England
Igirisu no	English (not the language)
namae	name
Nihon	Japan (also, occasionally, Nippon)

Nihon no	Japanese (not the language) (also, sometimes, Nippon no)
ga	but
kono	this (adjective)
muzukashii	difficult
yasashii	easy
keredomo	however
Igirisujin	English person
Amerikajin	American person
Nihonjin	Japanese person (also, sometimes, Nipponjin)
to	and
ni(wa)	for (plus attention-calling particle wa)
ne	final particle implying agreement: 'Isn't it!'
nê	more emphatic than ne
taihen	very
hatsuon	pronunciation
gaikokujin	foreigner

2.3 EXPLANATIONS

(a) 'This' and 'that'; 'here' and 'there'

Kono kaban	This briefcase near me.
Sono kaban.	That briefcase by you.
Ano kaban.	That briefcase over there near neither of us.

Three *words of place* have the same function:

koko	here, by me
soko	there, near you
asoko	over there

(b) Countries

Igirisu (or, sometimes, Eikoku) is the country – England, Britain, the UK.

Igirisu no kuruma	'A car of England', i.e. an English car.

Nihon no kuruma	A Japanese car.
Amerika no kuruma	An American car.

Some other countries:

Furansu	France
Furansu no kaban	A French briefcase
Doitsu	Germany
Doitsu no kuruma	a German car
Itarii or Itaria	Italy
Itarii or Itaria no keisu	an Italian suitcase
Chûgoku	China
Chûgoku no namae	a Chinese name

For some people, the word **Nippon** has unwelcome 'nationalistic' overtones; **Nihon** is perhaps the word generally preferred nowadays.

(c) But/However
keredomo (however) is slightly stronger than ga (but) as a word separating two sentences:

> **Kaban wa akai desu ga/keisu wa kuroi desu.**
> The briefcase is red but the suitcase is black.
> **Watakushi wa Igirisujin desu keredomo/kanai wa Amerika-jin desu.**
> I am English but my wife is American.

Note that in each case the 'break' comes *after the pivot-word*.

(d) Further notes

Sô desu ka?	A genuine question: 'Is that so?'
Sô desu ne.	No question about it: 'That's so, isn't it.'
Sô desu nê.	Even more emphatic!: 'That's so, *isn't* it!'

to is 'and' between nouns or pronouns:

anata to watakushi	you and I
kaban to keisu	the briefcase(s) and the suitcase(s)

Remember each Japanese word can be singular *or* plural!

ni means *for* or *in*, and comes *after* the noun or pronoun:

Nihonjin ni	for Japanese people or for a Japanese
Nihon ni	in Japan
Nihongo wa watakushi-tachi ni muzukashii desu.	Japanese is difficult for us.

-jin is a suffix meaning 'a human being':

Igirisu	England
Igirisujin	an Englishman or -woman
Amerikajin	an American
Furansujin	a Frenchman or -woman
Doitsujin	a German
Itariijin or Itariajin	an Italian

gai = outside; koku = country, and so gaikokujin = foreigner:

Nihongo wa gaikokujin ni muzukashii desu.
Japanese is difficult for foreigners.
Nihongo wa Nihonjin ni yasashii desu.
Japanese is easy for the Japanese.

2.4 EXERCISES

Section A
Exercise 1
Translate into Japanese:
1. This car is a Honda.
2. That car (near you) is a Mitsubishi.
3. That car over there is a Toyota.
4. Where is my case? It's here.
5. Where is my briefcase? It's there! (By you.)
6. Where is your car? It's over there.
7. The German car is red.
8. My American car is black.
9. Japanese names are difficult.
10. English names are easy.

16

Exercise 2

Contrast the following, using ga or keredomo (**Example**: My car is red. Your car is black – Watakushi no kuruma wa akai desu ga (*or* keredomo) anata no kuruma wa kuroi desu):

1. The Italian car is large. The French car is small.
2. My suitcase is black. Your suitcase is red.
3. My wife's car is small. It is not red.
4. My husband's despatch-case is large. It is not black.

Exercise 3

Answer the following questions:

1. Anata wa Igirisujin desu ka?

   .... (No, I'm French.)
2. Anata wa Nihonjin desu ka?

   .... (No, I'm Italian.)
3. Okusama wa Amerikajin desu ka?

   .... (No, my wife is Japanese.)
4. Goshujin wa Doitsujin desu ka?

   .... (No, my husband is English.)

Section B
Exercise 4

Re-read or listen again to the first two dialogues and then say whether the following statements are, or are not, correct:

1. Foster-san no okusama wa Nihonjin desu.
2. Foster-san no kaban wa chiisai desu.
3. Foster-san no keisu wa akai desu.
4. Itô-san no kuruma wa kuroi desu.
5. Foster-san no okusan no kuruma wa ôkiku wa arimasen.
6. 'Itô' wa Furansu no namae desu.
7. Itô-san no kuruma wa Austin desu.

Exercise 5 📼

Play the part of Mr Satô in the following dialogue:

Mr Kimura: Satô-san desu ka?

MrSatô: .... (Yes, I'm Satô.)

Mr Kimura: Hajimemashite.

MrSatô: .... (How do you do? This is my wife.)

Mr Kimura: Sô desu ka. Okusama wa gaikokujin desu ka?

MrSatô: .... (Yes, my wife is French.)

Mr Kimura: Ogenki desu ka?

MrSatô: .... (Yes, I'm fine. How are you?)

Mr Kimura: Genki desu. Arigatô. Ano . . . Anata no keisu wa doko desu ka?

MrSatô: .... (They're over there.)

Mr Kimura: Kore desu ka?

MrSatô: .... (No, my case is not large.)

Mr Kimura: Kore desu ka?

MrSatô: .... (No, that isn't black. My case is black.)

Mr Kimura: Kore desu ka?

Mr Satô: ....(Yes! That's it! Thank you.)

Mr Kimura: Okusama no keisu mo kuroi desu ka?

MrSatô: .... (No, my wife's case is red.)

Mr Kimura: Kono keisu wa akai desu. Okusama no keisu desu ka?

Mr Satô:.(Yes. That is my wife's case. Thank you. Is that your car over there?)

Mr Kimura: Hai, sô desu. Ano akai kuruma wa watakushi no desu.

MrSatô: .... (Is it a Japanese car?)

Mr Kimura: Iie, Igirisu no kuruma desu.

MrSatö: .... (My car is a Toyota.)

Mr Kimura: Nihon no kuruma desu ka?

MrSatô: .... (That's right!)

CHAPTER 3

EATING AT HOME

3.1 DIALOGUES 📼

Dialogue 1

   At Mr and Mrs Itô's house: Japanese food and drink.

Mrs Foster: Nihonjin wa nani o tabemasu ka?

Mrs Itô: Gohan o takusan tabemasu. Sakana mo tabemasu.
               Igirisujin wa gohan o tabemasu ka?

Mr Foster: Hai, tabemasu.

Mrs Foster: Tabemasu yo.

Mr Itô: Gohan o tabemasu keredomo sashimi wa tabemasen!

Mr Foster: Futsû tabemasen keredomo watakushi wa sashimi
              o tabemashita.
Mrs Itô: Sô desu ka? Igirisu de tabemashita ka?
Mr Foster: Iie. Nihon de tabemashita.
Mrs Itô: Okusama wa sashimi o tabemashita ka?
Mrs Foster: Iie, tabemasen deshita.
Mr Itô: Ano . . . yûhan ni nani o tabemasu ka?
Mrs Itô: Gohan ya sakana ya naganegi o tabemasu.
Mr Itô: Nani o nomimasu ka?
Mrs Itô: Osake matawa biiru o nomimasu.
Mr Foster: Kanai wa biiru o nomimasen. Omizu ga arimasu ka?
Mrs Itô: Ocha o nomimasu ka?
Mrs Foster: Sore wa nan desu ka?
Mr Foster: Ocha wa Nihon no nomimono desu. Karada ni ii
              desu nê!
Mrs Itô: Sô desu nê!

Dialogue 2 🔲

Talking about meals.
Mrs Itô: Sore wa ebi desu.
Mrs Foster: Ôkii desu nê!
Mr Itô: Nihon no ebi wa ôkii desu nê!
Mr Foster: Oishii desu ka?
Mrs Foster: Mmmmm! Oishii desu yo!
Mrs Itô: Igirisu no ebi wa ôkiku wa arimasen ka?
Mr Foster: Hai. Ôkiku wa arimasen. Chiisai desu.
Mrs Foster: Amerika no ebi mo ôkii desu nê.
Mr Itô: Sô desu nê. Amerika de ebi o tabemashita ka?
Mrs Foster: Hai.

Dialogue 3 🔲

More talking about meals
Mr Itô: Foster-san. Osake o nomimasu ka?
Mr Foster: Hai. Arigatô.
Mr Itô: Mary-san wa biiru o nomimasen ka?
Mrs Foster: Hai. Nomimasen.
Mrs Itô: Ocha o nomimasu ka?
Mrs Foster: Hai. Oishii desu.
Mrs Itô: Kore wa naganegi desu. Igirisu niwa naganegi ga
              arimasu ka?
Mr Foster: Arimasu yo.
Mr Itô: Igirisu de naganegi o tabemashita.

Mr Foster: Nihon no naganegi wa chiisai desu keredomo Igirisu no naganegi wa ôkii desu nê.
Mr Itô: Sô desu nê. Ôkii desu nê.
Mrs Itô: Ano . . . kudamono ga arimasu. Nani o tabemasu ka? Ringo? Momo?
Mrs Foster: Momo o kudasai.
Mrs Itô: Foster-san. Nani o tabemasu ka?
Mr Foster: Watakushi mo momo o tabemasu. Arigatô.

3.2   VOCABULARY

nani?	what?
o	particle showing the object of a transitive verb
tabemasu	present tense of the verb 'to eat' taberu
gohan	cooked rice
takusan	a great deal
sakana	fish
yo	emphatic conclusion to a statement
(o)sashimi	slices of fish eaten raw
tabemasen	negative of tabemasu = do/does not eat
futsû	usually
tabemashita	ate, past tense of the verb 'to eat'
de	particle showing where an action is done
tabemasen deshita	did not eat, past negative of the verb 'to eat'
yûhan	supper, dinner, evening meal

ya	and (when more than a couple of specific objects are implied)
naganegi	leeks, literally 'long onions'
nomimasu	present tense of the verb nomu 'to drink'
(o)sake	rice-wine, the national drink of Japan
matawa	or
biiru	beer
nomimasen	negative of nomimasu = do/does not drink
(o)mizu	water
ga	particle showing the subject of a verb
arimasu	present tense of the verb 'to be', meaning 'there is/are' (from aru)
ocha	Japanese tea
nan	nani (what) before t, d, and n
nomimono	drink (noun)
karada	body (hence 'general health')
ii	good
ebi	prawn
oishii	delicious
niwa	ni (in) plus the attention-calling particle wa
kudamono	fruit

ringo	apple
momo	peach
kudasai	please

3.3 EXPLANATIONS

(a) The Japanese house

Most Japanese houses have a genkan, an area on street-level just inside the front door. Here you leave your outdoor shoes, step up on to the ground-floor level and put on indoor slippers which are used inside the house for every room except those floored in tatami or rush mats: on these, stockinged or bare feet only must tread.

It is not customary to knock or ring. If the family is at home, the door is unlocked, the visitor opens it and calls out, waiting in the genkan until a member of the family comes to greet the visitor and offer a pair of slippers.

(b) Japanese food and drink

In the serving of Japanese food the 'look' of the dish is very important. Han (cooked rice) has the honorific go because gohan is the staple diet. The national drink is rice wine – (o)sake – usually given the honorific o because it is highly prized. Saké is drunk at just above blood-heat in china vessels about the size of egg-cups. Small decanters also of china stand in warm water until they are the correct temperature to be poured.

Thin, delicate slices of raw fish – (o)sashimi – are often served with a dash of soya-sauce (shôyu) and wasabi a kind of green horseradish.

> Breakfast is asahan, literally 'morning rice' (or, politely, asago-han).
> Lunch is hiruhan, literally 'noon rice'. (or, politely, hirugo-han).
> Dinner is yûhan, literally 'evening rice' (or, politely, yûgohan).

Ocha, the green tea of Japan, is drunk out of handle-less cups. It is slightly bitter and marvellously refreshing.

(c) The Object

The particle o is used after the word which is the *object* of a sentence.

> Satô-san wa gohan o tabemasu.
> Mr Satô eats rice.

Itô-san wa osake o nomimasu.
Mr Itô drinks saké.

Sometimes **wa** replaces **o**, either for emphasis or to imply contrast:

Gohan o tabemasu
They eat rice
Keredomo sashimi wa tabemasen.
However as for raw fish, they don't eat (that).

(d) Weak verbs (see Grammar Summary **1(c)**)
These verbs end in -eru or -iru (taberu, to eat, miru, to see), and
form their *present tense* by changing -ru to -masu:

Watakushi wa	I eat apples.
ringo o tabemasu.	
Anata wa	You eat
momo o tabemasu.	peaches.
Nihonjin wa	The Japanese
sashimi o tabemasu.	eat raw fish.

The *negative present ending* is -masen:

Igirisujin wa sashimi o	The English don't eat raw
tabemasen.	fish.

The *past tense* is formed by changing -ru to -mashita:

Foster-san wa	Mr Foster ate
ebi o tabemashita.	prawns.

The *past negative ending* is -masen deshita:

Mary-san wa ebi o	Mrs Foster didn't eat prawns.
tabemasen deshita.	

(e) 'There is', 'There are'
The verb aru, present tense arimasu, means 'There is' or 'There are'
and deals usually with *inanimate objects*. It is used in this sense with
ga:

Mizu ga arimasu.	There is water.
Ringo ga arimasu.	There are apples.

(f) De, Ni
Ni is used merely to show a *place*:

> Yokohama wa Nihon ni arimasu.
> Yokohama is in Japan.

De shows where an action is *performed*.

> Nihon de sashimi o tabemashita.
> I ate raw fish in Japan.

(g) Strong verbs
Details of strong verbs will be found in Chapter 4. (Also see Grammar Summary **1(d)**.)
Nomu, to drink, is a strong verb.

(h) Agreement with the other person
In English, we tend to say 'no' when we agree with someone who's said 'It's not raining', or 'You aren't French'.
 In Japanese, you *agree* with the speaker's *judgement*:

Anata wa Furansujin ja arimasen.	You aren't French.
Hai.	That's right! I'm not!
Doitsujin wa osake o nomimasen ka.	Don't Germans drink saké?
Hai. Nomimasen.	*No*, they don't.

(i) Yo
This puts *great emphasis* on the sentence it *concludes*:

Nihonjin desu yo.	He certainly is Japanese.
Osake o nomimasu yo.	I drink saké all right!

(j) And
To links specific *nouns* or *pronouns*.
Ya is used when other articles are implied *as well as the ones you are mentioning*.
Note that neither to nor ya can *link two sentences together*:

> Gohan to ebi o tabemashita. I ate (only) rice and prawns.

| Ocha ya biiru ya osake ga arimasu. | There are green tea and beer and saké and other drinks as well. |

3.4 EXERCISES

Section A
Exercise 1
Answer the following questions **Example**: Satô-san wa Igirisujin desu ka? –Iie Nihonjin desu (No, he's Japanese):

1. Anata wa Nihonjin desu ka?
   (No, I'm English.)
   ....

2. Okusama wa Nihonjin desu ka?
   (No, she's French.)
   ....

3. Greene-san wa Igirisujin desu ka?
   (No, he's American.)
   ....

4. Itô-san no okusan wa gaikokujin desu ka?
   (No, she's Japanese.)
   ....

5. Goshujin wa Igirisujin desu ka?
   (No, he's Italian.)
   ....

Exercise 2

Put in the appropriate particles (de, ga, ka, ja, matawa, ni, no, o, to, wa, ya):

1. Watakushi —— ringo —— tabemashita.
2. Nihonjin —— sashimi —— tabemasu.
3. Ebi —— sakana —— arimasu. (There are prawns or fish.)
4. Biiru —— osake —— arimasu. (There is only beer and saké.)
5. Ringo —— momo —— arimasu. (There may be other fruits.)
6. Nihon —— osake —— nomimashita.
7. Igirisu —— biiru —— nomimashita.
8. Igirisu —— naganegi —— ôkii desu.
9. Watakushi —— keisu —— kuruma —— arimasu.
10. Watakushi —— kuruma —— akaku —— arimasen.
11. Sore —— kanai —— keisu —— arimasen.

Exercise 3

End each sentence with the appropriate sound ka, ne, nê or yo:
1. Anata wa Igirisujin desu ——— . (Pure question.)
2. Okusama wa Furansujin desu ——— . (She is, isn't she?)
3. Ringo wa ôkii desu ——— . (They *are*, aren't they!)
4. Watakushi wa Igirisujin desu ——— . (I most certainly am!)

Exercise 4

Put into the negative:
1. Kudamono o tabemasu.
2. Doitsujin wa osashimi o tabemasu.
3. Momo o tabemashita.
4. Nihon de osashimi o tabemashita.

Exercise 5

1. The Japanese eat fish and rice (and other things).
2. Germans drink beer.
3. I ate (only) leeks and prawns.
4. I didn't eat raw fish in Japan.
5. My wife doesn't drink saké.

Section B 📼
Exercise 6
Invent replies in the following dialogue:
Anata wa nani o tabemasu ka?

....

Nani o nomimasu ka?

....

Osake o nomimasen ka?

.... (That's right. I don't.)

Exercise 7
Translate the following questions:
1. What is that?
2. Do you eat fruit?
3. Is that green tea?
4. Does Mr Itô drink beer?

5. Doesn't Mrs Itô drink saké?
6. Are English apples red?

Exercise 8
1. Ask if there is water.
2. Ask if there is green tea.
3. Ask if there is saké.
4. Say you drink saké in Japan.
5. Say it is delicious.

Exercise 9
Translate:
1. American leeks are big but Japanese ones are small.
2. I drink beer but my wife drinks saké.
3. My husband ate rice but Mr. Itô did not.
4. Japanese people drink saké but the English drink beer.

Exercise 10
Read or listen to Dialogues 3.1 again, and say whether or not these statements are true:
1. Nihonjin wa osake o nomimasu.
2. Igirisujin wa gohan o tabemasen.
3. Foster-san wa sashimi o tabemasen deshita.
4. Foster-san no okusan wa biiru o nomimasu.
5. Ocha wa karada ni ii desu.
6. Igirisu no ebi wa chiisai desu.
7. Ebi wa kudamono desu.
8. Osake wa nomimono desu.

CHAPTER 4

AFTER DINNER

4.1 DIALOGUES 🖭

Dialogue 1
The Japanese way of counting years.
Mr Itô: Foster-san. Itsu Nihon e kimashita ka?
Mr Foster: Sen kyûhyaku nanajûrokunen deshita.
Mrs Itô: Sen kyûhyaku nanajûrokunen . . . sore wa Shôwa
            gojûichinen deshita nê.
Mr Itô: Sô desu nê. Shôwa ichinen wa sen kyûhyaku
            nijûrokunen deshita. Desu kara Shôwa jûnen wa
            sen kyûhyaku sanjûgonen deshita.
Mrs Itô: Muzukashii desu nê!
Mr Itô: Yasashii desu yo! Shôwa nijûnen wa sen
            kyûhyakuyonjûgonen deshita.
Mr Foster: Shôwa sanjûnen wa . . .
Mrs Foster: Sen kyûhyaku gojûgonen deshita!
Mr Itô: Ojôzu desu nê, Mary-san!
Mrs Foster: Iie, heta desu yo!

Dialogue 2 🖭
Japanese weather.
Mrs Itô: Mary-san mo Shôwa gojûichinen ni Nihon e kimashita
            ka?
Mrs Foster: Iie, watakushi wa Nihon e kimasen deshita. Shujin
            wa hitori de koko e kimashita.
Mr Itô: Foster-san wa aki ni kimashita ka?
Mr Foster: Iie, natsu ni kimashita.
Mr Itô: Tôkyô no natsu wa atsui desu nê!
Mr Foster: Sô desu nê! Atsui desu nê!
Mrs Itô: Mushiatsui desu nê.
Mrs Foster: "Mushiatsui"? Nan desu ka? Wakarimasen.
Mrs Itô: Atsui desu. Ame ga furimasu. Kaze ja arimasen.
Mr Itô: Warui otenki desu nê.

Dialogue 3 🖭
Japanese and English.
Mrs Foster: Ima mushiatsuku wa arimasen! Ii otenki desu.
Mrs Itô: Suzushii desu ne.
Mrs Foster: Suzushii desu nê.
Mrs Itô: Ocha o mô ippai nomimasu ka?
Mrs Foster: Iie. Kekkô desu.
Mr Foster: Gochisôsama deshita!
Mrs Itô: Foster-san wa Nihongo o yoku hanashimasu nê!

Mr Foster: Heta desu yo!

Mrs Itô: Futaritomo yoku hanashimasu yo. Nihongo wa gaikokujin niwa muzukashii desu ka?

Mr Foster: Sô desu nê! Taihen muzukashii desu.

Mrs Foster: Itô-san. Eigo wa yasashii desu ka, muzukashii desu ka?

Mr Itô: Taihen muzukashii desu yo!

Mr Foster: Eigo wa Igirisujin niwa yasashii desu keredomo Nihongo wa muzukashii desu nê.

Mr Itô: Sô desu nê! Nihongo wa Nihonjin niwa muzukashiku wa arimasen keredomo gaikokujin niwa muzukashii desu.

4.2   VOCABULARY

itsu?	when?
e	to, towards
kimashita	came, past tense of the verb 'to come', kuru
sen	one thousand
kyûhyaku	nine hundred
nanajûroku	seventy-six
-nen	suffix meaning 'year'
deshita	past tense of 'desu', meaning 'was'/'were'
Shôwa	the current Imperial era
gojûichi	fifty-one
Shôwa ichinen	1926
nijûroku	twenty-six
desu kara	therefore
Shôwa jûnen	1935
sanjûgo	thirty-five
Shôwa nijûnen	1945
yonjûgo	forty-five
Shôwa sanjûnen	1955
gojûgo	fifty-five
(o)jôzu	skilled, clever, good (at)
heta	unskilled, clumsy, poor (at)
kimasen deshita	did not come, past negative of the verb 'to come', kuru
hitori	one person

hitori de	by him/herself
aki	autumn
natsu	summer
atsui	hot
mushiatsui	hot and humid, 'sticky'
wakarimasen	do not understand, present negative of the verb 'to understand', wakaru
ame	rain
furimasu	present tense of 'to fall' (of rain or snow), furu
kaze	wind
warui	bad
ima	now
(o)tenki	weather
suzushii	cool
mô	another
ippai	one cup
kekkô	fine, splendid
gochisôsama deshita	that was a marvellous meal
Nihongo	Japanese (language) or, sometimes, Nippongo
yoku	well
hanashimasu	present tense of the verb 'to speak', hanasu
hanashimasen	do not speak, present negative of the verb 'to speak', hanasu
futaritomo	both
Eigo	English (language)

4.3 EXPLANATIONS

(a) Counting years

Although 'officially' the year may be 1988 A.D., the Japanese have stuck to their traditional way of reckoning the year. Just as in the Middle Ages it was not '1405' but 'The sixth year of King Henry IV', so 1988 was the sixty-third year since the former emperor ascended the throne. He took the name Shôwa to signify his reign and so 1935, for example, was Shôwa 10. The current era is Heisei. (See p. 303.)

(b) Weather

The Japanese like talking about the weather – so much so that it usually carries an honorific: ii otenki desu nê (isn't it lovely weather) or warui otenki desu nê (isn't it horrible weather). The Japanese year has fairly well-defined seasons: spring (haru) is humid and tends to be misty; summer (especially on the Pacific coast) is hot and heavy with a 'rainy season' (tsuyu) in May and June; in early September storms, sometimes reaching typhoon strength, sweep away the muggy clouds and autumn is a bright, dry, clear season (there is a Japanese proverb: ten takaku, uma koeru – the sky is high and horses are getting fat). Winter (fuyu) is mainly dry and cold. Snow is rare in the Tokyo area where it may stay dry and fine for weeks on end, though, on the west coast, the famous Yukiguni or Snow Country has heavy snowfalls as the bitter winds sweep down from Siberia.

(c) Conversational expressions

As in other languages, there are many 'set phrases' to cover various social eventualities; it is useful if these are *memorised*. We have met SEVEN in the first four chapters:

Hajimemashite	How do you do?
Ogenki desu ka	How are you?
Genki desu	I'm fine.
Arigatô gozaimasu	Thank you very much.
Kekkô desu	literally, 'That's fine', used politely to refuse a second helping.
Gochisôsama deshita	That was delicious (literally, a feast).
Wakarimasen	I don't understand.

(d) Verbs in Japanese

There are *two* types of verbs in Japanese – *weak* verbs like taberu (Chapter 3) and *strong* verbs like nomu also met in Chapter 3.

1. *Strong verbs* end in -bu, -gu, -ku, -mu, -nu, -ru, -su, -tsu, or -u. nomu forms its tenses in this way:

nomimasu	(I) drink
nomimasen	do not drink
nomimashita	drank
nomimasen deshita	did not drink

2. hanasu forms them this way:

hanashimasu	(I) speak
hanashimasen	do not speak
hanashimashita	spoke
hanashimasen deshita	did not speak

3. kuru, to come
There are only three *irregular verbs* in Japanese, and kuru is one of them (see Grammar Summary 1(e)).

kimasu	(I) come
kimasen	do not come
kimashita	came
kimasen deshita	did not come

(e) Counting

1. Here are the numbers *from 1 to 10*:

ichi	1
ni	2
san	3
shi *or* yon	4
go	5
roku	6
shichi *or* nana	7
hachi	8
kyû	9
jû	10

2. Numbers *higher than 10*:

11	jûichi	10 and 1
12	jûni	10 and 2
13	jûsan	
14	jûyon (or jûshi)	
15	jûgo	
16	jûroku	
17	jûshichi (or jûnana)	
18	jûhachi	
19	jûkyû	

And 20?

```
20   nijû 2 and 10
21   nijûichi
22   nijûni,
```
and so on
```
30   sanjû
40   yonjû,
```
and so on
```
50   gojû
60   rokujû
70   shichijû
```
(*or* nanajû)
```
80   hachijû
90   kyûjû
100  hyaku
1000 sen
1985 sen kyûhyaku hachijûgo
```
A.D. 1985 sen kyûhyaku hachijûgonen (*or* Shôwa rokujûnen)

3. Counting *people*
Unfortunately not all Japanese counting is as easy as that.
To *count people*, this system is used:

hitori	one person, hence also 'alone'
futari	two people
sannin	three people
yonin	four people

Thereafter, the suffix -nin goes *on the number*. The famous film *Seven Samurai* is:

Shichinin no samurai.

10 people	jûnin
26 people	nijûrokunin
100 people	hyakunin, and so on.

4.   Counting *cupfuls or glasses*
To count cupfuls or glasses, there is another system:

ippai	one cupful, one glassful
nihai	two cupfuls
sambai	three cupfuls
yonhai (or shihai)	four cupfuls

Therefore mô ippai means 'another cup':

Mô ippai, Mary-san?	Would you like another cup, Mrs Foster?
Mô ippai kudasai.	Another cup, please.
Biiru desu ka?	Is it beer you're wanting?
Hai! Biiru o nihai kudasai.	Yes! Two beers please.

(Please refer to the Reference Material sections pp. 297–8 and 304–5 when necessary.)

(f)   Languages
The suffix -go is used after the name of the country to indicate the language. Thus:

Nihon, Japan; Nihongo, Japanese
Furansu, France; Furansugo, French

You will remember there was an alternative form for England –Igirisu or Eikoku. English (the language) is Eigo.

(g)   Adverbs (see Grammar Summary 7)
To form the adverb of a true adjective take off the final -i and put -ku. Thus:

yasashii, easy; yasashiku, easily
muzukashii, difficult; muzikashiku, with difficulty

ii, good, has an exceptional adverbial form: **yoku**, well. This form is also used for the *negative*:

    yoku wa arimasen   It is not good.

(h) Giving praise
To praise someone you say:

    Ojôzu desu nê!   You really are skilled!

The modest reply is:

    Iie! Heta desu yo!   No, I'm not!

(i) Rainfall and snowfall
The verb used is **furu**; the present tense is **furimasu** (negative **furimasen**), and the past tense is **furimashita** (negative **furimasen deshita**). The *subject* is either **ame** (rain) or **yuki** (snow) with **ga**:

Ame ga takusan furimasu. It rains a lot.
Sen kyûhyaku rokujûhachinen ni yuki ga takusan furimashita.
In 1968 it snowed a great deal.

4.4 Exercises

Section A
Exercise 1
Give the negative, and then the opposite, of the following (**Example: Ôkii desu ka? – Iie, ôkiku wa arimasen. Chiisai desu.**):
    1. Yasashii desu ka?
    2. Warui desu ka?
    3. Suzushii desu ka?
    4. Muzukashii desu ka?
    5. Ii desu ka?

Exercise 2

Answer the following questions (**Example: Igirisujin wa Eigo o hanashimasu.** English people speak English):
    1. Nihonjin wa?
    2. Doitsujin wa?
    3. Itariijin wa?
    4. Anata wa?

Exercise 3

Write out the following dates:
1920	1985
1937	Shôwa 19
1953	Shôwa 46

Exercise 4

Count from 50 to 71.

Exercise 5

Put into the negative:
1. Satô-san wa Eigo o hanashimasu.
2. Okusama wa biiru o nomimasu.
3. Watakushi wa sashimi o tabemasu.
4. Kore wa watakushi no keisu desu.
5. Yamada-san wa Bonn de Doitsugo o hanashimashita.
6. Anata wa osake o takusan nomimashita.
7. Ano Nihonjin wa naganegi o tabemashita.
8. Kuruma wa akai desu.

Exercise 6

Answer the following questions (**Example**: sen kyûhyaku sanjûgonen wa Shôwa jûnen deshita nê. – (1935 was Shôwa 10, wasn't it?):
1. Sen kyûhyaku nijûhachinen wa?
2. Sen kyûhyaku yonjûnen wa?
3. Sen kyûhyaku rokujûninen wa?
4. Sen kyûhyaku shichijûkyûnen wa?

Section B 🎴
Exercise 7
Play the part of Mr or Mrs Foster in the following dialogue:
Itsu Nihon e kimashita ka?	(I came in the summer of 1983.)
Ii otenki deshita ka?	(No. It was hot and sticky weather.)
Hitori de kimashita ka?	(No. My wife/husband came too.)

Anata wa Nihongo o yoku   (No, I'm not!)
hanashimasu nê. Ojôzu
desu nê!

Exercise 8

Translate:
1. I did not come to Japan in the autumn.
2. My husband came to Tokyo alone.
3. English is difficult for the French.
4. Mrs Yamamoto speaks German well.

Exercise 9

Re-read (or listen again to) the Dialogues 4.1 and say whether these statements are true, or false:
1. Foster-san wa 1960 ni Nihon e kimashita.
2. Shôwa 41 wa 1966 deshita.
3. 1976 ni Foster-san to okusan wa Nihon e kimashita.
4. Tôkyô no natsu wa suzushii desu.
5. Mary-san wa ocha o ippai nomimashita.
6. Nihongo wa gaikokujin niwa muzukashii desu.

Exercise 10 📼

Play the part of Mr Smith in the following dialogue:
Mr Itô: Ogenki desu ka?
MrSmith: .... (Yes, thank you. I'm fine. How are you?)
Mr Itô: Genki desu. Arigatô.
MrSmith: .... (Isn't it bad weather?)
Mr Itô: Sô desu nê.
MrSmith: .... (It's cool, isn't it.)
Mr Itô: Hai, sô desu.
MrSmith: .... (It rains a lot doesn't it!)
Mr Itô: Sô desu nê. Takusan furimasu nê.
MrSmith: .... (Would you like some beer?)
Mr Itô: Iie, biiru o nomimasen.
MrSmith: .... (Would you like some Japanese tea?)
Mr Itô: Hai. Arigatô.
MrSmith: .... (Is it good?)

Mr Itô: Oishii desu yo.
MrSmith: .... (Another cup?)
Mr Itô: Iie. Kekkô desu.

CHAPTER 5

THE NEXT MORNING

5.1 DIALOGUES 📼

Dialogue 1

London's weather compared with Tokyo's.

Mrs Itô: Ohayô gozaimasu!

Mrs Foster: Ohayô gozaimasu!

Mrs Itô: Yoku nemurimashita ka?

Mrs Foster: Hai Arigatô gozaimasu. Taihen yoku nemur-
imashita.
Mrs Itô: Ii otenki desu nê.
Mrs Foster: Sô desu. Mushiatsuku wa arimasen.
Mrs Itô: Ima kugatsu desu kara atsuku wa arimasen. Igirisu no
aki wa ii otenki desu ka?
Mrs Foster: Tokidoki ii otenki desu ga tokidoki ame ga takusan
furimasu.
Mrs Itô: Nihon dewa ame ga rokugatsu to shichigatsu ni
takusan furimasu ga futsû aki niwa furimasen.
Mrs Foster: Fuyu niwa yuki ga furimasu ka?
Mrs Itô: Nihon no kita to nishi niwa yuki ga takusan furimasu
keredomo Tôkyô dewa furimasen. Tôkyô no fuyu
wa taihen samui desu.
Mrs Foster: Sô desu ka? Futsû Rondon no fuyu wa samuku wa
arimasen. Ame ga takusan furimasu ga yuki
wa furimasen.
Mrs Itô: Kugatsu niwa taifû ga kimasu. Ki o tsukete kudasai!
Mrs Foster: Mainen kimasu ka?
Mrs Itô: Iie, mochiron mainen wa kimasen keredomo kyonen
ôkii taifû ga kimashita.

Dialogue 2 📻
School and office; telling the time; days of the week.
Mr Itô: Kyô wa doyôbi desu kara jimusho e ikimasen. Igirisu
demo doyôbi wa yasumi desu ka?
Mr Foster: Sô desu nê. Ima wa yasumi desu keredomo jûnen
mae niwa mainichi jimusho e ikimashita.
Mochiron nichiyôbi wa ikimasen deshita.
Mr Itô: Nihon demo sô deshita keredomo ima wa getsuyôbi
kara kin'yôbi made desu.
Mr Foster: Kodomotachi wa gakkô e ikimasu ka?
Mr Itô: Ikimasu yo. Doyôbi mo gakkô e ikimasu. Igirisu dewa?
Mr Foster: Jûnen mae niwa ikimashita ga ima wa ikimasen.
Nihon no kodomotachi wa nanji ni gakkô e
ikimasu ka?
Mr Itô: Asa hachiji ni ikimasu.
Mr Foster: Sô desu ka! Igirisu dewa kuji desu. Gogo yoji ni
uchi e kaerimasu.
Mr Itô: Nihon dewa gogo goji desu.
Mr Foster: Nanji ni asagohan o tabemasu ka?
Mr Itô: Asagohan o gozen shichiji ni tabemasu.
Mr Foster: Hirugohan wa?
Mr Itô: Futsû jûniji jûgofun desu.

Dialogue 3

Plans for Saturday.

Mr Itô: Kyô nani o shimasu ka?

Mr Foster: Ima nanji desu ka?

Mr Itô: Ima jûji desu.

Mr Foster: Iie, jûjijippun desu nê.

Mr Itô: Sô desu ka? Ano . . . kinô anata wa nanji ni Nihon e
         kimashita ka? Rokujihan deshita nê?

Mr Foster: Sô deshita. Rokuji sanjippun deshita yo.

Mrs Itô: Ii otenki desu nê.

Mr Itô: Taihen ii otenki desu nê. Kuruma de inaka e ikimashô.

Mrs Itô: Ichiji ni hirugohan o tabemashô. Sono ato sampo o
         shimashô. Ikaga desu ka?

Mr Foster: Ii desu nê! Sô shimashô.

5.2 VOCABULARY

Ohayô gozaimasu	good morning
nemurimashita	slept, past tense of
	nemuru, to sleep
ima	now
kugatsu	September
tokidoki	sometimes
rokugatsu	June
shichigatsu	July
futsû	usually
fuyu	winter
kita	north
nishi	west
samui	cold
Rondon	London
taifû	typhoon
ki o tsukete kudasai	please take care
mainen	each year
mochiron	of course
kyonen	last year
kyô	to-day
doyôbi	Saturday
kara	because
jimusho	office

ikimasen	do not go, present negative of iku, to go
yasumi	holiday
mae	before
mainichi	every day
ikimashita	went, past tense of iku, to go
nichiyôbi	Sunday
getsuyôbi	Monday
kara	from
kin'yôbi	Friday
made	until
kodomotachi	children
gakkô	school
nanji	what time
asa	morning
hachiji	eight o'clock
kuji	nine o'clock
gogo	p.m.
yoji	4 o'clock
uchi	house
kaerimasu	present tense of kaeru, to return
goji	five o'clock
gozen	a.m.
shichiji	seven o'clock
jûniji	twelve o'clock
jûgofun	fifteen minutes
shimasu	present tense of suru, to do
jûji	ten o'clock
jippun	ten minutes
kinô	yesterday
rokujihan	half past six
sanjippun	thirty minutes
de	by, of transport
kuruma de	by car
inaka	the country
ikimashô	let's go
ichiji	one o'clock
tabemashô	let's eat
sono ato	after that

sampo o suru	go for a walk (the o is sometimes omitted)
ikaga desu ka	how's that
shimashô	let's do

5.3 EXPLANATIONS

(a) l and r

The transcription of foreign words with 'l' in them presents some difficulty:

Rondon	London
Berurin	Berlin
Risuto	Liszt

(See Guide to Pronunciation.)

(b) The education system

Work starts earlier both at school and in the office. School is compulsory from the age of *six*, though many children go to private kindergartens (yôchien) before reaching that age. They attend primary school (shôgakkô) from six to twelve, middle school (chûgakkô) from twelve to fifteen and high school (kôtôgakkô) from fifteen to eighteen. A high percentage of Japanese go on to attend university – national universities such as Yokohama Kokuritsu Daigaku (kokuritsu, national; daigaku, university); city universities such as Yokohama Shiritsu Daigaku (shiritsu, municipal); or private universities, Shiritsu Daigaku (rather confusingly shiritsu also means 'private' but the Chinese character for shi is quite different).

(c) Take care!

Ki o tsukete kudasai! is a standard friendly warning.

(d) The days of the week

nichiyôbi	Sunday (nichi means sun)
getsuyôbi	Monday (getsu means moon)

kayôbi	Tuesday (ka means fire)
suiyôbi	Wednesday (sui means water)
mokuyôbi	Thursday (moku means tree)
kin'yôbi	Friday (kin means gold)
doyôbi	Saturday (do means earth)

(e) The months of the year
These are set out on pp. 301–3.

(f) Telling the time

ichiji	one o'clock
ichijihan	half past one
niji	two o'clock
nijihan	half past two
sanji	three o'clock
yoji	four o'clock
goji	five o'clock
rokuji	six o'clock
shichiji (or nanaji)	seven o'clock
hachiji	eight "
kuji	nine "
jûji	ten "
jûichiji	eleven "
jûniji	twelve "

The suffix -ji means o'clock). The suffix -fun means minute(s) but, like hai in Chapter 4, it undergoes some changes:

ippun	one minute
nifun	two minutes
sampun	three
yompun	four
gofun	five
roppun	six minutes
shichifun (or nanafun)	seven minutes
hachifun (or happun)	eight minutes

kyûfun	nine minutes
jippun	ten minutes

Thus, going round the clock at five minute intervals, we get:

ichiji gofun
ichiji jippun
ichiji jûgofun
ichiji nijippun
ichiji nijûgofun
ichiji han (or ichiji sanjippun)
ichiji sanjûgofun
ichiji yonjippun.

Nowadays, especially with digital watches, we can continue:

ichiji yonjûgofun
ichiji gojippun
ichiji gojûgofun
niji
niji gofun, etc.

But, traditionally, 1.45 is niji jûgofun mae (two o'clock fifteen minutes before); 1.50 is niji jippun mae, and 1.55 is niji gofun mae. Both forms are common.

Gozen and gogo (literally before noon and after noon) go *before the number*:

gozen goji	5 a.m.
gogo shichijihan	7.30 p.m.

Sometimes asa, morning, is used:

asa rokuji	6.00 in the morning

(g) Four more verbs
nemuru, to sleep, is a *strong* verb like aru:

nemurimasu	(I) sleep
nemurimasen	do not sleep
nemurimashita	slept

| nemurimasen de-shita | did not sleep |

kaeru to return, is one of the few verbs ending in -eru which are *strong* and it, too, goes like aru:

kaerimasu	(I) return
kaerimasen	do not return
kaerimashita	returned
kaerimasen deshita	did not return

iku is a slightly irregular verb, but fortunately not in any of its basic tenses where it behaves like other *strong* verbs:

ikimasu	(I) go
ikimasen	do not go
ikimashita	went
ikimasen deshita	did not go

suru, to do or to make, however, is very *irregular*:

shimasu	(I) do
shimasen	do not do
shimashita	did
shimasen deshita	did not

(h) mai-
mai means each or every

mainen	every year
maigetsu (or maitsuki)	every month
mainichi	every day

(i) let's!
By changing the present tense of a verb from -masu to -mashô, you get the 'Let's' form:

Tabemashô.	Let's eat.
Tôkyô e ikimashô.	Let's go to Tôkyo.
Mizu o nomimashô	Let's drink some water.

(j) gozaimasu
This verb is a polite version of desu.

Arigatô gozaimasu means literally 'is rarely (to be found)' – i.e., What you have just said or done is so nice it's rarely met with. Hence, thank you.

Ohayô gozaimasu means literally 'You are early', hence, good morning.

It is encountered in many polite set-phrases:

Omedetô gozaimasu.	Congratulations.
Sayô de gozaimasu ka.	Very polite form of Sô desu ka?
Nani mo gozaimasen.	Literally, 'There isn't any' this is a polite disclaimer uttered by a hostess usually before a groaning board!

Older people use de gozaimasu instead of desu when wishing to be very formal:

Watakushi wa Yamada de gozaimasu.	I am Yamada.

(k) Kuru

The verb used with taifû (literally, big wind – our word is of course derived from the Japanese) is kuru:

Kugatsu niwa taifû ga kimasu	There are typhoons in September.
Shôwa yonjûichinen ni ôkii taifû ga kimashita.	There was a big typhoon in 1966.

(l) Because

We have already come across the expression desu kara, therefore. Kara coming after the verb means 'because':

Doyôbi desu kara jimusho e ikimasen.
As it's Saturday, I don't go to the office.

Desu kara really means 'because it is'. Look at some other examples:

Ichiji desu kara tabemashô.
As it's one o'clock let's eat.
Ii otenki desu kara sampo o shimashô.
As the weather is nice let's go for a walk.

5.4 EXERCISES

Section A
Exercise 1
Ima nanji desu ka (what time is it?)

6.15 a.m.	9.30
8.00 in the morning	10.55
11.05	5.40
1.20 p.m.	a quarter to four
2.10	4.35
7.25	8.50

Exercise 2
Nani o shimashô ka? (what shall we do?)
1. Biiru o nomu
2. Sakana o taberu
3. Sampo o suru
4. Uchi e kaeru
5. Nihongo o hanasu
6. Jimusho e iku

Exercise 3
What did you do on each day of the week?
1. On Sunday I went back to Yokohama.
2. On Monday I went to the office.
3. On Tuesday I came home at 8 o'clock.
4. On Wednesday I ate some sashimi.
5. On Thursday I spoke Japanese.
6. On Friday I did not go to the office.
7. On Saturday I went for a walk.

Exercise 4 📼
Play the part of Mr or Mrs Potts in the following dialogue:

Mr Itô: Ohayô gozai-
masu.
Mr/s Potts:......................... (Good morning. Did you
Mr Itô: Arigatô. Yoku sleep well)?
nemurimashita. Anata
mo?
Mr/s Potts: .... (Yes, thank you. I slept
well. The weather's bad,
isn't it.)

Mr Itô: Sô desu nê.
Warui desu nê.

Mr/s Potts: .... (Yesterday the weather was cool.)

Mr Itô: Sô desu nê.

Mr/s Potts: .... (What is the time?)

Mr Itô: Ima hachiji han desu.

Mr/s Potts: .... (As it's Saturday I don't go to the office.)

Mr Itô: Nani o shimashô ka?

Mr/s Potts: .... (Let's go to Tôkyô. How's that?)

Mr Itô: Nanji ni kaerimasu ka?

Mr/s Potts: .... (At seven fifteen.)

Section B
Exercise 5
Answer the following questions about yourself:
1. Anata wa nanji ni asagohan o tabemasu ka?
2. Anata wa nanji ni hirugohan o tabemasu ka?
3. Anata wa nanji ni yûgohan o tabemasu ka?
4. Jimusho e mainichi ikimasu ka?
5. Gakkô e ikimasu ka?
6. Futsû nanji ni uchi e kaerimasu ka?
7. Nihon e ikimashita ka?
8. Nihongo o hanashimasu ka? (Hai . . . !)

Exercise 6
Without looking back, see how many of these conversational expressions you can remember:
1. How do you do?
2. Good morning.
3. Take care!
4. Congratulations.
5. Thank you very much.
6. That is delicious.
7. That's fine. (I don't want any more.)
8. I don't understand.

Exercise 7
Translate:
1. As it's February it's cold.
2. As it's July it's hot.
3. As it's October it's cool.
4. As it's June it's hot and sticky.
5. As it's Saturday let's go to the country.
6. As it's Sunday Mr Itô does not go the office.

Exercise 8
What do Japanese children do? Use a complete sentence for your answer.
1. Nihon dewa kodomotachi wa nanji ni asagohan o tabemasu ka?
2. Nanji ni gakkô e ikimasu ka?
3. Nanji ni hirugohan o tabemasu ka?
4. Nanji ni uchi e kaerimasu ka?
5. Doyôbi mo gakkô e ikimasu ka?

Exercise 9
Translate:
1. It rains from time to time.
2. Of course Mr Itô doesn't go to the office at 6.30 a.m.
3. Mr Satô usually comes home at 5.15.
4. He went to Japan last year.
5. He eats rice every day.
6. From Tuesday to Saturday it was fine.
7. From nine a.m. to four p.m. it is hot.

REVISION AND SELF-ASSESSMENT TESTS FOR CHAPTERS 1–5

Do the full test and mark it, using the mark scheme suggested. *If you made any mistakes, make sure you go back and revise the relevant chapter(s) before proceeding with Chapter 6.*

Section 1
Put in the appropriate particles:
1. Kore —— watakushi —— kaban —— arimasen.
2. Uchi —— ringo —— momo —— arimasu.
3. Nihon —— kodomotachi —— hachiji —— gakkô —— ikimasu.
4. Watakushi —— Yokohama —— ikimashita.
5. Foster-san —— Kyôto —— sashimi —— tabemashita.
6. Yuki —— takusan furimasu.
7. Getsuyôbi —— kin'yôbi —— jimusho —— ikimasu.
8. Samuku —— arimasen.

(Score: 20)

Section 2
'Is it easy?' 'No, it isn't easy. It's difficult.'
1. Yasashii desu ka?
2. Samui desu ka?
3. Chiisai desu ka?
4. Warui desu ka?
5. Ii desu ka?

(Score: 10)

Section 3
Write out the following numbers:

11	55
22	78
33	89
46	94
47	100

(Score: 10)

Section 4
Give the year A.D. for:
    Shôwa 40
    Shôwa 55

(Score: 10)

Section 5
Ima nanji desu ka?
    7.15 a.m.
    8.45 p.m.
    ten to four
    11.35
    9.20

(Score: 10)

Section 6
Translate the following:

leeks	your husband
fruit	September
car	Thursday
rain	today
your wife	of course

(Score: 10)

Section 7
Answer the following questions with complete sentences:
1. Rondon no haru wa mushiatsui desu ka?
2. Igirisu dewa fuyu wa atsui desu ka?
3. Nihonjin wa nani o tabemasu ka?
4. Nihongo wa gaikokujin ni muzukashii desu ka?
5. Nihon dewa kodomotachi wa futsû nanji ni uchi e kaerimasu ka?

(Score: 10)

Section 8 📼

Read the following conversation or listen to it on your cassette. If you have the cassette, do *not* read the text. Then answer the questions underneath.

Mr Jones: Watakushi no keisu wa akai desu.

Mr Kimura: Kore desu ka?

Mr Jones: Iie. Sore wa chiisai desu.

Mr Kimura: Kono ôkii keisu wa anata no desu ka?

Mr Jones: Hai, sô desu. Arigatô gozaimasu.

Mr Kimura: Ano . . . Uchi e ikimashô ka?

Mr Jones: Ima nanji desu ka?

Mr Kimura: Rokuji han desu.

Mr Jones: Anata no kuruma wa akai desu ka kuroi desu ka?

Mr Kimura: Kuroi desu.

Mr Jones: Nihon no kuruma desu ka?

Mr Kimura: Iie, Doitsu no kuruma desu.

Mr Jones: Ano . . . Nani o tabemashô ka?

Mr Kimura: Sakana ya gohan o tabemashô nê.

Mr Jones: Nomimono wa?

Mr Kimura: Osake matawa ocha desu. Osake o nomimasu ka?

Mr Jones: Iie, nomimasen.

Mr Kimura: Okusama wa Nihongo o hanashimasu ka?

Mr Jones: Iie, hanashimasen.

Mr Kimura: Okusama wa itsu Nihon e kimashita ka?

Mr Jones: Rokugatsu ni kimashita.

1. Describe Mr Jones's suitcase.
2. What time is it?
3. What colour is Mr Kimura's car?
4. Is it a Japanese car?
5. What are they going to eat for supper?
6. What are they going to drink?
7. Does Mr Jones drink saké?
8. Does Mrs Jones speak Japanese?
9. When did she come to Japan?

(Score: Total 10 – score 2 for Qu. 1)

Self-assessment grades: Maximum total score = 90

Over 70   Excellent

45 – 70   Satisfactory

Under 45   More revision needed

SHOPPING – 1
GOING TO THE BOOKSHOP

6.1 DIALOGUES

Dialogue 1
Making plans.
Mrs Foster: Kaimono o shitai desu.
Mrs Itô: Sô desu ka? Doko e ikitai desu ka?
Mrs Foster: Hon'ya e ikitai desu keredomo. Ii desu ka?
Mrs Itô: Ii desu yo. Watakushi mo hon'ya de jibiki o kaitai desu.
Mrs Foster: Hon'ya wa doko desu ka?
Mrs Itô: Yûbinkyoku no mae ni arimasu.

Mrs Foster: Sô desu ka. Sore wa ii desu nê. Watakushi wa kitte o kaitai desu kara issho ni yûbinkyoku e ikimashô ka?
Mrs Itô: Arukimashô. Jippun dake desu.
Mrs Foster: Ii otenki desu kara watakushi wa sampo shitai desu.
Mrs Itô: Watakushi mo. Ikimashô ka?
Mrs Foster: Sô desu. Watakushi wa Nihon no hon'ya o mitai desu yo.
Mrs Itô: Omoshiroi desu nê.
Mrs Foster: Sô desu. Taihen omoshiroi desu. Itsu otaku e kaerimasu ka?
Mrs Itô: Jûichiji han ni.

Dialogue 2 🔲

At the bookshop.

Mrs Itô: Hon'ya wa kudamonoya no yoko ni arimasu.
Mrs Foster: Kudamono o kaitai desu ka?
Mrs Itô: Iie. Kudamono o kaitaku wa arimasen keredomo kudamono wa totemo utsukushii desu nê.
Mrs Foster: Sô desu nê. Utsukushii desu nê. Momo ya nashi ya ringo no iro wa utsukushii desu nê.
Mrs Itô: Koko ga hon'ya desu. Hairimashô.
(They go into the shop.)
    Gomen kudasai!
Shopkeeper: Irasshaimase!
Mrs Itô: Watakushi no tomodachi wa Igirisujin desu.
Shopkeeper: Sayô de gozaimasu ka. Igirisu kara irasshaima-shita ka?
Mrs Foster: Sô desu. Watakushitachi wa kinô Nihon e kima-shita.
Shopkeeper: Ah! Nihongo ga wakarimasu ka? Ojôzu desu nê!
Mrs Foster: Iie! Totemo heta desu yo!

Dialogue 3 🔲

Buying a dictionary.

Mrs Itô: Watakushi wa Ei-wa jiten o kaitai desu keredomo. Arimasu ka?
Shopkeeper: Arimasu yo. Kore wa ii jibiki desu.
Mrs Itô: Takai desu ka?
Shopkeeper: Sukoshi takai desu keredomo taihen benri na jibiki desu yo.
Mrs Itô: Ikura desu ka?
Shopkeeper: Niman gosen happyaku-en desu.

Mrs Itô:　Sô desu ka. Niman gosen happyaku-en desu ka. Takai desu nê. Shikashi Eigo no hon o yomitai desu kara jibiki wa hitsuyô desu nê. Eigo no kotoba wa watakushi niwa taihen muzukashii desu kara. Samman-en de otsuri o itadakemasu ka.

Shopkeeper:　Dômo arigatô gozaimasu. Yonsen nihyaku-en no okaeshi desu.

Mrs Itô:　Arigatô gozaimasu.

6.2 VOCABULARY

kaimono	shopping (literally, 'buy-things')
kaimono (o) suru	to go shopping
kaimono (o) shitai desu	I want to go shopping
ikitai desu	I want to go
hon'ya	bookshop
jibiki	dictionary
kaitai desu	I want to buy (from **kau** to buy)
yûbinkyoku	post-office
mae	in front
kitte	postage-stamp
kara	because
issho ni	together
arukimashô	let's walk, (from **aruku**, to walk)
dake	only
sampo shitai	I want to go for a walk
kudamonoya	fruiterer's
mitai desu	I want to see (from **miru**, to see)
omoshiroi	interesting
otaku	your home (as opposed to uchi, my home)
yoko	beside
kaitaku wa arimasen	I do not want to buy
totemo	very
nashi	Japanese pear
iro	colour
utsukushii	beautiful

hairimashô	let's enter (from hairu, to go in)
gomen kudasai!	excuse me!
irasshaimase!	welcome! come in!
tomodachi	friend
sayô de gozaimasu ka	sô desu ka (very polite)
irasshaimashita	very polite verb equalling kimashita, came, have come
Ei-Wa jiten	English–Japanese dictionary
takai	high, expensive
sukoshi	a little
benri na	useful
ikura	how much
niman	twenty thousand
gosen	five thousand
happyaku-en	eight hundred yen
shikashi	still, however, yet
yomitai desu	I want to read (from yomu, to read)
hitsuyô	necessary
kotoba	word
samman-en	thirty thousand yen
otsuri	change
itadakemasu ka	very polite expression, meaning may I accept, may I take (from itadakeru)
dômo	very much
yonsen	four thousand
okaeshi	change

6.3 EXPLANATIONS

(a) Shops

Although supermarkets are becoming common, and concrete and plate-glass are replacing the traditional small Japanese wooden shop open on to the street, the housewife still prefers to choose fruit, fish, vegetables and rice from the little specialist shops. Shops selling ocha (Japanese tea) and traditional cakes and sweets are frequent, also delightfully-smelling craftsmen's ateliers where tatami mats are made, to form the floor of the traditional Japanese room.

Pavements are rare and the average Japanese shopping street is a cheerful, bustling sight. The customer calls out **Gomen kudasai!** on entering in order to attract attention, and the shopkeeper will always give the cry of welcome, **Irasshaimase!** Delivery boys on bicycles or mopeds weave in and out of the passers-by at noon and in the early evening, taking food to those who have ordered it by telephone. As in France and Italy, it is possible to buy stamps at a tobacconist's.

(b)   Wanting to do something
To say you want to do something, take off the **-masu** from the present tense of any verb and substitute **-tai desu**:

ikimasu	ikitai desu I want to go
yomimasu	yomitai desu I want to read
tabemasu	tabetai desu I want to eat
mimasu	mitai desu I want to see

Ikitai, yomitai, tabetai and mitai are now *true adjectives*. Therefore, to say *you do not want to do something*, take off the -i and substitute **-ku wa arimasen**:

shiroi desu	it is white
shiroku wa arimasen	it is not white
ikitai desu	I want to go
ikitaku wa arimasen	I do not want to go

(c)   keredomo
keredomo (however) frequently ends a sentence, trailing away in a kind of 'you see' meaninglessness. You will have noticed that Japanese speakers tend to dislike leaving their remarks baldly alone with the end-verb, preferring **nê** or **yo** or an unquestioning **ka** – or, as here, **keredomo**.

(d)   hon'ya de jibiki o kaitai desu
The **de** is used because it is *there that the transaction takes place*. It is not a mere question of geography. (See Grammar Summary **8(f)**.)

(e)   Expressing position
To express position, the construction . . . . **no** . . . **ni arimasu** is used (see Grammar Summary **9**). As explained in Chapter 1.3. (g) **no** equals 's in English:

Hon'ya wa doko desu ka?
Where is the bookshop?
(Hon'ya wa) yûbinkyoku no mae ni arimasu.
At the post-office's front – i.e., in front of the post-office.
                kudamonoya no yoko ni arimasu.
At the fruit-shop's side – i.e., next to the fruit-shop.

This is a good example of Japanese as a 'mirror-language' to English, as mentioned in the Introduction.

```
                 1        2    3   4    5
(Hon'ya wa) yûbinkyoku no mae ni arimasu.
                 5 4    3 2        1
(The bookshop) is in front of the post-office.
```

(f)   The suffix -ya
The suffix -ya means *shop*:

hon'ya	bookshop
kudamonoya	fruit-shop
sakanaya	fishmonger's
	but note:
sakaya	saké shop

(g)
aruku **and** sampo (o) suru
aruku is to perform *the act of walking*, as opposed to cycling or some other means of getting from place A to place B.
sampo (o) suru is to *enjoy the act of walking for its own sake*, like the French verb *se promener*

(h)   hairu
hairu, to enter, is a *strong* verb, even though it ends in -iru:

hairimasu	(I) enter
hairimasen	do not enter
hairimashita	entered
hairimasen deshita	did not enter

(i) wakaru
wakaru, to understand, takes the following construction:

Watakushi *wa* Nihongo *ga* wakarimasu.
I understand Japanese.

It really means, 'As for me, Japanese is understandable'.

(j) Wajin
Wajin is an old word for a Japanese. The Chinese character is the wa in Shôwa. In compounds, wa is often used: wahon, a Japanese book; wagaku, Japanese literature; or, as here, wa-ei, Japanese–English; ei-wa, English–Japanese.

(k) Adjectives that are not true adjectives
Adjectives that are not true adjectives – i.e., that do not end in the syllable -i (ta-ka-i; shi-ro-i) (see Chapter **1.3(b)**)) take the particle na before the noun:

benri na jibiki	a useful dictionary
hitsuyô na hon	a necessary book
genki na hito	a healthy person.

(l) Counting in thousands
-man is the suffix to count in *tens of thousands*.

ichiman-en	10 000 yen
niman-en	20 000 yen
samman-en	30 000 yen

Up to 9000, the suffix -sen is used:

sen-en	1000 yen (issen-en in combination with -man)
nisen-en	2000 yen
sanzen-en	3000 yen
yonsen-en	4000 yen
gosen-en	5000 yen
rokusen-en	6000 yen
shichisen-en (or nanasen-en)	7000 yen
hassen-en	8000 yen
kyûsen-en	9000 yen

Thereafter, in combination with -man:

ichiman issen-en	11 000 yen
ichiman nisen-en	12 000 yen

(m)   -hyaku
The complete listing of -hyaku is:

hyaku-en	100 yen
nihyaku-en	200 yen
sambyaku-en	300 yen
yonhyaku-en	400 yen
gohyaku-en	500 yen
roppyaku-en	600 yen
shichihyaku-en	700 yen (or nanahyaku-en)
happyaku-en	800 yen
kyûhyaku-en	900 yen

(n)   Change in shops
In shops, when you want change you use the following form:

Samman-en de otsuri o itadakemasu ka.	Here is 30 000 yen.

(Being a case of 30 000 yen, may I receive change?)

The reply, then, is:

Yonsen nihyaku -en no okaeshi desu.	4200 yen change.

(o)   otaku
otaku is the honorific form of uchi:

otaku e ikimasu ka?	Are you going home?
uchi e kaerimasu	I'm returning home

(p)   Japanese currency (See also p. 305.)
There are 1 yen, 5 yen, 10 yen, 100 yen and 500 yen *coins*.
There are 1000 yen, 5000 yen and 10 000 yen *bank-notes*.

6.4 EXERCISES
Section A
Exercise 1
Put in the appropriate particles (wa, ga, o, ni, de no, ka, e):
1. Yûbinkyoku ——— kitte ——— kaimashita.
2. Hon ——— kaitaku ——— arimasen.
3. Hon'ya ——— gakkô ——— mae ——— arimasu.
4. Issho ——— Yokohama ——— ikimashô ———?
5. Ano hito ——— Eigo ——— wakarimasu ———?
6. Gaikokujin ——— hon ——— omoshiroku ———
   arimasen.
7. Watakushi ——— tomodachi ——— Eigo ——— hon ———
   kaitai desu.

Exercise 2
Add the most logical verb.
1. Hon o ———————.
2. Sakana o ———————.
3. Osake o ———————.
4. Nihongo ga ———————.
5. Nihongo o ———————.
6. Ame ga ———————.
7. Kinô Tôkyô e ———————.
8. Nigatsu ni Nihon e ———————.
9. Nichiyôbi ni sampo o ———————.
10. Kinô Igirisujin wa Eikoku e ———————.

Exercise 3
Let's (**Example**: Let's read a Japanese book Nihon no hon o (yomu) – yomimashô.):
1. Let's walk. (Aruku).
2. Let's go on in. (Hairu).
3. Let's go back to the post-office. (Yûbinkyoku e kaeru).
4. Let's buy some Japanese pears. (Nashi o kau).

Exercise 4
My friend and I have different tastes (**Example**: Watakushi wa sampo shitai desu. I want to go for a walk. Tomodachi wa sampo shitaku wa arimasen. My friend does not want to go for a walk.):

I want to	1.	go to the post-office.
My friend doesn't want to	2.	see Japan.
	3.	eat sashimi.
	4.	read that book.
	5.	buy some peaches.
	6.	return to Yokohama.

Exercise 5
Where are they?
1. Yûbinkyoku wa gakkô no mae ni arimasu ka?
.... (No, it's beside it.)
2. Kudamonoya wa hon'ya no yoko ni arimasu ka?
.... (No, it's in front of it.)
3. Anata no kuruma wa jimusho no yoko ni arimasu ka?
.... (No, it's beside the post-office.)
4. Ringo wa nashi no mae ni arimasu ka?
.... (No, they're next to the peaches.)

Exercise 6
Ikura desu ka? Nihyaku-en desu.
Ikura desu ka?
1. It is 300 yen.
2. It is 2800 yen.
3. It is 3400 yen.
4. It is 5600 yen.
5. It is 10 000 yen.
6. It is 24 200 yen.
7. It is 38 000 yen.
8. It is 39 500 yen.

Exercise 7
My friend understands English –
Tomodachi wa Eigo ga wakarimasu.
1. That child understands French.
2. Your wife understands German.
3. My husband understands Japanese.
4. That foreigner understands Italian.
5. Does that Japanese person understand English?

Section B
Exercise 8
Translate into Japanese (**Example**: The post-office is in front of the fruiterer's – Yûbinkyoku wa kudamanoya no mae ni arimasu.):

1. The fruiterer's is next to the bookshop.
2. My car is in front of my house.
3. My suitcase is next to your briefcase.
4. The peaches are next to the apples.
5. The school is in front of my office.

Exercise 9
Work out the change!
1. Sen-en de otsuri o itadakemasu ka?
.... (It costs 850 yen.)
2. Nisen-en de otsuri o itadakemasu ka?
.... (It costs 1500 yen.)
3. Gosen-en de otsuri o itadakemasu ka?
.... (It costs 3200 yen.)
4. Ichiman-en de otsuri o itadakemasu ka?
.... (It costs 7000 yen.)
5. Niman-en de otsuri o itadakemasu ka?
.... (It costs 10400 yen.)

Exercise 10
Play the part of the purchaser in the following dialogue:
You: .... (Excuse me!)
Shopkeeper: Irasshaimase!
You: .... (Are there any dictionaries?)
Shopkeeper: Arimasu yo.
You: ..... (I want to buy a Japanese – English one, you see.)
Shopkeeper: Sô desu ka. Ano, kore wa ii jibiki desu.
You: .... (Is it expensive?)
Shopkeeper: Sukoshi takai desu keredomo benri na jibiki desu yo.
You: .... (How much is it?)
Shopkeeper: Ichiman nanahyaku-en desu.
You: .... (Is that so? It is dear but I want to read Japanese books. Here's 20 000 yen. May I have the change, please?)
Shopkeeper: Arigatô gozaimasu. Sanzen-en no okaeshi desu.
You: .... (Thank you very much.)

SHOPPING – 2
AT THE POST OFFICE

7.1 DIALOGUE 📼

Buying stamps.

Mrs Itô:　Nani o kaitai desu ka, Mary-san?

Mrs Foster:　Kitte o kaitai desu. Kesa tegami o kakimashita kara Igirisu e okuritai desu.

Mrs Itô:　Tegami o nammai kakimashita ka?

Mrs Foster:　Gomai kakimashita.

(They go up to the counter.)

Mrs Foster:　Sumimasen. Eigo ga wakarimasu ka?

Employee:　Iie. Wakarimasen.

(Mrs Foster turns in dismay to Mrs Itô.)

Mrs Foster: Itô-san! Watakushi no kitte o katte kudasaimasen ka?

Mrs Itô: Iie! Anata wa Nihongo ga yoku wakarimasu kara Nihongo de hanashite kudasai!

Mrs Foster: Ano ... Igirisu made kono tegami o okuritai no desu ga ikura desu ka?

Employee: Igirisu desu ka? Chotto matte kudasai.

Mrs Itô: Ikura desu ka?

Mrs Foster: Mada wakarimasen.

Employee: Eeto ... Igirisu nara sambyaku gojû-en desu.

Mrs Foster: Sambyaku gojû-en no kitte o gomai kudasai.

Employee: Sen nanahyaku gojû-en desu.

(Mrs Foster suddenly remembers.)

Mrs Foster: Ah! Omoidashimashita! Shujin wa ehagaki o nimai kakimashita. Ehagaki nara ikura desu ka?

Employee: Igirisu made desu ka?

Mrs Foster: Sô desu. Igirisu desu.

Employee: Chotto matte kudasai.

Mrs Itô: Sono kitte wa takai desu ka?

Mrs Foster: Iie, takaku wa arimasen. Yasui desu.

Mrs Itô: Ehagaki mo yasui desu ka?

Mrs Foster: Mada wakarimasen.

Employee: Ehagaki nara hyaku gojû-en desu.

Mrs Foster: Nimai kudasai.

Employee: Sambyaku-en desu. Ano ... Sen nanahyaku gojû-en to sambyaku-en de nisen gojû-en desu.

Mrs Foster: Sumimasen. Ichiman-en satsu shika arimasen ga ii desu ka?

Employee: Kekkô desu yo. Nanasen kyûhyaku gojû-en no otsuri desu. Arigatô gozaimasu. Otsugi no kata. Dôzo.

(Mrs Itô steps up to the counter.)

Mrs Itô: Hyaku gojû-en no kitte o jûmai kudasai.

Employee: Sen gohyaku-en desu.

Mrs Itô: Hai. Nisen-en desu.

Employee: Arigatô gozaimasu. Ano ... gohyaku-en no okaeshi desu.

Mrs Itô: Arigatô gozaimasu.

7.2 VOCABULARY

kesa	this morning
tegami	letter
kakimashita	past tense of kaku, to write
okuritai (no) desu	I want to send (from okuru, to send) (see 19.3(j))
nammai	how many (referring to flat objects)
gomai	five (flat objects)
sumimasen	I'm sorry to bother you
katte kudasaimasen ka	would you be so kind as to buy (from kau, to buy)
hanashite kudasai	please speak (from hanasu, to speak)
made	to, up to, as far as
chotto	just a moment
matte kudasai	please wait (from matsu, to wait)
mada (with negative)	not yet
eeto	let's see, well . . .
nara	if it's a case of
omoidashimashita	remembered (past tense of omoidasu, to remember or recollect)
ehagaki	picture postcard
nimai	two (flat objects)
yasui	cheap
satsu	bank-note
shika (with negative)	only
(o)tsugi	next
kata	person (marginally politer than hito)
dôzo	please
jûmai	ten (flat objects)

7.3 EXPLANATIONS

(a) More about counting

We have already met ways of counting *people* (hitori, futari, sannin, etc. in Chapter 4), of counting *cupfuls* (ippai, nihai, sambai, etc., also in Chapter 4), of counting in *hundreds* and *thousands* (hyaku, nihyaku, sambyaku, etc. and sen, nisen, sanzen, etc. in Chapter 6). The system with years and with yen is, as we have seen, simpler (merely adding the appropriate suffix -nen or -en: ichinen, ninen, sannen; ichi-en, ni-en, san-en).

Counting in Japanese is a complicated affair – or rather, because each language has its own way of doing certain things, represents a different way of looking at life from the English way. In Japan, objects that are *flat* (pieces of paper, stamps, bank-notes, tickets, slices of bread or fish or meat, plates, records, postcards, letters) require the suffix -mai: ichimai, nimai, sammai, yommai or yomai, gomai, rokumai, shichimai (or nanamai), hachimai, kyûmai, jûmai, jûichimai, etc.

Therefore, when you both know what you are talking about, the word for the *object* is unnecessary. In a station, Nimai kudasai means two tickets. In the post-office, Nimai kudasai means two stamps.

(b) More strong verbs
kaku to write, goes like aruku:

(present)	kakimasu	(I) write
(present negative)	kakimasen	do not write
(past)	kakimashita	wrote, have written
(past negative)	kakimasen deshita	did not write

A new verb, matsu, to wait:

machimasu	(I) wait
machimasen	don't wait
machimashita	waited
machimasen deshita	didn't wait

omoidasu, to recollect or remember, goes like hanasu:

omoidashimasu	(I) recollect
omoidashimasen	don't remember
omoidashimashita	remembered
omoidashimasen deshita	didn't recollect

okuru, to send, goes like aru, furu, kaeru, hairu:

okurimasu	(I) send
okurimasen	don't send
okurimashita	sent
okurimasen deshita	did not send

(c)   The -te form (1): giving instructions

We meet in this chapter a most important part of the Japanese verb, and will deal now with one of its uses.

Verbs ending in -u have a -te form -tte:

kau, to buy, katte

Verbs ending in -su have a -te form -shite:

hanasu, to speak, hanashite

Verbs ending in -tsu have a -te form -tte:

matsu, to wait matte

In order to give a *polite command* or *recommendation*, you use the -te form and add kudasai:

kitte o katte kudasai	please buy some stamps
Nihongo de hanashite kudasai	please speak Japanese
chotto matte kudasai	please wait a moment

To be very polite indeed, you add kudasaimasen ka:

katte kudasaimasen ka	would you be so kind as to buy

(d)   nara

This is a useful word, meaning 'let's take', or 'supposing', or 'if it's a case of':

Igirisu nara sambyaku gojû-en desu. For England it's 350 yen.
(Literally, if we're talking about England then it's 350 yen.)

(e) Two adverbs with the negative:

mada wakarimasen	I do not yet understand
mada ikimasen	I haven't been there yet
mada kakimasen	I haven't written yet
Ichiman-en satsu shika arimasen.	I've only got a 10 000 yen note.
Nigatsu wa nijûhachinichi shika arimasen.	February has only 28 days.

(f) Otsugi no kata: 'next, please'
Here, the honorific o- is used with the slightly politer word for person – kata, not hito; dôzo, by all means, can be used by itself in reponse to a request:

tegami o kakitai desu	I want to write some letters
dôzo	please do!
hon'ya e ikitai desu	I want to go to the bookshop
dôzo	fine! off you go!

7.4 EXERCISES

Section A
Exercise 1
Ask favours using the -te form (**Example**: (Kitte o kau)–kitte o katte kudasai):
1. (Chotto matsu)
2. (Eigo de hanasu)
3. (Ehagaki o kau)
4. (Omoidasu)

Exercise 2
Nani o kaitai desu ka? (**Example:** Nani o kaitai desu ka? Ehagaki o nimai kaitai desu – What do you want to buy? (I want to buy two postcards.)

1. Nani o kaitai desu ka?	(three stamps)
2.	(five postcards)
3.	(eight stamps)
4.	(ten postcards)
5.	(eleven stamps)

Exercise 3
Igirisu e ikimashita ka? Iie, mada ikimasen – Have you been to England? No, not yet.
1. Ringo o kaimashita ka?
2. Shujin wa kaerimashita ka?
3. Osake o nomimashita ka?
4. Yuki ga furimashita ka?

Exercise 4
Put in the appropriate particles (wa, ga, e, made, no, na, ni, o, de):
1. Igirisu —— ikitai desu.
2. Furansu —— kono ehagaki —— okuritai desu.
3. Benri —— jibiki desu ka?
4. Hyaku-en —— kitte —— kaitai desu.
5. Kanai —— Itariigo —— wakarimasu.
6. Hon'ya —— uchi —— mae —— arimasu.
7. Kudamonoya —— ringo —— kaimashita.

Exercise 5
Add 100 yen each time:
1. Kore wa kyûhyaku-en desu. Sore wa?
2. Kore wa nihyaku-en desu. Sore wa?
3. Kore wa kyûsen kyûhyaku gojû-en desu. Sore wa?
4. Kore wa nisen kyûhyaku nanajûgo-en desu. Sore wa?
5. Kore wa shichihyaku-en desu. Sore wa?
6. Kore wa gohyaku-en desu. Sore wa?
7. Kore wa hachijû-en desu. Sore wa?

Exercise 6
Without looking back, see if you can recognise these words and say in Japanese where you can buy the articles mentioned:
1. Doko de kitte o kaimasu ka?
2. Doko de ringo o kaimasu ka?
3. Doko de jibiki o kaimasu ka?
4. Doko de osake o kaimasu ka?
5. Doko de nashi o kaimasu ka?
6. Doko de sakana o kaimasu ka?
7. Doko de momo o kaimasu ka?
8. Doko de jiten o kaimasu ka?

Section B
Exercise 7
Change the response, using the English information in brackets to
modify your reply:
1. Ii otenki deshita ka? (No, it rained)
2. Kitte o gomai kaimashita ka? (No, I bought six)
3. Hachiji ni kaerimashita ka? (No, at nine)
4. Kin'yôbi Tôkyô e ikimashita ka? (No, on Saturday)
5. Anata no kaban wa kuroi desu ka? (No, it's red)
6. Kinô ringo o tabemashita ka? (No, Japanese pears)
7. Hon'ya e ikitai desu ka? (No, to the Post-Office)
8. Goshujin wa tegami o sammai kakimashita ka? (No, he
   wrote two postcards)

Exercise 8
Nani o shimashita ka? What did you do?
1. Yesterday I wrote three letters.
2. This morning I drank two cups of Japanese tea.
3. On Friday I saw two Japanese.
4. At twenty past three I bought five postcards.
5. At seven o'clock I wrote four letters.

Exercise 9
Play the part of Mr Smith in the following dialogues
Dialogue 1
Mr Itô: Nani o shitai desu ka?
MrSmith: .... (Go to the post-office)
Mr Itô: Kuruma de ikimashô ka?
MrSmith: .... (No, let's walk)
Mr Itô: Yûbinkyoku de nani o shitai desu ka?
MrSmith: (I wrote some postcards this morning and therefore
   I want to send them to America)
Mr Itô: Ehagaki o nammai kakimashita ka?
MrSmith: .... (I wrote three)

Dialogue 2
MrSmith: .... (Excuse me. Do you speak English?)
Post office employee: Iie. Wakarimasen.
MrSmith: .... (Well . . . I want to send three postcards to
   America. How much is that?)
Employee: Amerika nara hyaku gojû-en desu.
MrSmith: .... (Three 150 yen stamps please.)
Employee: Yonhyaku gojû-en desu.

MrSmith: .... (I've only got a 5000 yen note. Is that all right?)

Employee: Kekkô desu yo. Yonsen gohyaku gojû-en no okaeshi desu.

MrSmith: .... (Thank you very much.)

Employee: Arigatô gozaimasu. Otsugi no kata. Dôzo.

AT MR MAEDA'S OFFICE

8.1 DIALOGUES 📼

Dialogue 1
   Waiting to see Mr Maeda.
Mr Itô: Maeda-san to ohanashi shitai no desu ga ima oiso-
           gashii desu ka?
Secretary: Ima denwa de hanashite imasu.

Mr Itô: Ah sô desu ka. Foster to iu tomodachi ga Maeda-san to ohanashi shitai no desu.Igirisu kara kimashita. Ototoi Nihon e kimashita.

Secretary: Onamae o kono kami ni kaite kudasaimasen ka?

Mr Foster: Ah sumimasen. Pen ga arimasen. Kyô mô ippon kaitai no desu ga mada katte imasen.

Secretary: Foster-san wa Nihongo ga ojôzu desu nê!

Mr Foster: Sukoshi hanashimasu keredomo jôzu ja arimasen.

Mr Itô: Kinô ano Nihonjin to yoku hanashite imashita nê!

Mr Foster: Biiru o nonde imashita kara Nihongo de hanashi-mashita yo!

Mr Itô: Biiru o nambon nomimashita ka?

Mr Foster: Nihon dake deshita.

Mr Itô: Nihon dake deshita ka? Hontô desu ka?

Mr Foster: Wasuremashita!

Dialogue 2 📷

Tea while they wait.

Mr Itô :   Shimbun wa arimasu ka?

Secretary: Arimasu keredomo Yamamoto-san ga yonde ima-su.

Mr Itô: Asahi Shimbun desu ka?

Secretary: Sô desu.

Mr Itô: Ah, kesa yomimashita keredomo. Zasshi wa arimasu ka?

Mr Foster: Hai. Mite kudasai. Kono isu no ushiro ni zasshi ga arimasu yo.

Secretary: Ocha o onomi ni narimasu ka soretomo kôcha desu ka?

Mr Foster: Kôcha o nomitai desu. Arigatô.

Mr Itô: Watakushi mo kôcha ni shimasu. Ah. Supuun wa arimasu ka?

Mr Foster: Hai! Teeburu no ue ni supuun ga gohon arimasu.

Mr Itô: Gohon desu ka? Arigatô! Ippon dake de ii desu yo!

Mr Foster: Nampun gurai machimasu ka?

Secretary: Jippun dake deshô. Kôcha o mô ippai? Ikaga desu ka?

Mr Foster: Iie. Kekkô desu.

Dialogue 3 📷

Making an appointment.

Mr Foster: Kyô wa nannichi desu ka?

Mr Itô: Jûshichinichi desu ne.

Mr Foster: Desu kara asatte wa jûkunichi desu nê. Asatte mô ichido kimashô ka? Maeda-san wa ima oísogashii deshô. Maeda-san wa hataraite imasu ga watakushi wa hataraite imasen.

Mr Itô: Kyô gozenchû watakushi wa yasunde imasu keredomo asatte wa hatarakimasu.

Mr Foster: Sô desu ka. Ano, raishû no kayôbi ni shimashô ka? Nijûgonichi desu nê.

Mr Itô: Suiyôbi wa nijûrokunichi desu kara watakushi wa isogashiku wa arimasen.

Mr Foster: Sô shimashô. Raishû no suiyôbi ni mata kimashô.

8.2 VOCABULARY

ohanashi shitai no desu	would like to speak (polite form of hanashitai desu)
(o)isogashii	busy
denwa	telephone
hanashite imasu	is speaking (from hanasu, to speak)
imasu	is (from iru, to be, to exist)
iu	to call
ototoi	the day before yesterday
(o)namae	name
kami	paper
kaite kudasaimasen ka	would you please write (kaite is the -te form of kaku)
pen	pen
ippon	one (cylindrical object)
mada katte imasen	haven't yet bought
wasuremashita	I forgot (past tense of wasureru)
hanashite imashita	you were speaking (from hanasu, to speak)
nonde imashita	was drinking (nonde is the -te form of nomu, to drink)
nambon	how many (cylindrical objects)
nihon	two (cylindrical objects)
hontô	true, the truth
shimbun	newspaper

yonde imasu	is reading, (from yomu, to read)
zasshi	magazine
mite kudasai	look! (from miru)
isu	chair
ushiro	behind
ue	on top
onomi ni narimasu	polite form of nomimasu (from nomu, to drink)
soretomo	or else
kôcha	Indian tea (literally, 'red tea')
ni shimasu	I'll decide on (from suru, to do)
supuun	spoon
teeburu	table
gohon	five (cylindrical objects)
gurai	roughly, about
nampun	how many minutes
deshô	probably is/are
nannichi	what day of the week
jûshichinichi	17th day of the month
jûkunichi	19th day of the month
asatte	the day after to-morrow
mô ichido	once more, one more time
hataraite imasu	is working (from hataraku, to work)
gozenchû	all morning
yasunde imasu	am not working (from yasumu, to rest, to be on holiday)
raishû	next week
nijûgonichi	25th day of the month
nijûrokunichi	26th day of the month
mata	again

8.3 EXPLANATIONS

(a) Hospitality
In offices, common-rooms and waiting-rooms, ocha, kôcha or coffee are always offered to visitors.

(b) Newspapers and magazines

The Japanese are compulsive readers of newspapers and magazines. The Yomiuri Shimbun has the largest circulation of any newspaper in the world.

The range of material available is enormous, and you do see adults devouring comics as well as specialist magazines of all kinds.

(c) Politer language

You will have noticed that more and more *polite forms* are being introduced. For a foreigner, especially at the beginning, these are very important to *recognise* as you will be hearing them all the time. But at the moment, you need not worry too much about *using* them yourself. Mr Itô starting a conversation in a strange office does not say hanashitai desu but uses the honorific o- followed by the verb-stem hanashi and the appropriate form of the verb suru ending with no desu, but it would be perfectly acceptable for a foreigner merely to use the straightforward form. As always with a foreign language, sympathy is shown towards the non-native – and, of course, gratitude towards someone who has taken the trouble to master the basic forms of communication in another language. But it must be stressed that, though you yourself will probably mostly be using the straightforward form, what you will be hearing will be, as here, various socially necessary forms of the verb.

(d) The -te form (2): continuous actions:

Nihonjin wa gohan o tabemasu.
Japanese people generally eat rice.
Ano hito wa Eigo o hanashimasu.
That person speaks English.

The *present tense* of the verb deals with *general statements*. In order to express actions that are being done *at the present time*, you use the -te form of the verb with imasu:

Ima denwa de hanashite imasu.
He is at this moment speaking on the phone.
Maeda-san wa hataraite imasu.
Mr Maeda is working.

The same applies to *past continuous actions*:

Biiru o nonde imashita.
I was drinking beer.

and to *actions in the negative*:

Hataraite imasen.	I am not working.
Hataraite imasen deshita.	I was not working.

Verbs ending in -ku have a -te form -ite:

kaku, to write, kaite
hataraku, to work, hataraite

Verbs ending in -mu have a -te form -nde:

nomu, to drink, nonde
yomu, to read, yonde
yasumu, to rest, yasunde

All *weak verbs make the* -te form by changing the -ru to te:

miru, to see, mite
taberu, to eat, tabete

(e)   The verb iu

The verb iu, to call, takes to before it:
Watakushi wa Foster to iimasu. I am called Foster.

Hence the useful expression '. . . to iu' person or place:

Foster to iu tomodachi. My friend called Foster.

Hanasu, as well, takes to:

Maeda-san to hanashitai desu. I want to speak to Mr Maeda.

(f)   Counting cylindrical things

Counting pens, pencils, umbrellas, leeks, spoons, knives, forks, cigarettes, toothbrushes, bottles, prawns, chrysanthemums – anything shaped in a roughly cylindrical fashion – you use the following system:

ippon	1
nihon	2
sambon	3
yonhon (or shihon)	4

gohon	5
roppon	6
shichihon (or nanahon)	7
happon (or hachihon)	8
kyûhon	9
jippon	10
jûippon, etc.	11, and so on

(g) Two more expressions of position (see Grammar Summary **9**)
As in Chapter **6.3(e)**:

teeburu no ue ni = on top of the table
isu no ushiro ni = behind the chair

(h) ni suru

ni suru is a useful expression, meaning 'to decide on':

kôcha ni shimasu	I decide on tea (I'll have tea)
kayôbi ni shimashô	Let's make it Tuesday

(i) Dates (1)

To express the *day of the month*, you add the suffix -nichi to the numbers you learnt in **4.3(e)**, but *only* for the following dates:

11th – 13th	jûichinichi, jûninichi, jûsannichi
15th – 19th	jûgonichi, etc. (*but* jûkunichi)
21st – 23rd	nijûichinichi, etc.
25th – 31st	nijûgonichi, etc. (*but* nijûkunichi)

The other dates will be learnt in Chapter 11.

(j) deshô

deshô modifies the more definite statement desu:

isogashii desu.	I am busy.
oisogashii deshô.	You are probably busy.

(k) -chû

-chû is a suffix indicating *length of time*:

gozenchû   throughout all the a.m., all morning

(l)   Before and after today

ototoi	the day before yesterday
kinô	yesterday
kyô	today
ashita	tomorrow
asatte	the day after tomorrow

(m)   Once and more than once

ichido, nido, sando, etc. once, twice, three times, and so on.

8.4   EXERCISES

Section A
Exercise 1
What are you doing? (**Example**: (Ringo o taberu) Ringo o tabete imasu.)
   1.   (Hon o kau)
   2.   (Tegami o kaku)
   3.   (Shimbun o yomu)
   4.   (Denwa de hanasu)
   5.   (Matsu)
   6.   (Ocha o nomu)
   7.   (Jimusho de hataraku)

Exercise 2
Kyô wa kayôbi desu (Today is Tuesday)
   1.   Ashita wa? (Tomorrow is?)
   2.   Asatte wa?
   3.   Kinô wa?
   4.   Ototoi wa?

Exercise 3
Kyô wa sangatsu nijûkunichi desu.
1. Ashita wa?
2. Asatte wa?
3. Kinô wa?
4. Ototoi wa?

Exercise 4
Kyô wa jûgatsu jûgonichi getsuyôbi desu. (Today is Monday October 15.)
1. Raishû no getsuyôbi wa?
2. Raishû no kayôbi wa?
3. Raishû no mokuyôbi wa?
4. Raishû no kin'yôbi wa?

Exercise 5
Ask people to do things (**Example**: (Zasshi o yomu) Zasshi o yonde kudasai.):
1. (Hon o miru)
2. (Nihongo de hanasu)
3. (Momo o taberu)
4. (Ehagaki o kau)
5. (Kono kami ni kaku)
6. (Kôcha o nomu)

Exercise 6
Use ni suru in its appropriate form to express the following:
1. Let's make it Sunday.
2. I'll have beer.
3. Let's make it the thirteenth of June.
4. I'll have ocha.
5. Let's make it Saturday.

Exercise 7
Nani o kaimashita ka?
1. Two bottles of beer.
2. Ten prawns.
3. Three leeks.
4. Five spoons.
5. Six pens.
6. One umbrella.

Exercise 8

Nampun gurai machimashita ka?
1. Five minutes.
2. Ten minutes.
3. Fifteen minutes.
4. Twenty minutes.
5. Thirty minutes.

Exercise 9

Put in the appropriate particles (o, de, wa, to, ni, mô, no, ka, ga):
1. Eigo —— hanashimasu.
2. Satô-san —— hanashimashita.
3. Teeburu —— ue —— nani —— arimasu —— ?
4. —— ippai?
5. Kôcha —— shimasu.
6. Itô —— iu tomodachi desu.
7. Sono hon —— omoshiroku —— arimasen.
8. Hon'ya —— jibiki —— kaimashita.

Section B
Exercise 10

Invent answers to the following questions:
1. Nani o nomitai desu ka?
2. Nani o kakitai desu ka?
3. Nani o tabetai desu ka?
4. Nihon de nani o mitai desu ka?
5. Kudamonoya de nani o kaitai desu ka?
6. Nani o yomitai desu ka?

Exercise 11

What is Mr Yamada doing?
1. Kyô yasunde imasu ka? (No, he's working.)
2. Kôcha o nonde imasu ka? (No, he's drinking ocha.)
3. Sakana o tabete imasu ka? (No, prawns.)
4. Zasshi o yonde imasu ka? (No, a newspaper.)
5. Ehagaki o kaite imasu ka? (No, a letter.)
6. Kitte o katte imasu ka? (No, a postcard.)
7. Denwa de hanashite imasu ka? (No, he's reading a magazine.)

Exercise 12

Translate the following:
1. There are three pens in front of the telephone.

2. There are two stamps behind the book.
3. There are five pieces of paper on the chair.
4. There are six bottles of beer on the table.
5. There are five leeks next to the apples.

Exercise 13

Play the part of Mr Foster in the following dialogue:

Mr Maeda: Oisogashii deshô ka?
Mr Foster: ....(No, I'm not.)
Mr Maeda: Pen o kaimashita ka?
Mr Foster: .... (I forgot.)
Mr Maeda: Shimbun wa arimasu ka?
Mr Foster: .... (Yes there is, but Mr Itô is reading it.)
Mr Maeda: Zasshi wa arimasu ka?
Mr Foster: .... (Yes, on the table.)
Mr Maeda: Kôcha o onomi ni narimasu ka soretomo ocha
            desu ka?
Mr Foster: .... (I'd like kôcha. Thank you.)
Mr Maeda: Dôzo.
Mr Foster: .... (Oh, is there a spoon?)

ON THE GINZA

9.1 DIALOGUES 📼

Dialogue 1

Mr Itô and Mr Foster have elevenses.

Mr Itô: Okusama wa kyô nani o shite imasu ka?

Mr Foster: Kaimono o shite imasu. Ima nanji desu ka?

Mr Itô: Ima jûichiji jûgofun desu.

Mr Foster: Chôdo kanai wa kôhii o nonde okashi o tabete imasu.

Mr Itô: Sô desu ka? Mainichi kôhii o nonde okashi o tabete imasu ka?

Mr Foster: Mainichi kôhii o nomimasu ga okashi wa tokidoki shika tabemasen.

Mr Itô: Anata wa biiru o nomitai desu ka?

Mr Foster: Hai! Kyô yasunde imasu kara biiru o ippon nomitai desu yo. Anata mo?

Mr Itô: Iie! Ima hataraite imasen ga niji ni jimusho e ikimasu kara biiru o nomimasen. Zannen desu ga.

Mr Foster: Jimusho e itte nani o shimasu ka?

Mr Itô: Hagaki o kaite tegami o yonde denwa de hanashimasu yo. Foster-san wa hirugohan o tabete nani o shimasu ka?

Mr Foster: Ginza e itte kanai ni aimasu.

Mr Itô: Okusama ni atte kaimono o shimasu ka?

Mr Foster: Sô deshô nê! Kanai wa mainichi kaimono o shitai desu!

Dialogue 2 📼

Mr Foster and Mrs Foster and Mrs Itô discuss their morning.

Mr Foster: Konnichi wa!

Mr Itô: Konnichi wa!

Mr Foster: Kesa nani o shimashita ka?

Mrs Foster: Tôkyô e kite Itô-san no okusama to issho ni iroiro na omoshiroi mono o mimashita.

Mrs Itô: Sô desu nê. Asakusa e itte otera o mimashita. Subarashii desu nê. Nihon no otera wa hontô ni utsukushii desu nê.

Mr Foster: Sô desu. Ninen mae ni Kyôto e itte Kiyomizudera to iu otera e ikimashita.

Mrs Itô: Ah. Sono otera wa kirei desu nê.

Mrs Foster: Watakushi wa Kyôto e ikitai desu yo.

Mr Foster: Saraishû ikimashô ka?

Mrs Foster: Sô shimashô. Raishû anata wa hatarakimasu ga saraishû yasumimasu ne.

Mr Foster: Ano, Yûrakuchô e ikimashô ka? Kasa ga arimasu ka?

Mrs Foster: Arimasu yo.

Dialogue 3 📼

Telephoning and smoking.

Mrs Itô: Chotto matte kudasai. Denwa de shujin to hanashitai no desu ga . . . Denwa wa arimasu ka?

Mr Foster: Hai, asoko ni arimasu. Kusuriya no mae ni futatsu arimasu.

Mrs Foster: Ah! Omoidashimashita. Hamigaki o kaitai desu.

Mr Foster: Kusuriya no yoko ni tabakoya ga arimasu kara watakushi ni tabako o katte kudasai.

Mrs Foster: Hito hako?

Mr Foster: Futa hako katte kudasai.

Mrs Itô: Mainichi nambon suimasu ka?

Mrs Foster: Takusan suimasu.

Mr Foster: Iie! Gohon ka roppon dake suimasu.

Mrs Itô: Shujin wa sanjippon gurai suimasu. Ima jimusho de sutte imasu yo!

Mrs Foster: Karada ni warui desu nê.

Mrs Itô: Sô desu nê.

9.2 VOCABULARY

shite imasu	is doing (shite is the -te form of suru, to do)
kaimono (o) suru	to go shopping
kaimono	a purchase

chôdo	at this moment, just, precisely
kôhii	coffee
(o)kashi	cakes, sweets, sweetmeats
zannen desu ga	it's a pity but (there it is)
hagaki	card, post-card
itte (see Chapter **9.3(e)**)	-te form of iku, to go
aimasu	meet (present tense of **au**)
atte (see Chapter **9.3(e)**)	-te form of au, to meet
kite (see Chapter **9.3(e)**)	-te form of kuru to come
konnichi wa	Good day!
iroiro na	all sorts of
(o)tera	Buddhist temple
subarashii	splendid
hontô ni	in truth, really, truly
kirei	pretty
kasa	umbrella
saraishû	the week after next
kusuriya	chemist's shop
futatsu	two
hamigaki	toothpaste (from ha, a tooth, migaku, to clean or polish)
tabakoya	tobacconist's
tabako	a cigarette, cigarettes
hito hako	one box, case, packet
futa hako	two boxes, cases, packets
suu	to smoke
sutte	-te form of suu
takusan	a great deal, a lot

9.3 EXPLANATIONS

(a) The Ginza

The Ginza is the *shopping and entertainment centre* of Tokyo. Originally the street of the silversmiths, it is now an area of big department-stores, cinemas, bars and night-clubs. The Kabuki Theatre is here. Many of the streets are pedestrian precincts and, though it is always crowded, on Sunday afternoons it is packed.

Asakusa is to the north of the Ginza, near the bank of the Sumida River. There is a park by the temple and, leading up to the temple itself, are many stalls selling sweets and toys and souvenirs.

(b) On and kun

Buddhist missionaries came to Japan from China in the 6th century A.D. The Japanese had no written language and *Chinese characters* were used to transcribe Japanese – not very appropriately, as Chinese is largely monosyllabic and Japanese polysyllabic. Also, the Chinese ideograph brought its own sound with it, so that for every character in modern Japanese there are *at least* two different ways of pronouncing it. The first character of Tôkyô means 'east' (Tokyo is the eastern capital, as Peking is the northern capital and Nanking the southern); by itself it can be pronounced higashi, and this is the kun or Japanese reading. In combination with the character for city it is pronounced tô and this is the on or Chinese reading. Another example:

> Fuji-san wa yama desu.
> Mt Fuji is a mountain.

The san and the yama are the same Chinese character but san is the on reading and yama is the kun reading:

富士山は山です

(c) Kyoto

Kyoto was the capital of Japan from 794 until 1869. There are many magnificent Buddhist temples in and around the city, Kiyomizudera being one of the most spectacular, sited as it is on a high platform over woods to the south-east of the city.

(d) Telephones

The Japanese love telephoning, and there are public telephones available everywhere – not only in booths but in the open air, on shelves outside shops, on railway sweet-stalls and newspaper stands.

(e) The -te form (3): joining two sentences together

Every Japanese sentence ends with a *verb* (usually with a *qualifying noise* after it.) If you wish to link a sentence with another, you end the first sentence with a verb in the -te form and carry on. The final verb may be present or past. This does not affect the use of the -te form, which is *constant*:

> Tôkyô e itte kaimono o shimasu.
> I'm going to Tokyo to do some shopping.

Tôkyô e itte kaimono o shimashita.
I went to Tokyo and did some shopping.

One can think of the -te form in this construction as a kind of *participle*:

Going to Tokyo I'll do some shopping.
Having gone to Tokyo I did some shopping.

Suru, kuru and iku have irregular -te forms:

suru	shite
kuru	kite
iku	itte
Nani o shite imasu ka?	What are you doing?
Koko e kite kudasai.	Please come here.

In the dialogues at the beginning of this chapter there are a number of examples of this use of the -te form:

Kôhii o nonde okashi o tabete imasu.
She is drinking coffee and eating cakes.
Jimusho e itte nani o shimasu ka?
When you get to the office what will you do?
Hagaki o kaite tegami o yonde denwa de hanashimasu.
I'll write cards, read letters and speak on the phone.
Okusama ni atte kaimono o shimasu ka?
When you've met your wife will you go shopping?

(f) Meeting someone
The verb au, to meet, takes ni:

Tomodachi ni aimashita.   I met a friend.

(g) Counting 'unclassifiable' objects
Here and in the next Chapter we meet an 'all-purpose' method of counting – what in fact are the *old Japanese numerals* (because ichi, ni, san, shi, go, etc. derive from the Chinese). Hitotsu, futatsu, etc. are used to count 'unclassifiable' objects, like telephones, chairs, stations, tables or doors and windows in a room. You *can* sometimes 'get away with' using these numerals if you cannot remember the correct form – but there are strict disciplinarians among Japanese

shopkeepers who will refuse to understand you even if you point to a
pair of objects and say, hopefully, **futatsu kudasai**!

(h) hako
hako means a box or packet or case:

hito hako	one box
futa hako	two boxes
mi hako	three
yo hako	four
go hako	five
roppako	six

(i) suu
The verb **suu** is used with **tabako** (nomu is also sometimes
used):

shujin wa tabako o suimasu/nomimasu
my husband smokes

9.4 EXERCISES

Section A
Exercise 1
Link these sentences using the -te form (**Example**: Okashi o tabemashita. Shimbun o yomimashita–Okashi o tabete shimbun o
yomimashita.):
1. Tôkyô e ikimashita. Kaimono o shimashita.
2. Kaimono o shimashita. Kôhii o nomimashita.
3. Kôhii o nomimashita. Okashi o tabemashita.
4. Yokohama e kimashita. Tomodachi ni aimashita.
5. Tomodachi ni aimashita. Uchi e kaerimashita.
6. Tegami o kakimashita. Yûbinkyoku e ikimashita.
7. Otera o mimashita. Ginza e kimashita.

Exercise 2
Which Japanese expression is appropriate in sentences (a)-(f) below?

Dôzo.
Zannen desu ga.
Sumimasen.
Irasshaimase.

Gomen kudasai.
Chotto matte kudasai.

(a) You reject an invitation with regret.
(b) You want to attract attention on entering a shop.
(c) You tell a friend you want to help yourself to a cup of tea. He says?
(d) You ask someone to wait for a moment.
(e) You hear this welcome from a shopkeeper.
(f) You apologise for not having brought a pen.

Exercise 3
Put the appropriate word in the blanks:

sukoshi; shikashi; matawa; soretomo; tokidoki; futsû; mochiron; ikaga; ikura; mada; mata; shika.

1. Takai desu nê! ————— benri na hon deshô.
2. ————— takai desu keredomo taihen ii desu.
3. ————— tabako o nomimasu ga mainichi wa nomimasen.
4. Shimbun ————— zasshi o yomitai desu ka?
5. Shimbun o yomitai desu ka ————— zasshi desu ka?
6. ————— natsu wa atsui desu.
7. Kyô wa mokuyôbi desu kara ————— ashita wa kin'yôbi desu.
8. ————— wakarimasen.
9. Raishû no getsuyôbi ni ————— kimashô.
10. Sen-en satsu ————— arimasen.
11. Yokohama e ikimashô ka? ————— desu ka?
12. Sono naganegi o kaitai desu. ————— desu ka?

Exercise 4
Revising adjectives. Translate the following:
1. That red temple is beautiful.
2. That black book is interesting.
3. Japanese is easy but English is difficult.
4. That small dictionary is cheap.
5. Today it's hot and sticky. Yesterday it was cool.

Section B
Exercise 5

Tell us about yourself:

1. Anata wa mainichi nani o shimasu ka?
2. Ima nani o shite imasu ka?
3. Tabako o nomimasu ka?
4. Ima kôhii o nonde imasu ka?
5. Doko de hatarakimasu ka?
6. Tôkyô e ikitai desu ka?
7. Kyôto e ikimashita ka?
8. Mainichi shimbun o yomimasu ka?
9. Kinô kaimono o shimashita ka?
10. Nanji ni asagohan o tabemashita ka?

Exercise 6

Translate the following:

1. He's free all morning.
2. He's speaking on the phone.
3. What day of the week shall we make it?
4. Let's come again the day after tomorrow.
5. I met Mr Kimura the day before yesterday.

Exercise 7 📼

Play the part of Mr or Mrs Smith in the following dialogue:

Mr Maeda: Ima nanji desu ka?
Mr/sSmith: .... (It's half past ten)
Mr Maeda: Ima Itô-san wa nani o shite imasu ka?
Mr/sSmith: .... (He's working at the office at this moment)
Mr Maeda: Anata wa nani o shitai desu ka?
Mr/sSmith: .... (Go to the Ginza and do some shopping)
Mr Maeda: Nani o kaitai desu ka?
Mr/sSmith: .... (Some toothpaste. Is there a chemist's?)
Mr Maeda: Hai, tabakoya no yoko ni arimasu.
Mr/sSmith: .... (Ah! I've remembered! I want to buy some cigarettes)
Mr Maeda: Watakushi ni tabako o katte kudasaimasen ka?
Mr/sSmith: .... (One packet?)
Mr Maeda: Sô desu. Arigatô.
Mr/sSmith: .... (How many do you smoke a day?)
Mr Maeda: Nijippon gurai suimasu. Anata wa?
Mr/sSmith: .... (About fifteen. It's bad for the health, isn't it!)
Mr Maeda: Sô desu nê!

BY TAXI AND BY TRAIN

10.1 DIALOGUES 📼

Dialogue 1

On the pavement.

Mrs Itô: Ame ga futte imasu kara takushii de ikimashô ka?

Mrs Foster: Densha wa nanji ni demasu ka?

Mrs Itô: Jippun oki ni demasu. Mite kudasai. Ano depaato no mae ni takushii ga imasu.

Getting into the taxi.

Mrs Itô: Yûrakuchô e itte kudasai. Massugu itte ano ôkina tatemono no tokoro o migi e magatte kudasai. Sore kara mittsume no kado o hidari e magatte kudasai.

Taxidriver: Hai. Wakarimashita.

Mr Foster: Mary, nimotsu ga arimasu ka?

Mrs Foster:Hitotsu, futatsu, mittsu, yottsu, itsutsu, muttsu . . . arimasu yo!

Mr Foster: Mô hitotsu arimasu!

Mrs Foster: Ah, sore mo motte kite kudasai. Arigatô!

Mr Foster: Sayonara. Ki o tsukete kudasai.

In the taxi.

Mrs Itô: Mochiron chikatetsu wa motto hayai desu keredomo anata wa nimotsu ga takusan arimasu kara takushii wa benri desu nê.

Mrs Foster: Yûrakuchô wa tôi desu ka?

Mrs Itô: Iie, amari tôku wa arimasen. Chikai desu.

Mrs Foster: Nampun gurai kakarimasu ka?

Mrs Itô: Untenshu-san? Nampun gurai?

Taxidriver: Kuruma ga konde imasu kara nijippun gurai kakaru deshô.

At the end of the taxi-ride.

Mrs Itô: Ikura desu ka?

Taxidriver: Nanahyaku-en desu.

Mrs Itô: Sen-en de otsuri o itadakemasu ka.

Taxidriver: Sambyaku-en no okaeshi desu. Arigatô.

Mrs Foster: Chikatetsu nara ikura deshô ka?

Mrs Itô: Hyaku nijû-en desu.

Mrs Foster: Sô desu ka. Amari takaku wa arimasen.

Mrs Itô: Sô desu ne. Yasui desu ne. Takushii wa chikatetsu yori takai desu ga ima chikatetsu wa konde imasu kara takushii no hô ga ii desu.

Dialogue 2 📼

At the station ticket-office.

Mrs Itô: Nagahara made nimai kudasai.

Clerk: Gohyaku yonjû-en itadakimasu.

Mrs Itô: Roppyaku-en de otsuri o kudasai.

Clerk: Arigatô gozaimasu. Rokujû-en no okaeshi desu.

Mrs Itô: Arigatô.

In the train.

Mrs Itô: Gotanda de norikaemasu.

Mrs Foster: Yûrakuchô kara Gotanda made eki wa ikutsu arimasu ka?

Mrs Itô: Eeto ... Shimbashi, Hamamatsuchô, Tamachi, Shinagawa, Ôsaki, Gotanda. Muttsu arimasu.

Mrs Foster: Gotanda kara Nagahara made wa?

Mrs Itô: Itsutsu arimasu.

Mrs Foster: Eki no namae o mimashita. Eigo deshita!

Mrs Itô: Sô desu ne. Eki no namae o yomu koto ga dekimasu nê. Kiite kudasai! Eki e tsuku mae ni shashô-san ga eki no namae o iimasu. Desu kara gaikokujin nimo wakarimasu.

Mrs Foster: Benri desu nê.

Mrs Itô: Ah! Hidari o mite kudasai. Fune ga imasu. Tôkyô-wan desu. Migi ni chiisana jinja ga arimasu. Akai torii o miru koto ga dekimasu ka? Ano ôkina ki wa sugi to iimasu.

Mrs Foster: Kirei desu ne. Jinja e ikitai desu.

Mrs Itô: Ano, uchi e kaette tonari no jinja e ikimashô ka? Omoshiroi deshô. Ima ame ga yande imasu kara uchi e kaette kara sampo shimashô ka?

10.2 VOCABULARY

takushii	taxi
futte	(-te form of furu, to rain)
densha	train
demasu	leave (present tense of deru)
oki	every
depaato	department store
massugu	straight ahead
ôkina	colloquial form of ôkii, large
tatemono	building
tokoro	place
migi	right-hand
magatte	(-te form of magaru, to turn)
mittsume	third
kado	corner
hidari	left-hand
nimotsu	packages
hitotsu	one
mittsu	three

yottsu	four
itsutsu	five
muttsu	six
motte	(-te form of motsu, to hold)
motte kitte kudasai	please bring
sayonara	good-bye
chikatetsu	underground railway
motto	more
hayai	quick
tôi	far
amari (with negative)	(not) very
chikai	close, near
kakarimasu	(present tense of kakaru, to take (time))
untenshu	driver (unten suru, to drive)
konde	(-te form of komu, to crowd, be crowded)
yori	than
. . . no hô ga ii	is preferable
itadaku	take, accept (a polite verb)
norikaemasu	(present tense of norikaeru (a weak verb)) to change (station)
eki	station
ikutsu	how many
. . . koto ga dekimasu	are able to (from dekiru, a weak verb)
kiite	(-te form of kiku, to hear)
tsuku	arrive
shashô	conductor
fune	ship
wan	bay
chiisana	colloquial form of chiisai
jinja	Shintô shrine
torii	shrine gate
ki	tree
sugi	Japanese cedar, cryptomeria
kaette	(-te form of kaeru, to return)
tonari no	neighbouring, nearby
yande	(-te form of yamu, to stop)
kara (after -te form)	after

10.3 EXPLANATIONS

(a) Transport

Taxis are plentiful and relatively inexpensive. What is surprising, though, is that few drivers know their way around! It is essential for the passenger to know where he or she is headed and to be able to express simple directions. You never tip the driver (tipping is *very* uncommon in Japan) and at the end of the journey he will open the door for you automatically.

The underground railway system is highly efficient, though at peak-hours it becomes tremendously crowded. The names of all stations are written up in rômaji (Roman script) and you can get a map of the subway system in rômaji as well.

There is an overhead 'ring-railway' round Tokyo called the Yamanote-sen. This links all the main termini and all the stations that send out lines into the suburbs and surrounding dormitory-towns. Mrs. Itô and Mrs Foster are circling round the eastern side of the city to take a suburban line out to the south. This happens to be another privately-owned railway though in different hands from JR (Japan Railways), but you can buy one ticket at any station whether you are 'mixing your lines' or not. All stations now have automatic ticket-dispensers and you must consult the map above them to see what *price you have to pay.*

Public transport of all kinds is swift, regular and reliable. Japanese trains *never* leave a second after the scheduled time and if they are held up (which rarely ever happens) an apology is handsomely made.

The conductor announces the name of each station as the train pulls in.

The word for a long-distance train is kisha (literally, steam-train).

The word used in this exercise, densha (literally, electric train – compare denwa, electric speech, i.e. telephone), refers to *local* or *suburban trains.*

(b) Shrines

Shintô (the Way of the Gods) is the age-old religion of Japan. Technically, the *entire land is sacred*, but the innumerable shrines celebrate particularly holy places. Each shrine has an *open gate*, usually painted red, called a torii (a place for birds to perch – tori, a bird, i, to be or exist – you have met this in the word imasu) and a courtyard usually planted with trees – the sugi, a tall evergreen of characteristic shape, especially being regarded as a sacred tree.

(c) -oki

The suffix -oki means every (other):

jippun oki   every ten minutes

(d) Directions

massugu iku   to go straight ahead
migi e magaru   to turn right
hidari e magaru   to turn left

You use the particle o with magaru, referring to *street-corners*:

Ano kado o hidari e magatte kudasai
Please turn right at that corner.
Ano tatemono no tokoro o migi e magatte kudasai.
Turn right at that building over there (literally, at the place of that building please turn right).

(e) More 'all-purpose' counters

As promised in Chapter 9, here are some more 'all-purpose' counters:

hitotsu   1
futatsu   2
mittsu   3
yottsu   4
itsutsu   5
muttsu   6
ikutsu   how many

(f) The -te form (4): linked verbs

This usage is really the same as **(iii)(9.3(e))** except that *two verbs* are joined rather than whole sentences. In order to say 'bring' in Japanese, you say 'hold and come', or, 'holding, come':

Ano nimotsu o motte kite kudasai.
Please bring that package (literally, holding the package, please bring it).

In order to say 'take away', you use motte with iku (hold and go), so 'Take away that bauble!' would be:

Ano (*or* sono!) mono o motte itte kudasai.

(g) amari with the negative

Amari tôku wa arimasen. It is not very far.

(h) deshô after the infinitive
Like the construction given in Chapter **8.3(j)** this gives the feeling of *probability* rather than certainty:

Nijippun gurai kakaru deshô.
It will probably take about twenty minutes.

(i) Comparatives (see Grammar Summary **6(d)**)
Yori means 'than', but that is all you need to do to make the comparative:

takushii wa takai desu   taxis are expensive
takushii wa chikatetsu yori takai desu.
Taxis are more expensive than the tube.
Kyôto wa tôi desu.   Kyoto is a long way away.
Kyôto wa Yokohama yori tôi desu.
Kyoto is further than Yokohama.

motto is used when there is no 'than':

motto hayai desu it's quicker

(j) ... no hô ga ii
This is another useful comparative construction. hô means 'side' or 'direction', hence:

takushii no hô ga ii desu   Taxis are preferable (i.e.,
the taxi's side is good
(= better))

(k) ôkii and chiisai
Although ôkii and chiisai are true adjectives, in spoken Japanese they are more often treated like benri or genki which are not (**see chapter 6.3(k)**):

ôkina tatemono   a large building
chiisana jinja   a small shrine

(Although, of course, ôkii tatemono and chiisai jinja are perfectly correct.)

(l) To be able to do something
Use the infinitive followed by koto ga dekimasu. koto means 'an abstract thing' (unlike mono which means 'a concrete thing'), so by adding koto to a verb you get a verb-noun: miru koto = the act of seeing. dekiru means to be possible, to be capable, hence:

> miru koto ga dekimasu   you can see

(m)   mae ni after the infinitive

> eki e tsuku mae ni before arriving at the station

(n)   Strong verbs ending in -ru
Strong verbs ending in -ru have a -te form -tte:

aru	atte
kaeru	kaette
hairu	haitte

(o)   The -te form (5): after
The word kara used with the -te form means 'after doing something':

> uchi e kaette kara   after we get home
> ame ga futte kara   after it stops raining

Be careful not to confuse this construction with kara *after the present* or *past tense of the verb*:

> ame ga futte imasu kara   because it is raining
> ame ga yande imasu   as it's stopping raining
> kara
> tegami o kakimashita   as I wrote a letter
> kara

(p)   *imasu*
With people, animals and means of transport this verb is used instead of *arimasu*:

kodomo ga imasu   there's a child
tori ga imasu   there's a bird
takushii ga imasu   there's a taxi

10.5 EXERCISES

Section A
Exercise 1
Make comparative sentences (**Example**: Takushii wa takai desu.
(Chikatetsu) – Takushii wa chikatetsu yori takai desu.):
1. Depaato wa tôi desu. (Yûbinkyoku)
2. Nihongo wa omoshiroi desu. (Eigo)
3. Furansugo wa yasashii desu. (Doitsugo)
4. Natsu wa atsui desu. (Aki)
5. Shimbun wa yasui desu. (Zasshi)

Exercise 2
Use kara with the -te form (**Example**: Uchi e (kaeru) sampo o
shimashô – Uchi e kaette kara sampo o shimashô.):
1. Gohan o (taberu) nani o shimashô ka?
2. Tegami o (kaku) yûbinkyoku e ikimasu.
3. Tomodachi ni (au) Tôkyô e ikimashita.
4. Migi e (magaru) jinja o mite kudasai.
5. Hon o (yomu) ocha o nomitai desu.

Exercise 3
Nani o suru koto ga dekimasu ka? What can you do?
(**Example**: (see Mt Fuji) – Fuji-san o miru koto ga dekimasu.)
1. (Read Japanese)
2. (Speak German)
3. (Drink saké)
4. (Go to Tokyo to-morrow)
5. (Buy an expensive dictionary)

Exercise 4
How many are there? (**Example**: Kippu ga (1) arimasu – Kippu ga
ichimai arimasu.)
1. Kami ga (2) arimasu.
2. Naganegi ga (6) arimasu.
3. Eki ga (5) arimasu.
4. Ebi ga (5) arimasu.
5. Gaikokujin o (7) mimashita.
6. Kitte o (3) kaimashita.

7. Tabako ga (3) arimasu.
8. Denwa ga (3) arimasu.
9. Teeburu ga (4) arimasu.
10. Pen ga (1) arimasu.

Exercise 5
Probability not certainty. (**Example**: Ano hito wa koko e kimasu, That fellow will be coming here – Ano hito wa koko e kuru deshô, He will probably come.)
1. Mainichi sampo shimasu.
2. Jippun kakarimasu.
3. Massugu ikimasu.
4. Tomodachi wa ehagaki o kakimasu.
5. Ano Nihonjin wa Eigo de hanashimasu.

Exercise 6
Give the opposite. (**Example**: (Tôi) – Amari tôku wa arimasen. Chikai desu.)
1. (Chiisai)
2. (Yasashii)
3. (Takai)
4. (Muzukashii)
5. (Ii)

Exercise 7
How long will it take? (**Example**: About ten minutes – Jippun gurai kakarimasu.)
1. About five minutes.
2. About fifteen minutes.
3. About twenty minutes.
4. About thirty minutes.
5. About forty minutes.
6. About fifty minutes.

Section B
Exercise 8
Densha wa nanji ni demasu ka? What time does the train leave? (**Example**: At ten o'clock – Jûji ni demasu.)
1. At half past two.
2. At five to three.
3. At seven fifteen.
4. Every five minutes.
5. Every thirty-five minutes.

Exercise 9
Translate:
1. Osake o nonde kara sakana o tabemashita.
2. Osake wa oishii desu kara nomimashô.
3. Tôkyô e itte kara kaimono o shimashita.
4. Tôkyô e ikimasu kara Satô-san ni au koto ga dekimasu.
5. Yuki ga futte imasu kara kaerimashô.
6. Yuki ga yande imasu kara sampo o shitai desu.
7. Denwa de hanashite kara hatarakimashita.
8. Kuruma ga konde imasu kara chikatetsu de ikimashô.

Exercise 10
Give directions:
1. Go straight ahead.
2. Turn left.
3. Take the second turning on the right.
4. Turn left at that big post-office.
5. Turn right at the tobacconist's.

Exercise 11
Translate into Japanese:
1. I went to the station by taxi.
2. I came to Japan by boat.
3. I returned to Yurakucho by underground.
4. I want to go to Kyoto by train.
5. I went to the department-store by car.

REVISION AND SELF-ASSESSMENT TESTS FOR CHAPTERS 6–10

Do the full test and mark it, using the mark-scheme suggested. *If* you made any mistakes, make sure you go back and revise the relevant chapter(s) before proceeding with Chapter 11.

Section 1
Put in the appropriate counters:
1. Kitte o (10) kaimashita.
2. Teeburu ga (2) arimasu.
3. Naganegi o (10) kaimashita.
4. Ocha o (3) nomimashita.
5. Nimotsu o (5) motte kimashita.

(Score: 5)

Section 2
What are you doing at this moment?
1. Tegami o kaku.
2. Kaimono o suru.
3. Ebi o kau.
4. Nihongo de hanasu.
5. Tôkyô e kuru.

(Score: 5)

Section 3
Link the two sentences together:
1. Jimusho de hatarakimashita. Tegami o kakimashita.
2. Tôkyô e ikimashita. Kaimono o shimashita.
3. Uchi e kaerimashita. Gohan o tabemashita.
4. Gohan o tabemashita. Shimbun o yomimashita.
5. Shimbun o yomimashita. Osake o nomimashita.

(Score: 5)

Section 4
Put in the appropriate particles:
1. Otera wa Kiyomizudera —— iimasu.
2. Teeburu —— ue —— nani —— arimasu —— ?
3. Watakushi —— Nihonjin —— aimashita.
4. Kôcha —— shimashô.
5. Otera —— mimashita.
6. Yûrakuchô —— Gotanda —— eki —— muttsu
arimasu.
7. Benri —— hon deshô.
8. Ano hito —— Nihongo —— yoku wakarimasu.

(Score: 15)

Section 5.
Translate into Japanese:
1. Go straight ahead. (2)
2. Turn left. (2)
3. Turn right at the third corner. (4)
4. Turn left at that big building. (2)

(Score: Total 10)

Section 6

Read the following conversation or listen to it on your cassette. If you
have the cassette, do *not* read the text. Then answer the questions
underneath.

Mr Itô: Nihyaku gojû-en no kitte o sammai kudasai.
Clerk: Nanahyaku gojû-en desu.
Mr Itô: Ah omoidashimashita! Kesa tegami o nimai kakima-
shita. Doitsu made kono tegami o okuritai no desu
ga ikura desu ka?
Clerk: Doitsu desu ka? Chotto matte kudasai. Eeto . . . Doitsu
nara sambyaku gojû-en desu.
Mr Itô: Gomai kudasai. Ashita mo tegami o kakimasu kara.
Clerk: Sô desu ka? Ano . . . nanahyaku gojû-en to sen nana-
hyaku gojû-en de nisen gohyaku-en desu.
Mr Itô: Sumimasen. Ichiman-en satsu shika arimasen ga ii
desu ka?
Clerk: Kekkô desu yo. Nanasen gohyaku-en no otsuri desu.
Mr Itô: Arigatô gozaimasu. Ah sumimasen. Pen wa arimasu
ka?
Clerk: Hai. Ano teeburu no ue ni pen ga nihon arimasu.
Mr Itô: Arigatô. Kyô wa nannichi desu ka?

Clerk: Jûgatsu jûsannichi desu.
Mr Itô: Ima nanji desu ka?
Clerk: Ima niji nijûgofun desu.
Mr Itô: Sô desu ka. Arigatô.

1. How many stamps does Mr Itô first ask for?
2. How much does the first purchase come to?
3. Which foreign country does he enquire about?
4. How much do the two purchases come to?
5. What amount of money does he apologise for handing over?
6. What is the change?
7. Where are the pens and how many are there?
8. What is the date?
9. What is the time?

(Score: Total 20–score 4 for Qu.7)

Section 7
Translate into Japanese:
1. There is a chemist's next to the post office. (5)
2. There is a telephone in front of the fruit shop. (5)

(Score: Total 10)

Section 8
Write out in full:
25 000 yen
36 000 yen
360 yen
645 yen
3700 yen

(Score: 10)

Section 9
Give the opposite:
1. Hatarakimashita.
2. Yasui desu.
3. Chikai desu.
4. Karada ni warui desu.
5. Nihongo wa muzukashii desu.

(Score 5)

Section 10
Translate into English:
1. Ame ga yande imasu kara sampo o shimashô ka?
2. Ikura desu ka? Mada wakarimasen.
3. Raishû no kin'yôbi ni mata kimashô.
4. Sukoshi muzukashii desu ga omoshiroi desu.
5. Tôkyô e kite kara jinja o mimashita.

(**Score: 10**)

Self assessment grades: Maximum total score = 95.
Over 80: Excellent
45 – 80: Satisfactory
Under 45: More revision needed

CHAPTER 11

FEELING ILL

11.1 DIALOGUES

Dialogue 1

Mr Foster tells Mrs Itô about his wife's health.

Mrs Itô: Ohayô gozaimasu, Foster-san. Ame ga yande otenki
ga yoku narimashita ne.

Mr Foster: Sô desu nê.

Mrs Itô: Kinô anata wa onaka ga sukoshi itaku narimashita ne. Kyô wa ikaga desu ka? Mô genki ni narimashita ka?

Mr Foster: Watakushi wa yoku narimashita ga kanai wa atama ga itai desu.

Mrs Itô: Sô desu ka. Sore wa ikemasen ne. Netsu ga demashita ka?

Mr Foster: Sukoshi demashita. Nodo mo itaku narimashita.

Mrs Itô: Tabun kaze o hikimashita nê.

Mr Foster: Sô desu ne. Yokka ni ame ga takusan furimashita keredomo kanai wa kaimono o shitakute mise e aruite ikimashita.

Mrs Itô: Futsuka mae ni samuku narimashita nê. Ki o tsukena- kereba narimasen. Samukute otenki ga warui desu kara.

Mr Foster: Kokonoka ni watakushitachi wa Kyôto e ikitai node kanai wa genki ni naranakereba narimasen nê.

Mrs Itô: Sô desu nê.

Dialogue 2

A little later.

Mr Foster: Sumimasen. Kanai wa nodo ga itai node mizu o ippai nomitai yô desu.

Mrs Itô: Sô desu ka. Sore dewa watakushi ga mizu o motte ikimashô.

Mr Foster: Iie, watakushi ga motte ikimasu yo. Daidokoro e itte mizu o motte kimasu.

Mrs Itô: Anata wa soko ni kakete itte kudasai. Watakushi ga okusama o mi ni ikimasu yo.

Mr Foster: Itô-san wa shinsetsu desu ne. Arigatô gozaimasu.

Dialogue 3

In Mrs Foster's bedroom.

Mrs Itô: Ohayô gozaimasu. Goshujin no ohanashi dewa anata wa guai ga warui sô desu ne. Hontô desu ka?

Mrs Foster: Hontô desu yo. Nodo ga itai node amari hanasu koto ga dekimasen.

Mrs Itô: Atama mo itai desu ka?

Mrs Foster: Sakuban yori ii desu keredomo mada itai desu.

Mrs Itô: Oishasan e ikanakereba narimasen ne. Foster-san wa aruku koto ga dekimasu ka?

Mrs Foster: Dekimasu yo. Oishasan no ie wa tôi desu ka?

Mrs Itô: Iie, aruite tatta no gofun desu. Asagohan o tabete kara ikimashô. Ano . . . nani o tabetai desu ka? Tamago? Pan?

Mrs Foster: Nani mo tabetaku wa arimasen. Nanika nomitai desu.

Mrs Itô: Nani o nomitai desu ka? Kôhii? Kôcha?

Mrs Foster: Ocha no hô ga ii deshô. Arimasu ka?

Mrs Itô: Mochiron arimasu. Chotto matte kudasai. Daidokoro e itte, gofun go ni ocha o motte kimasu.

Mrs Foster: Arigatô gozaimasu.

11.2 VOCABULARY

narimashita	became, has become (from naru)
onaka	stomach
itai	painful
atama	head
mô	already
sore wa ikemasen	that's too bad, that's a shame
netsu	fever
demashita	started, has broken out (from deru)
nodo	throat
kaze	a cold
hiku	catch (of colds)
yokka	the fourth day, four days
mise	shop(s)
futsuka	the second day, two days
samui	cold
ki o tsukenakereba narimasen	you must take care
kokonoka	the ninth day, nine days
node	on account of, since, as
genki ni naranakereba narimasen	she must get better
yô desu	seems to
daidokoro	kitchen
mitsukeru	look for, fetch, find
kakeru	sit down (on a chair) (weak verb)
mi ni iku	go and see
shinsetsu	kind, considerate

no (o)hanashi dewa	according to what someone has said
guai	condition, state, health
sakuban	yesterday evening
mada (without negative)	still
(o)isha(san)	doctor
ie	house
tatta	only, just
tamago	egg
pan	bread
nanika	anything
go ni	after (as in gogo, p.m.)

11.3 EXPLANATIONS

(a) Doctors and medicine

A doctor is so important that he merits two honorifics. Isha is the word for 'doctor' but one says oishasan. Ha is 'a tooth' or 'teeth', and so haisha is 'tooth-doctor' or 'dentist'.

The basic phrases relevant to illness are kaze o hiku, 'to catch a cold', and netsu ga deru, 'to start a fever', 'break out in a fever'. Byôki is the opposite of genki and means 'ill', but this is, as it were, an impersonal word and is not used when talking to a person. Guai, 'a state' or 'condition', is used:

guai ga warui/ii desu.

itai, 'painful', is used to express aches and pains:

nodo ga itai desu	I have a sore throat
atama ga itai desu	I have a headache
onaka ga itai desu	I have a stomach-ache
ha ga itai desu	I have toothache

Japanese doctors tend not to make house-calls. They very often issue their own medicines there and then. There is a National Insurance system in Japan but this is on a repayment basis, so the patient must be prepared to pay the doctor or dentist after treatment. Doctors tend to specialise rather – for children, for women, for certain complaints – and so it is as well to check before making an appointment or visiting a surgery.

There is a good deal of 'alternative medicine' – acupuncture and its somewhat more alarming counterpart 'moxa cautery', when the

specialist sets fire to little cones of herbs on the patient's bare skin!
Advertisements for doctors of all varieties are clearly visible in the
street, and so it is advisable yet again to master the written language.

(b)   naru
After the adverbial form of a true adjective – remember, you substitute -ku for the final -i (**warui, waruku**) except with ii which has
the irregular form **yoku** – or after ni after any other word, **naru**
means *to become*:

otenki ga yoku narima-shita	it has become fine
samuku narimashita	it has got cold
genki ni narimashita	I feel better (literally, I have become well)

(c)   The -te form of adjectives
Adjectives, too, have their -te form: take off the final -i and put
-kute:

> **Samukute otenki ga warui desu.**
> The weather is cold and unpleasant (literally, being cold the
> weather is unpleasant).

As verbs in the -tai form have become true adjectives, they have their
-te form also in -kute:

Kaimono o shitakute mise e aruite ikimashita. She wanted to go
shopping and she walked to the shops. (see Grammar summary **15**)

(d)   the . . . wa . . . ga pattern
This is a near equivalent of the English 'I have' . . . ; 'you have' . . .
The **wa** tells us *who we are thinking about* and the **ga** is the *subject of
the verb*.

watakushi wa nodo ga itai desu	I have a sore throat (literally, as for me the throat is sore)

Compare the following examples:

Goshujin wa atama ga itai desu.	Your husband has a head-ache.

Itô-san wa me ga utsukushii desu.	Mrs Itô has beautiful eyes.
Watakushi wa okane ga arimasu	I've got some money.
Itô-san wa kippu ga arimasu.	Mr Itô has the tickets.

(e) Dates (2)

You have learnt the days of the month from the 11th to the 31st, omitting the 14th, 20th, 24th. Here are the other ones:

tsuitachi	1st
futsuka	2nd
mikka	3rd
yokka	4th
itsuka	5th
muika	6th
nanoka	7th
yôka	8th
kokonoka	9th
tôka	10th
jûyokka	14th
hatsuka	20th
nijûyokka	24th

(f) Negative infinitives

To form the negative infinitive of a *weak* verb, you substitute -nai for the final -ru – e.g., taberu, to eat; tabenai, not to eat.

To form the negative infinitive of a *strong* verb, you alter the final vowel to -a and add -nai – e.g.

iku, to go; ikanai, not to go
naru, to become, naranai, not to become

Do not worry too much about this at the moment, but it is very important because we use this negative to form 'must' ideas.

tabenai	not to eat
tabenakereba	if you do not eat
tabenakereba narimasen	you or I or he must eat (literally, if you do not eat, it will not do)
iku	to go
ikanai	not to go

ikanakereba narimasen	you or I or he must go
ki o tsukenakereba nari-masen	you must take care
genki ni naranakereba narimasen	she must get better

(g) node

node meaning 'because', 'on account of', 'since', 'as', is practically interchangeable with kara, but with node there tends to be an *intenser connection* between the two clauses:

Kyôto e ikitai node kanai wa genki ni naranakereba narimasen.
As we want to go to Kyoto my wife simply must get well.
Kanai wa nodo ga itai node mizu o nomitai desu
As she has a sore throat my wife wants a drink of water.

(h) . . . yô desu . . . sô desu

If you want to distance yourself somewhat from a direct statement (something on the whole the Japanese prefer doing whenever possible!) you conclude the sentence with . . . yô desu, to imply 'it seems that', and with . . . sô desu to imply you have been told something:

mizu o ippai nomitai yô desu
it would seem she wants a drink of water
anata wa guai ga warui sô desu
I've been told you're not feeling too good

(i) According to . . . :

| Itô-san no hanashi dewa. | According to what Mr Itô said. |
| Goshujin no ohanashi dewa. | According to your husband. |

The honorific is used when referring to somebody connected to the person you are speaking to.

11.4 EXERCISES

Section A
Exercise 1
Give the date in Japanese:
1. July 1
2. October 6
3. January 14
4. May 9
5. June 3
6. February 2
7. March 7
8. April 10
9. August 5
10. September 20

Exercise 2
Translate linking the adjectives and using their -te form:
1. The car is big and red.
2. The book is small and black.
3. Japanese is easy and interesting.
4. My throat is painful and inflamed (red).

Exercise 3
Convert the following statements (**Example:** Samui desu – Samuku narimashita.):
1. Taihen atsui desu.
2. Nihongo wa muzukashii desu.
3. Kodomo wa ôkii desu.
4. Onaka ga itai desu.
5. Warui desu.

Exercise 4
Translate the following:
1. Mr Itô has a car.
2. I've got some stamps.
3. Mr Yamada's throat hurts.
4. Mrs Satô has a headache.
5. He's got a large house.

Exercise 5

What must you do? (**Example:** Kyôto e iku – Kyôto e ikanakereba narimasen.)

1. Osake o nomu.
2. Fuji-san o miru.
3. Uchi e kaeru.
4. Denwa de hanasu.
5. Ki o tsukeru.
6. Yasumu.
7. Genki ni naru.
8. Asahan o taberu.
9. Gotanda de norikaeru.
10. Biiru o mitsukeru.

Exercise 6

What is wrong with Mr Kawakami? (**Example:** Kawakami-san wa te ga itai desu. – Mr Kawakami's hand hurts.)

1. Kawakami-san wa onaka ga itai desu.
2. Kawakami-san wa atama mo itai desu.
3. Kawakami-san wa kaze o hikimashita.
4. Kawakami-san wa netsu ga demashita.
5. Kawakami-san wa nodo ga itai desu.

Section B
Exercise 7

Itsu Nihon e kimashita ka?

1. Yesterday.
2. Four days ago.
3. In 1977.
4. On November 8.
5. Ten days ago.
6. On December 24.
7. At 9.30 a.m.
8. The day before yesterday.
9. Yesterday evening.
10. This morning.

Exercise 8 📼

Play the part of Mr Smith in the following dialogue:

Mr Yamada: Ame ga futte imasu ka?
MrSmith: .... (No, it's stopped.)
Mr Yamada: Atsui desu ka?
MrSmith: .... (No, it's turned cold.)

Mr Yamada: Itô-san no hanashi dewa okusama wa nodo ga itai sô desu. Kyô wa ikaga desu ka?
MrSmith: .... (She has caught a cold.)
Mr Yamada: Sô desu ka. Sore wa ikemasen nê.
MrSmith: .... (She has a fever.)
Mr Yamada: Sô desu ka? Oishasan e ikimashita ka?
MrSmith: .... (Not yet.)
Mr Yamada: Oishasan e ikanakereba narimasen nê. Oishasan no ie wa tôi desu ka?
MrSmith: .... (No, not far. It is close.)
Mr Yamada: Anata wa ikaga desu ka? Ogenki desu ka?
MrSmith: .... (I have a headache.)
Mr Yamada: Hontô desu ka?
MrSmith: .... (Yes, really.)
Mr Yamada: Otaku e kaeritai desu ka?
MrSmith: .... (I'm sorry. Yes. I must go home.)
Mr Yamada: Ki o tsukete kudasai.
MrSmith: .... (Thank you very much.)

Exercise 9
Translate into Japanese:
1. I want to eat an egg and drink some Indian tea.
2. I want to go to Yokohama and buy a despatch-case.
3. Mrs Itô went into the kitchen and fetched some cakes.
4. My wife wants to go for a walk and do some shopping.
5. We met a Japanese and spoke Japanese.

AT THE DOCTOR'S

12.1 DIALOGUES 📼

Dialogue 1

Mrs Itô introduces her friend.

Mrs Itô: Kono kata wa Foster-san to iu tomodachi desu. Tôka mae ni Nihon e kite ima uchi ni irasshaimasu.

Doctor: Sô desu ka? Igirisu no kata desu ka? Anata wa Nihongo ga wakarimasu ka?

Mrs Foster: Sukoshi wakarimasu keredomo anata no hanashi ga wakaranakereba Itô-san ga yakushite kudasaimasu.

Mrs Itô: Watakushi wa Eigo o yoku hanasu koto wa dekimasen ga tonikaku setsumei shimashô.

Mrs Foster: Arigatô gozaimasu. Ano . . . yukkuri hanashite kudasai!

Doctor: Dô shimashita ka?

Mrs Foster: Atama ga itai desu. Netsu ga sukoshi dete nodo mo itaku narimashita.

Doctor: Taion ga sanjû hachido sambu arimasu. Hidoku wa arimasen keredomo otaku e kaette yasumanakereba narimasen.

Mrs Foster: Asatte shujin to issho ni Kyôto e ikimasu. Daijôbu desu ka?

Doctor: Heinetsu ni naranakereba Kyôto e iku koto wa dekimasen keredomo kono aoi kusuri o nomeba hayaku genki ni narimasu yo.

Dialogue 2 🔲
They discuss the medicine.

Mrs Foster: Itsu sono aoi kusuri o nomanakereba narimasen ka?

Doctor: Shokuzen ni nonde kudasai. Mainichi sando desu. Asagohan no mae, hirugohan no mae, yûgohan no mae desu. Wakarimashita ka?

Mrs Foster: Yoku wakarimashita. Nani o taberu koto ga dekimasu ka?

Doctor: Nan demo kekkô desu keredomo nodo ga itai yô desu kara takusan nonde kudasai.

Mrs Itô: Nani ga hoshii desu ka, Foster-san?

Mrs Foster: Mizu ga hoshii desu.

Doctor: Kono kusuri wa oishii desu ka?

Mrs Foster: Iie! Dai kirai desu! Totemo mazui desu.

Doctor: Taihen ii kusuri desu ga aji wa hontô ni warui desu. Okinodoku desu ne.

Mrs Foster: Demo, daijôbu desu yo.

Dialogue 3 🔲
Afterwards.

Mrs Itô: Sâ, hayaku kaeranakereba narimasen. Anata wa hirugohan o tabete kara beddo e ikanakereba narimasen yo. Beddo de hirugohan o tabetai desu ka?

Mrs Foster: Iie, Itô-san. Hirugohan o tabete kara yasumimasu keredomo ima wa beddo e ikitaku wa arimasen.

Mrs Itô: Terebi o mitai desu ka?

Mrs Foster: Hai. Terebi ga suki desu.

Mrs Itô: Koshikakete ocha o nominagara terebi o mite kudasai. Nihongo desu kara anata no tame ni narimasu yo.

Mrs Foster: Mâ Itô-san! Watakushi wa byôki desu yo. Benkyô shitaku wa arimasen!

Mrs Itô: Mainichi benkyô shite kudasai! Benkyô sureba ojôzu ni narimasu!

12.2 VOCABULARY

irasshaimasu	here, the polite form of imasu, is
yakushite	(-te form of yakusu, to translate)

kudasaimasu	will be so kind as to
tonikaku	anyway
setsumei suru	explain
yukkuri	slowly
dô	how, in what way
dô shimashita ka	what's wrong
taion	temperature
-do	degree
-bu	decimal tenth
hidoku wa arimasen	is not serious (from hidoi, serious, severe)
daijôbu	all right
heinetsu	normal temperature
aoi	pale green
kusuri	medicine
shokuzen	before meals
-do	times
sando	three times
takusan	a lot, a great deal
hoshii	want
kirai	dislike
dai kirai	very much dislike
totemo	extremely, thoroughly
mazui	unpleasant, unsavoury
(o)kinodoku	too bad, I'm sorry to hear that
taihen	very
aji	taste
beddo	Western-style bed
terebi	television
suki	like
koshikakeru	sit down
sâ	come on!
-nagara	while
tame ni naru	be beneficial to, be useful to
benkyô suru	study
mâ	hey! hold on a minute!

12.3 EXPLANATIONS

(a) More polite phrases

The verb irassharu is used as a polite substitute for iku, to go, kuru, to come and iru, to be.

We have met kudasai, which means 'please', after the -te form of a verb: kono kusuri o nonde kudasai, please drink this medicine, *or* please take this medicine (because you always use the verb nomu, even if the medicine is in tablet form). Kudasaimasu is used when you are asking someone to do you a favour:

> Itô-san ga yakushite kudasaimasu ka?
> Would Mrs Itô be so kind as to translate?

(b) More on the Japanese house
In a traditional Japanese house, one sleeps on a padded mattress called a futon spread out on the tatami floor. As the tatami mats (three feet by six feet and bordered with black or dark brown ribbon) are suspended over the floor proper so that they 'give' slightly, this is a deliciously comfortable way to sleep. In the morning, the bed-clothes and the futon are hung out of the window on dry sunny days and, when they are aired, they are rolled up and stowed in a wall-cupboard with sliding panel doors called fusuma. Thus, the 'bedroom' becomes another room, and all the waste space that a Western bed represents in the daytime does not exist.

There is always a raised alcove in a room floored with tatami called the tokonoma. Here, a prized scroll – a landscape or an example of calligraphy – will hang and there will probably be a beautiful vase with a flower arrangement. Such is the Japanese concept of politeness that an honoured guest will always be seated with his or her back to the tokonoma lest it be thought that the host or hostess is 'showing off' a precious painting or an ability to arrange flowers.

It must sadly be confessed that nowadays one sees a television set in the tokonoma of some houses!

(c) The media
Television is very popular in Japan and there are many channels to choose from.

NHK (Nihon Hôsô Kyokai, Japan Broadcasting Company) is the government-run organisation. Its two channels are nationwide – one for general viewing and one educational. This latter channel often transmits operas and concerts given by visiting artists.

The other channels are all *commercially run*, and have programmes interrupted by advertisements. These are regionally organised so that each district in Japan has different commercial stations.

Serials are extremely popular – often tales of the Middle Ages more or less true to recorded history. Some are drawn from novels concerning nineteenth-century Japan. Many serials last a whole year.

The situation with *radio* is similar. NHK is the one station that has nationwide coverage. Western music of all kinds is well known and well liked but traditional Japanese singing is hugely popular and the singers, male and female, have star status.

(d) wa **and** ga

In each chapter so far you have seen many examples of the use of these rather tricky particles. It must be confessed that foreigners find their correct use extremely difficult – so often when one says **wa**, a Japanese friend will courteously suggest that **ga** is better, and vice versa.

However . . . basically, **wa** is an *attention-calling* particle (and as such is frequently tacked on to ni or de as in Nihon dewa or uchi niwa) whereas **ga** seems to be slightly stronger and *controls the verb as its subject*:

Kore wa isu desu.	This is *a chair*.
Kore ga isu desu.	*This* is a chair.

Negative sentences usually take **wa**, as the emphasis tends to fall on what a thing is *not*:

Zasshi wa omoshiroku wa arimasen	The magazine is uninteresting
Ame wa furimasen	It doesn't rain

Certain verbs and constructions (almost always) take **ga**:

Nihongo ga wakarimasu ka?	Do you understand Japanese?
Atama ga itai desu.	I've a headache.
Uchi no mae ni gakkô ga arimasu.	There's a school in front of my house.

But if you look back over the preceding chapters, you will find exceptions to these rules. So the best course to follow is to learn how to use **wa** and **ga** in context as they happen – and not to worry too much!

(e) If

In Chapter 11 we met the -nakereba form:

Anata no hanashi ga wakaranakereba.	If I do not understand what you say.
Heinetsu ni narana-kereba	If your temperature does not become normal.

To say 'if' *without the negative*, you merely take off the last -u of any verb and put -eba instead:

kono kusuri o nomeba	if you take this medicine
Tôkyô e ikeba	if you go to Tokyo
gohan o tabereba	if you eat rice
benkyô sureba	if you study (see Grammar summary 13(j))

There is a close connection between true adjectives and verbs. In fact, akai means 'is or are red', and the desu is actually unnecessary. The negative infinitive is also an adjective, as is the -tai form. Adjectives. too, have their 'if' form. If you take off the final -i and put -kereba, there it is:

akakereba kaimasu	if it's red I'll buy it
omoshirokereba yomi-masu	if it's interesting I'll read it
Yokohama e ikitakereba asoko de kippu o kau koto ga dekimasu.	If you want to go to Yokohama you can get a ticket over there.

(f) aoi

aoi is a curious word. It means the green of foliage, the blue of the sky, the colour *GO* at traffic-lights, the colour of unripe fruit, a sickly complexion – and is also used to mean 'raw' or inexperienced.

(g) hoshii, (dai) suki, (dai) kirai

In Chapter 11, we looked in some detail at the . . . wa . . . ga pattern of sentences. Here we meet three new words that are used in the same way: hoshii, (dai) suki and (dai) kirai:

Watakushi wa mizu ga hoshii desu.
I want water (I'd like some water).

Watakushi wa kono hon ga (dai) suki desu.
I like this book (a lot).
Watakushi wa kono kusuri ga (dai) kirai desu.
I (thoroughly) dislike this medicine.

(h) -nagara
This is a useful verb-ending which is really an emphatic way of linking two sentences together to describe *simultaneous actions*:

Ocha o nominagara terebi o mite kudasai.
Do watch television while drinking some ocha.

You take off the -masu ending of the present tense, and replace it with -nagara.

(i) -mashô
The ending -mashô can often be used where the English would require a *future tense*:

watakushi ga setsumei shimashô
I'll explain
Yokohama e ikimashô
I'll be going to Yokohama

The implication is that something will *probably take place*. If you use the -masu form, you are being much more definite. Hence, as in the first example, if you are doing something for another person, you use a less certain verb-form to imply deference.

(j) To be useful/beneficial
... no tame ni means 'for the sake of'. With the verb naru, to become, we get the construction 'to be useful' or 'beneficial' to someone:

Nihongo desu kara anata no tame ni narimasu.
As it's in Japanese it'll be useful for you.

(k) Reactions
As in any other language there are many 'noises' which people make to signify their reactions. These are not really 'words' but mutually agreed sounds – in English, 'Oh?', 'Aha!', 'Hmmm!' for example. As Japanese is more rigorously organised than English, these sounds can

perhaps be more easily put into categories. You will have noticed that 'set phrases' are far more common in Japanese than in English:

Ii otenki desu nê.   Sô desu nê.

A simple exchange like that can be rendered in a number of ways:

Ii otenki desu nê.
$\begin{cases} \text{Nice day.} \\ \text{Fine weather we're having.} \\ \text{All right today isn't it?} \\ \text{Lovely weather, don't you think?} \end{cases}$

Sô desu nê.
$\begin{cases} \text{It is, isn't it.} \\ \text{We certainly are.} \\ \text{Sure is.} \\ \text{It's lovely, all right.} \end{cases}$

Similarly the 'social noises' referred to above are used in defined circumstances:

Ano	a prefatory noise, equalling 'Well . . . '
Ano nê	slightly more emphatic, 'Look here!'
Eeto	summing things up, 'Let's see . . .
Sâ	introductory noise, 'Come on!'
Mâ	mild protest, 'Hey! Hold on a minute!'

12.4 EXERCISES

Section A
Exercise 1
Put in the appropriate particles, wa or ga:
1. Watakushi — biiru — suki desu.
2. Anata — mizu — hoshii desu ka?
3. Shujin — ocha — dai kirai desu.
4. Kodomo — atama — itai desu.
5. Itô-san — okane — arimasu yo.

Exercise 2

Link the following sentences together using the -nagara form:
1. Biiru o nomimashita. Terebi o mimashita.
2. Terebi o mimashita. Okashi o tabemashita.
3. Okashi o tabemashita. Hon o yomimashita.
4. Tôkyô e ikimashita. Tomodachi to hanashimashita.
5. Sampo shimashita. Nihongo de hanashimashita.

Exercise 3

Put the verb in brackets into the 'if' form, and translate the sentence (**Example**: Tôkyô e (iku) kaimono suru koto ga dekimasu – Tôkyô e ikeba kaimono suru koto ga dekimasu, If you go to Tokyo you can go shopping.):
1. Kusuri o (nomu) genki ni narimasu.
2. Kyôto e (iku) subarashii otera o miru koto ga dekimasu.
3. Nihongo o (hanasu) jôzu ni narimasu.
4. Gohan o (taberu) ôkiku narimasu.
5. Koko e (kuru) Fuji-san o miru koto ga dekimasu.

Exercise 4

Put in the appropriate 'noises', ano, ano nê, eeto, sâ, mâ:
1. — oisha-san e ikitaku wa arimasen.
2. — . . . Hon'ya wa doko desu ka?
3. — anata wa Kyôto e ikitai desu ka?
4. — okusama wa byôki desu kara Kyôto e iku koto wa dekimasen.
5. — hayaku kaerimashô.

Exercise 5

Say the opposite (**Example**: Shiroi desu ka? – Kuroi desu.):
1. Yukkuri hanashimashita ka?
2. Oishii desu ka?
3. Suki desu ka?
4. Igirisu e ikitai desu ka?
5. Muzukashii desu ka?

Exercise 6

Play the part of Mr Smith in the following dialogue:
Mr Itô: Kyôto e ikimashita ka?
MrSmith: .... (No, I haven't)
Mr Itô: Ototoi Nihon e kimashita ka?
MrSmith: .... (No, yesterday)

Mr Itô: Amerika e itsu ikimasu ka?
MrSmith: .... (On the third)
Mr Itô: Mokuyôbi desu ka?
MrSmith: .... (No, Friday)
Mr Itô: Okusama to issho ni ikimasu ka?
MrSmith: .... (No, alone)
Mr Itô: Itsu kaerimasu ka?
MrSmith: .... (On the twentieth)
Mr Itô: Sâ, nomimashô ka? Nani ga hoshii desu ka?
MrSmith: .... (Anything)
Mr Itô: Ocha? Kôcha?
MrSmith:.. (Ocha would be preferable)

Section B
Exercise 7
Translate the following sentences:
1. If you get better you can go to Nikkô.
2. If you do not get better you cannot go to Kyôto.
3. If you go to Yokohama you can buy a German dictionary.
4. If you do not go to Japan you cannot see Mt Fuji (Fuji-san).
5. If you take this medicine you will get better.
6. If you do not study you will not improve (ojôzu ni naru).
7. If you go to the department store you can buy some chairs.

Exercise 8
Answer the following questions about yourself:
1. Nani o tabetai desu ka?
2. Nani ga hoshii desu ka?
3. Nani o nomitai desu ka?
4. Nani ga suki desu ka?
5. Nani ga kirai desu ka?

Exercise 9
Ask someone to help you: (**Example:** Yakusu – Yakushite kudasaimasu.)
1. Setsumei suru.
2. Depaato e iku.
3. Ehagaki o kaku.
4. Koko e kuru.
5. Jibiki o kau.

Exercise 10 📼

Play the part of Mr Smith in the following dialogue:

Doctor: Dô shimashita ka?

MrSmith: .... (I have a headache and a sore throat)

Doctor: Netsu ga demashita ka?

MrSmith: .... (Slightly. My temperature is 37.9)

Doctor: Sô desu ka. Onaka ga itai desu ka?

MrSmith: .... (No. It began to hurt yesterday but it is all right to-day)

Doctor: Kinô nani o tabemashita ka?

MrSmith: .... (Some prawns, some rice)

Doctor: Takusan nomitai desu ka?

MrSmith .... (Yes. As I have a sore throat I drink a lot of water)

Doctor: Nodo ga taihen itai desu ka?

MrSmith: .... (It's better than last night but it still hurts)

Doctor: Kaze desu. Ki o tsukete kudasai.

MrSmith: .... (Is it serious?)

Doctor: Hidoku wa arimasen keredomo otaku e kaette yasu-manakereba narimasen.

MrSmith: .... (I'm going to Matsushima on the tenth. Is that all right?)

Doctor: Heinetsu ni naranakereba Matsushima e iku koto ga dekimasen keredomo kono kusuri o nomeba genki ni narimasu yo.

MrSmith: .... (When should I take that medicine?)

Doctor: Shokuzen ni nonde kudasai.

MrSmith: .... (Thank you very much. Goodbye)

Exercise 11

Without looking back, see if you can remember what these words mean:

1. Tonikaku
2. Shinsetsu
3. Tamago
4. Daidokoro
5. Okinodoku
6. Kokonoka
7. Mitsukeru
8. Aji
9. Totemo
10. Setsumei

Exercise 12
Translate the following phrases:
1. Sore wa ikemasen ne.
2. Nan demo kekkô desu.
3. Aruite tatta no jippun desu.
4. Gomen kudasai.
5. Oisogashii deshô.
6. Hidari e magatte kudasai.
7. Benkyô shinakereba narimasen.
8. Kakete kudasai.
9. Ohayô gozaimasu.
10. Dô shimashita ka?

CHAPTER 13

SHOPPING

AND

BUSINESS TRIPS

13.1 DIALOGUES

Dialogue 1
Mrs Itô and Mrs Foster discuss some shopping.
Mrs Itô: Sono kusuri o nomeba genki ni narimasu yo.
Mrs Foster: Mô naorimashita yo! Ima totemo genki desu.

Mrs Itô: Kyô dekakenakereba ashita Kyôto e iku koto ga dekimasu.

Mrs Foster: Itô-san wa kaimono o suru tsumori desu ka?

Mrs Itô: Ee. Jûichiji ni dekakemasu.

Mrs Foster: Watakushi ni ume o katte kite kudasaimasen ka? Moshi kudamonoya e iku nara ume o tô katte kudasaimasen ka?

Mrs Itô: Mochiron katte kimasu yo. Jûnijihan ni kaereba yoi desu ka?

Mrs Foster: Ii desu tomo. Isoganaide kudasai. Moshi kudamonoya ni ume ga nakereba ii desu yo. Sore hodo jûyô ja arimasen kara.

Mrs Itô: Ume ga nakereba nashi o kau tsumori desu.

Mrs Foster: Arigatô. Watakushi wa nashi ga dai suki desu.

Mrs Itô: Moshi kôhii o nomu nara daidokoro ni okashi ga yattsu arimasu.

Mrs Foster: Yattsu desu ka! Moshi okashi o yattsu mo tabereba futorimasu ne!

Dialogue 2 📼

Mr Itô and Mr Foster discuss business trips.

Mr Itô: Rainen hikôki de Igirisu e ikeba Foster-san no kaisha o tazuneru koto ga dekimasu ka?

Mr Foster: Itsu demo dekimasu yo. Sore wa tanoshimi desu ne. Igirisu e kureba watakushi to issho ni iroiro na omoshiroi mono o miru koto ga dekimasu ne. Itsu kuru tsumori desu ka? Natsu desu ka, aki desu ka?

Mr Itô: Rainen no haru niwa taihen isogashiku narimasu kara natsu no hô ga ii deshô. Shichigatsu wa ikaga desu ka?

Mr Foster: Ii desu yo. Rokugatsu ni Furansu e ikanakereba narimasen ga watakushitachi no seihin o uru koto ga dekinakereba hayaku Eikoku e kaerimasu yo. Shikashi takusan uru koto ga dekireba mô ichido Furansu e ikanakereba narimasen.

Mr Itô: Sô deshô ne. Futsû ikutsu uru koto ga dekimasu ka?

Mr Foster: Arutoki niwa nanatsu, tokiniwa jûshichi, mata tokiniwa nanahyaku. Zenzen wakarimasen. Moshi Furansujin ga atarashii mono o kaitakereba takusan uru koto ga dekimasu. Kyonen takusan urimashita ga ninen mae niwa hitotsu mo uru koto ga dekimasen deshita.

Mr Itô: Ima dekakemasu ka?
Mr Foster: Dekakemasu yo. Ginkô e ikitai desu. Anata wa?
Mr Itô: Hai. Ginkô de jippun mateba ii desu ka?
Mr Foster: Ii desu yo. Go yukkuri!

13.2 VOCABULARY

mô	already
naorimashita	(from naoru, to get well, recover)
dekakenakereba	if you do not go out (from dekakeru, to go out)
tsumori desu	intend to
ee	oh yes
ume	plum
moshi	if
tô	ten
yoi	rather formal for ii
tomo	certainly
isoganaide kudasai	please do not hurry (from isogu)
nakereba	if there is not/are not
sore hodo	that much, to that extent
jûyô	importance, matter of consequence
yattsu	eight
futorimasu	I'll get fat (from futoru, to get fat)
rainen	next year
hikôki	aeroplane
kaisha	firm, company
tazuneru	visit (weak verb)
itsu demo	any time
tanoshimi	pleasure, enjoyment, delight
haru	spring (the season)
seihin	product(s)
uru	sell
ikutsu	how many
arutoki	sometimes
tokiniwa	at times
nanatsu	seven
zenzen	never (with negative)
atarashii	new

kyonen	last year
subarashii	splendid
ginkô	bank
mateba	if we wait (from matsu, to wait)
go yukkuri	take your time

13.3 EXPLANATIONS

(a) Mô naorimashita
Mô naorimashita means 'By now I have completely recovered', and is the normal response to an enquiry after one has suffered from an illness

(b) To intend to
If you put tsumori desu after the infinitive of a verb (what we can call the 'dictionary form'), it means 'to intend to':

kaimono o suru tsumori desu.
I intend to go shopping.
Itsu kuru tsumori desu ka?
When do you intend to come? (see Grammar summary (13f)).

(c) Would you be a dear . . .
Watakushi ni ume o katte kite kudasaimasen ka?
(Literally, having bought some plums for me, would you be so kind as to come?) i.e. Would you be a dear and buy me some plums?

(d) Moshi
Moshi emphasises the if-clause:

Moshi kudamonoya e iku nara
If you're going to the fruiterer's (literally, if it's a case of . . .).
Moshi okashi o tabereba.
If I eat some cakes.

(e) -tomo
-tomo is used at the end of a sentence to express *polite willingness*:

Ii desu tomo.　　　　　　That'd be fine, really.

(f) Negative requests

To give a negative request, you add -de to the negative form you learnt in **11.3(f)**:

isogu	to hurry
isoganai	not to hurry
isoganaide kudasai	please don't hurry

taberu	to eat
tabenai	not to eat
tabenaide kudasai	please don't eat

Please now look back at the 'available Japanese syllables' given in the Guide to Pronunciation. This pattern will help you to see the logic in the way strong verbs form their 'if' forms and their negatives.

As you learnt in Chapter 12.3 (e), to form the 'if' form you alter the final -u to -eba:

hanasu	hanaseba
yomu	yomeba
au	aeba
kaku	kakeba

If you consult the list of syllables in the Guide to Pronunciation you will see that the 't' sounds go:

ta	chi	tsu	te	to

so a verb like motsu or matsu is not at all irregular. Just as -su becomes -seba, and -mu becomes -meba, -tsu becomes -teba:

motsu	moteba
matsu	mateba

Similarly, as you learnt in Chapter **11.3(f)**, to form the *negative infinitive* you alter the -u to -anai:

hanasu, to speak	hanasanai
yomu, to read	yomanai
kaku, to write	kakanai

Verbs ending in -au are slightly irregular in that they take a **w** for the sound:

au, to meet	awanai
kau, to buy	kawanai

But motsu and matsu are perfectly regular if once again you consult the *syllabic scheme* – -tsu becomes -ta:

motsu, to hold	motanai
matsu, to wait	matanai

With *weak verbs*, no such complications arise, as they form their negatives by changing their -ru to -nai:

miru,to see	minai
taberu, to eat	tabenai

(g)   nai
nai is the negative infinitive of aru:

moshi momo ga areba
if there are peaches
moshi ume ga nakereba
if there aren't any plums

(h)   As it's not that important . . .

Sore hodo jûyô ja arimasen kara (literally, as it is not a matter of importance to that extent).

(i)   More 'all-purpose' counters
The other 'all-purpose' counters up to 10 (following on from Chapter **10.3(e)**) are:

nanatsu	7
yattsu	8
kokonotsu	9
tô	10

Thereafter, use jûichi, jûni, jûsan, etc.

(j) Referring to years

When referring to years past, present and future, the system is:

ototoshi	the year before last
kyonen	last year
kotoshi	this year
rainen	next year
sarainen	the year after next

13.4 EXERCISES

Section A
Exercise 1

Ask someone to get you things (**Example**: Watakushi ni (plums) o katte kite kudasaimasen ka? – Watakushi ni ume o katte kudasaimasen ka?):

1. Watakushi ni (leeks) o katte kite kudasaimasen ka?
2.   (a dictionary)
3.   (apples)
4.   (eggs)
5.   (stamps)

Exercise 2

What do you intend to do? (**Example**: (go out) Dekakeru tsumori desu.)

1. (study)
2. (go to the station)
3. (go shopping)
4. (read a magazine)
5. (visit Mr Itô's firm)

Exercise 3

Tell someone not to do something. (**Example**: Terebi o mite kudasai – Terebi o minaide kudasai.)

1. Gohan o tabete kudasai.
2. Tegami o kaite kudasai.
3. Osake o nonde kudasai.
4. Eigo de hanashite kudasai.
5. Momo o katte kudasai.
6. Matte kudasai.
7. Yokohama e itte kudasai.
8. Tomodachi o tazunete kudasai.

Exercise 4
This year is Shôwa 50. Next year?
1. Kotoshi wa Shôwa gojû-nen desu. Rainen wa?
2. Kotoshi wa Shôwa gojû-nen desu. Sarainen wa?
3. Ototoshi wa Shôwa rokujûsan-nen deshita. Kyonen wa?
4. Kyonen wa sen kyûhyaku hachijûroku-nen deshita. Ototoshi wa?

Exercise 5
Nani o kaimashita ka? What have you bought? (**Example**: 2 chairs – Isu o futatsu kaimashita.)

1. 10 apples.
2. 7 cakes.
3. 5 eggs.
4. 9 peaches.
5. 8 tables.
6. 11 telephones.

Exercise 6
Put into the negative (**Example**: Ume o kaeba motte kaerimasu. – Ume o kawanakereba motte kaerimasen.):
1. Yokohama e ikeba tomodachi ni aimasu.
2. Kusuri o nomeba genki ni narimasu.
3. Okashi o tabereba futorimasu.
4. Shimbun o yomeba yoku wakarimasu.
5. Ehagaki o kakeba yûbinkyoku e ikimasu.
6. Isogeba jûniji ni tsukimasu.

Exercise 7
Nani o shitai desu ka? What do you want to do? (**Example:** Eat some fish – Sakana o tabetai desu.)
1. Go to the bank.
2. Go out.
3. Go for a walk.
4. Return home.
5. Write a letter.
6. Meet a friend.

140

Section B
Exercise 8
What can you buy where? (**Example**: Moshi kudamonoya e iku nara ume o kau koto ga dekimasu.)
1. Hon'ya?
2. Eki?
3. Sakanaya?
4. Yûbinkyoku?
5. Sakaya?

Exercise 9

Play the part of Mr Smith in the following dialogue:

Mr Itô: Sono kusuri o nomeba genki ni narimasu yo.
MrSmith: .... (I'm fine now, honestly. I'm completely cured.)
Mr Itô: Kyô dekakemasu ka?
MrSmith: .... (Yes, I'm going out at half past ten.)
Mr Itô: Doko e iku tsumori desu ka?
MrSmith: .... (I intend going to the bank.)
Mr Itô: Sono ato wa?
MrSmith: .... (After going to the bank I shall go to the post-office.)
Mr Itô: Watakushi ni kitte o katte kite kudasaimasen ka?
MrSmith: .... (Of course. How many stamps will it be?)
Mr Itô: Hyaku gojû-en no kitte o jûmai katte kudasai.
MrSmith: .... (Do you intend going to Tokyo to-day?)
Mr Itô: Sô desu.
Mr Smith: (As I am rather busy would you be so kind as to visit my firm?)
Mr Itô: Mochiron tazunemasu yo.
MrSmith: ..... (If you go to my firm could you possibly bring my letters back with you?)
Mr Itô: Hai.
MrSmith: (If there aren't any letters that's all right – as it's not all that important.)

Exercise 10
Translate the following.
1. That will be a pleasure.
2. You never know.
3. July would probably be preferable.
4. If I go out at two will that be all right?
5. I'll have to go to Germany again.
6. Take your time!

THE YOUNG PEOPLE ARRIVE

14.1 DIALOGUES 📼

Dialogue 1 📼
Simon and Nobuo discuss likes and dislikes.
Nobuo: Ongaku ga suki desu ka?
Simon: Sô desu ne. Rekôdo o kiku koto ga suki desu yo.
Nobuo: Rekôdo ga takusan arimasu ka?
Simon: Hyakumai gurai arimasu keredomo konogoro wa teepu dake o kaimasu.
Nobuo: Rekôdo yori yasui desu ka?
Simon: Iie, onaji desu.
Nobuo: Eiga ga suki desu ka?
Simon: Ane wa eiga ga suki desu keredomo boku wa eigakan e tama ni shika ikimasen. Kimi wa?
Nobuo: Suki desu yo. Moshi samurai no eiga ga areba tonde ikimasu yo!
Simon: Kimi wa terebi ga suki desu ka?
Nobuo: Boku wa terebi ga kirai desu. Chiisasugimasu ne. Boku wa ôkina sukuriin no hô ga suki desu.
Simon: Hon o yomu koto ga suki desu ka?
Nobuo: Amari suki ja arimasen. Gakkô de takusan yomanakereba narimasen kara uchi dewa tama ni shika yomimasen.

Dialogue 2 📼
Jenny and Yoshiko have elevenses.
Yoshiko: Kôhii to jûsu to dochira ga ii desu ka?
Jenny: Kôhii no hô ga ii desu. Arigatô.
Yoshiko: Osatô ya miruku ga irimasu ka?
Jenny: Osatô mo miruku mo irimasu. Anata wa?

エデンの東

ビデオテープ（WHV）レーザー（WHV）VHD（日本ビクター）

TREASURE ISLAND

3月10日発売

誰でも知ってる名作『宝島』を
誰でも知ってる名優オーソン・ウエルズが
脚本を書き自ら主演した
マニア垂涎のビデオ化

宝島 オーソン・ウエルズ

レーモンド・

ジュリー・
ハリス

EAST OF EDEN

今月の新発売

今月の SPECIAL SELEC

荒野の用心棒　Per un Pugno di Dol

マカロニ・ウェスタン・ブー
となった記念碑的作品。主演の
ーストウッドは当時34歳、TV で
の人気者だった。監督セルジョ
（『ワンス・アポン・ア・タイム
リカ』）、音楽エンニオ・モルリコ
とっても出世作となった一本。
・マリア・ボロンテ。まさに待望の

スター

1930年
サンフラ
れ。現在
長も兼ね
スター。
ピカー。
のみの

クリント・
イーストウッド

日本コロムビア　3/1　97分
CMH　14,800円

Yoshiko: Watashi wa kôhii ga suki desu keredomo osatô wa irimasen.
Jenny: Miruku wa?
Yoshiko: Miruku wa irimasu. Burakku kôhii ga dai kirai desu. Eeto . . . Miruku wa . . . Ah! Omoidashimashita! Daidokoro ni arimasu. Chotto matte kudasai.
Jenny: Watashi mo ikimasu yo.
Yoshiko: Iie, konaide kudasai. Daijôbu desu. Miruku o motte kimasu.
Yoshiko: Okashi mo dôzo.
Jenny: Arigatô, itadakimasu. Nihon no okashi ga dai suki desu.
Yoshiko: Igirisu no okashi mo suki desu ka?
Jenny: Suki desu keredomo sukoshi chigaimasu ne.
Yoshiko: Kyô nani o shitai desu ka? Eiga o mi ni ikimashô ka?
Jenny: Hai, watashi wa eiga ga dai suki desu keredomo Nihongo ga yoku wakarimasen kara Nihon no eiga wa sukoshi muzukashii deshô.

Dialogue 3 📼
Gents and Ladies.
Jenny: Sumimasen. Otearai e ikitai no desu ga doko deshô ka?
Yoshiko: Asoko desu. Kanji o yomu koto ga dekimasu ka?
Jenny: Iie, yomu koto ga dekimasen.
Yoshiko: Mite kudasai. Sono kanji no yomikata wa danshi 男子 desu. Otoko to iu imi desu. Ano kanji wa joshi 女子 to yomimasu. Onna no hito no koto desu. Wasurenaide kudasai!
Jenny: Ima naraimashita kara oboemasu yo.
Yoshiko: Kanji o naraeba Nihongo wa dandan yasashiku narimasu ne. Mainichi atarashii kanji o oboereba Nihongo ga yoku wakaru deshô.
Jenny: Sô desu ne. Kanji o wasurenakereba ashita mo otearai o mitsukeru koto ga dekimasu. Benri desu ne.
Yoshiko: Benkyô shinakereba narimasen!

14.2 VOCABULARY

ongaku	music
rekôdo	a record
kiku	listen

koto	thing, matter, affair (but abstract as opposed to **mono**, a concrete thing)
kiku koto	the verb-noun 'listening'
konogoro	these days
teepu	tape
onaji	the same
eiga	film (in cinema)
ane	elder sister
boku	I (used by men)
eigakan	cinema
tama ni shika	rarely (with negative)
kimi	you (used by men)
tonde ikimasu	rush (from **tobu**, to fly)
-sugimasu	suffix meaning 'too much'
chiisasugimasu	it's too small
sukuriin	screen
jûsu	juice
dochira	which one
(o)satô	sugar
miruku	milk
irimasu	need, be needed (from **iru**, a strong verb)
watashi	I, alternative to **watakushi**
burakku	black (used with chocolate, coffee, etc.)
konaide kudasai	please don't come
itadakimasu	always said when beginning to eat, literally 'I accept', a polite verb
chigaimasu	are different (from **chigau**, to differ)
otearai	toilet
kanji	Chinese character(s)
yomikata	(literally) way to read
danshi	gentlemen
otoko (no hito)	man, male person
imi	meaning
joshi	ladies
onna (no hito)	woman, female person
naraimashita	learnt (from **narau**, to learn)

dandan	gradually
oboeru	remember (a weak verb), the opposite of **wasureru**
benkyô shinakereba narimasen	you must study (from **suru**)

14.3 EXPLANATIONS

(a) Names
Japanese names consist of a surname or family name like Itô or Yamada or Kawaguchi, which comes *first*, and then a *given name*. Mr and Mrs Itô's son is Itô Nobuo and their daughter is Itô Yoshiko.

Common male names are Ichirô (first son), Jirô (second son), Hideo, Takashi. Common female names often end in -ko like Sachiko, Yukiko, Keiko or Hideko.

The surnames often derive from place: **yama**, a mountain; **kawa**, a river; **ta**, a rice-field; **hayashi**, a wood; **mori**, a forest; **shima**, an island. So Yamashita is Underhill; Kobayashi is Littlewood; Yamada is Hillfield.

Great care is taken over the choosing of a given name. Priests are consulted and the 'look' of the name (i.e., which **kanji** are chosen to represent the sound) is of prime importance. You often see a Japanese being introduced to a stranger and writing his name on his palm because the **kanji** his parents chose are so unusual. When simplified **kanji** were introduced after the war many Japanese objected because their names were 'misspelt' in the telephone directory.

(b) The cinema
The Japanese cinema has produced so many masterpieces it is hard to choose representative names but directors like Ozu Yasujirô who made poignant studies of Japanese family life, Mizoguchi Kenji (**Ugetsu Monogatari**) and Kurosawa Akira (**Rashomon, Ran**) are perhaps the most famous.

(c) Language for men or women
The question of male and female language will be dealt with in greater detail in Chapter 18, but it is important to realise that this is a characteristic of Japanese. Things are changing and the distinction between the two languages is less clear than it was. Nevertheless, it exists. A man referring to himself uses **boku** or **ore**, a woman, **watashi** or **atashi**. 'You' for a man is **kimi** and for a woman **anata** or

anta. There are different endings for sentences depending on the *sex* of the speaker, different *verb-forms*, different 'social noises'. In this book up till now the 'neutral' form has been used, a polite impersonal form of language suitable for either sex and especially for foreigners who are 'outside' the nuances of class and age and gender.

(d) Foreign words in Japanese

The influence of English and American English has been immense. The language of advertising is sprinkled with more or less accurate borrowings that gradually filter down into everyday speech. Kuroi is 'black' just as gyûnyû is 'milk' but burakku and miruku are as common as basu, takushii, teepu, depaato, sando (from 'sandwich'), teeburu, sukuriin, suto (from sutoraiki, a strike), terebi, rajio (radio), nekutai (from 'necktie') or keisu.

(e) Gents and Ladies

The politest word for 'lavatory' is otearai, literally 'the place where one washes (arau, to wash) one's hands (te)'. In descending order of politeness there are also otoire, toire (both from 'toilet', see above!), obenjo, gofujô, habakari ('the place one hesitates to mention') and benjo.

(f) Before eating or drinking

Just before you take your first mouthful, you always say itadaki-masu. Itadaku is a polite verb meaning 'take', or 'accept'.

(g) suru and kuru

There are two irregular verbs, suru and kuru, which form their negative infinitives like this:

suru	to do
shinai	not to do
shinaide kudasai	please don't
shinakereba narimasen	you must do
kuru	to come
konai	not to come
konaide kudasai	please don't come
konakereba narimasen	you must come

(h) To do something rarely

tama ni shika ikimasen	I rarely go

| osake o tama ni shika nomimasen | I rarely drink saké |

(i) Strong verbs ending in -bu
Strong verbs ending in -bu have their -te form in -nde:

tobu	to fly
tonde imasu	is flying
tonde ikimasu	rush (literally, go flying)

(j) -sugimasu (from sugiru, a weak verb)
-sugimasu is an emphatic ending for verbs or adjectives used to express *excess*. With *verbs*, it replaces the -masu or -mashita:

tabesugimashita	I've eaten too much
nomisugimashita	I've drunk too much
gofun hayaku kisugimashita	I've come 5 minutes too early

With *adjectives*, it replaces the final -i:

| chiisasugimasu | it's too small |
| muzukashisugimashita | it was too difficult |

(k) Preference and need

.... ka ... ka } dochira ga ii desu ka? Which do you prefer?
.... to .... to }
Kôhii to (*or* ka) jûsu to (*or* ka) dochira ga ii desu ka? Which do you prefer, coffee or juice?
Miruku wa irimasu ka? Do you need milk? (literally, is milk needed?)

irimasu, from iru, to need, want, require. *Not* to be confused with iru, to be, exist (different kanji). Also iru, to be, is a *weak* verb.

(l) The way to do something
yomikata is 'the way to read' (kakikata is 'the way to write'):

| sono kanji no yomikata | the way to read those kanji |

... to yomimasu

you read them like ...

ano kanji wa joshi to yomimasu

you read those kanji as joshi (ladies)

(m) To recall/bring to mind

omoidasu means 'to bring to mind'

Omoidashimashita!

I've suddenly recalled. (As in Chapter 7)

oboeru, to remember, is the opposite of wasureru, to forget:

wasurenaide kudasai = oboete kudasai

do not forget   please remember

(n) Probability

deshô can be used after the dictionary form to imply *probability*:

Nihongo ga yoku wakaru deshô.
You'll probably understand Japanese well.
Ashita Kyôto e ikimasu.
I shall definitely go to Kyoto tomorrow.
Ashita Kyôto e iku deshô.
I shall probably go to Kyoto tomorrow.

(o) Koto and the infinitive

By putting koto after the infinitive form of a verb you make a *verb-noun*, the equivalent of our '-ing' in the sentence 'I like listening to music':

Ongaku o kiku koto ga suki desu.

I like listening to music.

Benkyô suru koto ga dai kirai desu.

I loathe studying.

Kaimono o suru koto ga suki desu ka?

Do you like shopping?

14.4 EXERCISES

Section A

Exercise 1

Revision of verbs: nani o shite imasu ka? (**Example:** Benkyô suru – Benkyô shite imasu.)

1. Yasumu.
2. Terebi o miru.
3. Matsu.
4. Tomodachi o tazuneru.
5. Naoru.
6. Ongaku o kiku.
7. Nihongo o narau.
8. Eigo o hanasu.
9. Eki e iku.
10. Yokohama kara kuru.

Exercise 2
Nani o shinakereba narimasen ka? (**Example**: Benkyô suru – Benkyô shinakereba narimasen.)

1. Oboeru.
2. Matsu.
3. Yokohama e iku.
4. Gakkô kara kuru.
5. Te o arau.
6. Hidari e magaru.
7. Mizu o nomu.
8. Denwa de hanasu.

Exercise 3
Nani o shitai desu ka? (**Example**: Benkyô suru. Benkyô shitai desu – Benkyô shitaku wa arimasen!)

1. Aruku.
2. Gohan o taberu.
3. Hon o yomu.
4. Takushii de kuru.

Exercise 4
Use tama ni shika to convert the following sentences (**Example**: Tegami o kaku – Tegami o tama ni shika kakimasen.):

1. Tôkyô e iku.
2. Koko e kuru.
3. Nihongo de hanasu.
4. Kôcha o nomu.
5. Ebi o taberu.
6. Eiga o miru.

Exercise 5

'Probably rather than definitely' (**Example**: Yoku hanashimasu! – Yoku hanasu deshô.):

1. Ocha o nomimasu.
2. Kanji o oboemasu.
3. Ongaku o kikimasu.
4. Benkyô shimasu.
5. Uchi e kaerimasu.
6. Furansugo ga wakarimasu.
7. Kaisha kara kimasu.
8. Kuruma ga konde imasu.

Section B
Exercise 6

Answer the questions as instructed

1. Nani o suru koto ga suki desu ka? (I like walking.)
2. Byôki ni nareba nani o shimasu ka? (I go to the doctor's.)
3. Eki made aruku koto ga dekimasu ka? (No, you must take a taxi.)
4. Biiru to osake to dochira ga ii desu ka? (I'd prefer beer.)

Now invent *questions* for the following *answers*:

5. Terebi o miru koto ga kirai desu.
6. Haisha e ikimasu.
7. Iie, hikôki de ikanakereba narimasen.
8. Kôhii no hô ga ii desu. Arigatô.

Exercise 7

Translate the following:

1. Those leeks are too expensive.
2. Those kanji are too difficult.
3. I ate too many cakes.
4. I arrived fifteen minutes too early.

Exercise 8

Translate the following:

1. Ano kanji o yomu koto ga dekimasu ka?
2. Ano kanji no yomikata wa hon'ya desu.
3. Ano kanji o oboemasu.
4. Ano kanji wa isha to yomimasu.

Exercise 9
Put the appropriate word into the blank: (dandan; zenzen; rainen; kyonen; otoko; onna)
1. Eiga e ——————— ikimasen.
2. Otenki wa ——————— yoku natte imasu ne.
3. Yoshiko wa ——————— no namae desu.
4. ——————— Igirisu e iku deshô.
5. ——————— no fuyu wa samusugimashita nê.
6. ——————— wa boku to iimasu.

Exercise 10
Give directions:
1. Otearai e ikitai desu ga doko deshô ka? (Behind the station)
2. Kusuriya e ikitai desu ga doko desu ka? (In front of the department store)
3. Denwa de hanashitai desu ga denwa ga arimasu ka? (Over there, beside the bank)
4. Okane mo arimasen kara ginkô e ikitai desu ga doko deshô ka? (Go straight ahead, take the first turning on the right. It's a big building. It is beside the station)

Exercise 11
Translate the following:
1. I learned some new kanji today.
2. I went to the cinema and saw a Japanese film.
3. This small red book is too easy.
4. My friend called Mr Satô had to rush to the station.

Exercise 12
Play the part of the guest in the following dialogue:
Host: Ocha to kôcha to dochira ga ii desu ka?
Guest: .... (I'd prefer Indian tea)
Host: Osatô ya miruku ga irimasu ka?
Guest: .... (I take milk but I don't take sugar.)
Host: Okashi o dôzo.
Guest: .... (No! If I eat too many cakes I'll be ill!)
Host: Hitotsu dake?
Guest: .... (I'll take one. Thank you.)
Host: Kyô nani o shitai desu ka?
Guest: .... (I have a headache so I won't go out)

Host: Guai ga warui desu ka?
Guest: .... (I've caught a cold)
Host: Ki o tsukete kudasai! Kôcha o mô ippai?
Guest: .... (No, that's fine thank you)

PLANNING A TRIP

15.1 DIALOGUES 📼

Dialogue 1
Planning the trip.
Mr Itô: Kodomotachi wa eiga o mi ni ikitasô desu.
Mrs Itô: Nobuo wa ureshisô desu ne. Igirisu no tomodachi to hanashitai yô desu ne. Gakkô ni tomodachi ga hitori ka futari iru deshô ga tokidoki sabishisô desu ne.
Mr Itô: Kanai no hanashi dewa Nobuo wa sabishii yô desu ga boku niwa Nobuo wa itsumo ureshisô desu. Mochiron gakkô de benkyô shinakereba narimasen ga maishû nichiyôbi ni tomodachi to issho ni Tôkyô e eiga o mi ni ikimasu.

Dialogue 2 📼
Zoo? Museum? Theatre?
Mr Itô: Simon o tsurete itte kudasai. Futari tomo Tôkyô e itte kudasai. Eigakan e iku mae ni jikan ga arimasu kara Simon wa iroiro na omoshiroi mono o mitai deshô.
Simon: Sô desu ne.
Nobuo: Dôbutsuen ka hakubutsukan ka gekijô ka doko ga ii desu ka?
Simon: Dôbutsuen ga ichiban omoshirosô desu ne. Boku wa dôbutsu ga dai suki desu. Igirisu no uchi niwa shiroi neko ga ippiki, inu ga nihiki imasu.
Nobuo: Sô desu ka. Demo inu wa neko ga kirai deshô.
Simon: Iie, sonna koto wa arimasen yo. Sambiki tomo naka ga ii desu yo.

Dialogue 3 📼
Learning to speak Japanese.
Simon: Nihongo de hanashitai desu keredomo hazukashii desu.
Nobuo: Hazukashigaranaide Nihongo de hanaseba boku ga kimi no Nihongo o naoshimasu. Ii desu ka?
Simon: Ii desu yo. Shikashi motto yukkuri hanashite kudasai. Tokidoki boku wa kimi no Nihongo ga yoku wakarimasu ga mata toki niwa chittomo wakarimasen.
Nobuo: Mado o akete kudasai!
Simon: Mô ichido itte kudasai! Wakarimasen deshita!
Nobuo: Jôdan deshô! Boku wa hakkiri iimashita yo!

Simon: Boku ni oshiete kudasai. Nihongo de hanashitai desu
yo. Moshi machigaeba naoshite kudasai.
Nobuo: Ano ... nani o shinakereba narimasen ka?
Simon: Mado o shimenakereba narimasen!

15.2 VOCABULARY

ureshii	happy, cheerful
sabishii	lonely
itsumo	always
maishû	every week
tsurete	(-te form of **tsureru**, to take, bring (a person))
tsurete itte kudasai	please take
tomo	both, alike
futari tomo	both (people)
jikan	time
dôbutsuen	zoo
ka	or
hakubutsukan	museum
gekijô	theatre
dôbutsu	animal
shiroi	white
neko	cat
ippiki	one (animal)
inu	dog
nihiki	two (animals)
sonna	that sort of
sambiki	three (animals)
sambiki tomo	all three (animals)
naka	relationship, terms
hazukashii	shy, embarrassed
hazukashigaranaide	without being embarrassed
naoshimasu	I'll correct (from **naosu**, to correct)
chittomo	(not) at all, (not) in the least
mado	window
akete kudasai	please open (-te form of **akeru**, to open)
itte kudasai	please speak (-te form of **iu**, to speak)
jôdan	joke

hakkiri	clearly
oshiete kudasai	please teach (-te form of oshieru, to teach)
machigaeba	'if' form of machigau, to make a mistake
shimenakereba	negative 'if'-form of shi-meru, to close, shut
shimenakereba narimasen	I must close

15.3 EXPLANATIONS

(a) Entertainment

Tokyo is one of the largest cities in the world and the entertainments offered are immensely varied. There are countless cinemas, some very small, and as well as the latest films from around the world, classic films are constantly shown to crammed houses. The National Theatre shows major Japanese plays, there are music-halls, theatres specialising in *avant-garde* performances, theatre-groups that put on foreign plays in translation as well as the Kabuki and Noh theatres. Several times a year the wonderful Bunraku or Puppet Theatre from Osaka comes – the puppets are half life-size, their handlers are in full view on the stage but such is their art that in minutes you are completely involved in their dramatic problems. The narration is sung to an accompaniment of samisen or Japanese guitar and is marvellously exciting.

Tokyo Museum has a fine collection of Oriental art. It is situated in Ueno Park to the north of the big business district. Literally tens of thousands of people visit this park in spring to see the brief season of cherry-blossom. From this park on a hill Tokyoites used to be able to see Mt Fuji but now, alas, since twentieth-century pollution has come to thicken the air, you can see Mt Fuji (about seventy miles to the south-west) for only three days at the New Year when the factories close down, or sometimes in the late autumn when fierce winds sweep away the smog. It is worth seeing – an almost perfect cone reddish in colour, capped in winter with snow.

Baseball is immensely popular and so is sumo, or ritual Japanese wrestling when oversized athletes try to shove each other out of a ring. Sumo wrestlers eat vast quantities of rice and chicken – but no four-legged animal as they have to stay on two legs. All major sporting events are televised. *Golf* is popular but enormously expensive – Japan is short of courses – so there are many rooftop or indoor golf-tees where you can practise driving or letting your inhibitions go by whacking a ball against a high mesh. *Indoor bowling rinks* are also common. Many thousands of people go skiing in the Japanese Alps during the winter.

Coffee-shops and *bars* abound. There are no licensing hours. A foreigner will occasionally find a bar is for Japanese only and will be, very politely, shown the door. But the vast majority of places are openly welcoming. When you take your place you are given a hot towel in winter and a cold one in summer to wipe your face and hands before ordering. This is called an oshibori.

(b)   Wild life

Deer are not uncommon, though most of the ones you will see are in temple precincts. There are *wild boar* in the deeper forests. *Monkeys* are frequent in certain parts. Brightly coloured, loudly screeching jays or onagadori (long-tails) haunt the Tokyo suburbs. The uguisu or Japanese warbler is found in high heathland and has a most ravishing song. In Kochi on the southern coast of Shikoku there are extraordinary chickens with tails over six feet long.

(c)   -sô desu

-sô desu, replacing the final -i of the true adjective, means 'to look', or 'to seem':

> Kodomotachi wa Tôkyô e ikitasô desu
> It seems the young people want to go to Tokyo.
> Nobuo wa ureshisô desu.
> Nobuo looks happy.

Do not confuse this construction with sô desu as used in Chapter **11.3** (h).

(d)   mai-

mai- means 'every':

mainichi	every day
maishû	every week
maigetsu or maitsuki	every month
mainen or maitoshi	every year

(e) tsureru

Tsureru is to 'take' or 'bring' a person: used with kuru it means to bring, with iku to take:

> Simon o tsurete itte kudasai.
> Please take Simon.
> Okusama o tsurete kite kudasai.
> Please come with your wife.

(f) jikan

jikan means 'length of time':

> Jikan ga arimasu ka? Is there time? Have we enough time?

Used as a *suffix*, it means 'number of hours':

> Nanjikan kakarimasu ka?
> How many hours will it take?
> Ichijikan-han kakarimasu.
> It takes an hour and a half.
> Gojikan gojippun kakarimasu.
> It takes five hours and fifty minutes.

(g) Comparative and superlative

We met the comparative in Chapter **10.3 (i)**:

> Tôkyô wa Rondon yori ôkii desu.
> Tokyo is bigger than London.

The *superlative* is formed by putting ichiban (number one) before the word:

> Dôbutsuen ga ichiban omoshiroi desu.
> The zoo is the most interesting (see Grammar Summary **6 (e)**).

(h) Counting animals

To count *animals*, you use this form:

ippiki	1
nihiki	2
sambiki	3
yonhiki	4
gohiki	5
roppiki	6

shichihiki (*or* nanahiki)	7
happiki	8
kyûhiki	9
jippiki	10

Igirisu no uchi niwa neko ga ippiki imasu. In our house in England there is one cat.

(imasu, not arimasu, because an *animate creature* is referred to).

(i) Kinds of things
donna, konna, sonna: What kind, this kind, that kind

Donna iro desu ka?	What (sort of) colour is it?
Konna hon ga suki desu	I like this kind of book.
Sonna koto wa	That is not the case
arimasen.	(literally, It is not such a thing).

(j) -garu
The suffix -garu replacing the final -i of the true adjective means 'to feel', or 'be inclined to':

ureshigaru	to feel joyful
hazukashigaru	to feel embarrassed

Hence (remembering Chapter **13.3 (f)**):

hazukashigaranaide kudasai.
Please don't feel embarrassed.

(k) naoru
naoru (remember Chapter **13.2**) is to be cured, to get better. naosu is to cure, to correct:

Mô naorimashita yo!	I'm completely cured.
Boku no Nihongo o naoshite kudasai.	Please correct my Japanese.
Oishasan no kusuri wa watakushi o naoshimashita.	The doctor's medicine cured me.

(l) oshieru
oshieru, to teach, a *weak* verb

watakushi ni Eigo o oshiete kudasai.
Please teach English to me.

(m) machigau
We met chigau in Chapter **14.2**. Machigau is to make a mistake:

Igirisu no okashi wa chigaimasu.	English cakes are different.
Machigaimashita!	I've made a mistake!
Moshi machigaeba	If I make a mistake

Chigaimasu on its own frequently means 'No, that's wrong':

Anata wa Nihonjin desu ka?	Are you Japanese?
Chigaimasu.	No.

15.4 EXERCISES

Section A
Exercise 1
Change 'is' to 'seems' **Example**: Itô-san wa ureshii desu – Itô-san wa ureshisô desu:
1. Ano hon wa omoshiroi desu.
2. Nobuo wa Eigo o hanashitai desu.
3. Yoshiko wa mizu ga hoshii desu.
4. Ane wa sabishii desu.
5. Tomodachi wa hazukashii desu.

Exercise 2
Put in the missing particles (o, ni, to, ka, ga, de, wa, no):
1. Ane ⎯⎯ issho ⎯⎯ eiga ⎯⎯ mi ⎯⎯ ikimashô.
2. Momo ⎯⎯ ringo ⎯⎯ dochira ⎯⎯ suki desu ka?
3. Gakkô ⎯⎯ tomodachi ⎯⎯ futari imasu.
4. Kusuri ⎯⎯ nonde kara kanai ⎯⎯ naorimashita.
5. Gakkô ⎯⎯ Eigo ⎯⎯ naraimasu.
6. Kusuri ⎯⎯ watakushi ⎯⎯ tomodachi ⎯⎯ naoshimashita.
7. Kanai ⎯⎯ genki ⎯⎯ narimashita.

Exercise 3
Nihongo ga wakarimasu ka? Do you understand Japanese?
1. I don't understand it at all.
2. I'm not very good at it.
3. I understand a little.
4. I understand it well.
5. I can speak it but I cannot write it.

Exercise 4
You have learnt quite a number of words by now. See how many appropriate words you can remember in filling in the following blanks. For example, you could have eaten prawns, fish, apples, peaches; you could have gone to the bank, the station, the post office, etc.
1. —————— o tabemashita.
2. —————— o nomimashita.
3. —————— o kikimashita.
4. —————— o kakimashita.
5. —————— o yomimashita.
6. —————— e ikimashita.
7. —————— de hatarakimashita.

Exercise 5
Translate the following:
1. Please bring your wife.
2. Please speak more slowly.
3. Please shut the window.
4. Please drink this medicine.
5. Please don't forget.
6. Please don't open that letter.
7. Please say that again.

Exercise 6
Answer the following questions:
1. Itsu Nihon e kimashita ka? (Last month)
2. Nannichi deshita ka? (June 24th)
3. Doko kara kimashita ka? (From England)
4. Fune de kimashita ka? (No, by plane)
5. Itsu kaeru tsumori desu ka? (October 10th)

Section B
Exercise 7
Translate the following:
1. Itô-san wa maishû Tôkyô e ikanakereba narimasen.

2. Momo wa nashi yori takai desu ga ringo wa ichiban takai desu.
3. Tomodachi wa watakushi ni Nihongo o oshiemashita.
4. Jikan ga arimasu ka?
5. Inu ka neko ka dochira ga suki desu ka?

Exercise 8 🎴

Play the part of Mr Jones in the following dialogue:

Mr Satô: Okusama wa ureshisô desu ne.
MrJones: .... (My wife likes Japan very much)
Mr Satô: Nihongo ga wakarimasu ka?
MrJones: .... (She doesn't speak it yet but she wants to learn)
Mr Satô: Anata wa ojôzu desu ne.
MrJones: ...... (No, I'm not good at it but I do want to speak it)
Mr Satô: Watakushi ga anata no Nihongo o naoshimasu. Ii desu ka?
Mr Jones: (Indeed it would. I am rather embarrassed, however)
Mr Satô: Hazukashigaranaide Nihongo o mainichi hanashite kudasai.
MrJones: .... (It's difficult but it is gradually getting easier)
Mr Satô: Kanji o yomu koto ga dekimasu ka?
Mr Jones: (Not yet but I have learned those Chinese characters)
Mr Satô: Ano kanji o yonde kudasai.
MrJones: .... (Those characters are read as 'Nihon')
Mr Satô: Sô desu nê! Ojôzu desu nê! Kono kanji no yomikata wa nan deshô ka?
MrJones: .... (I do not understand those characters)

Exercise 9

Translate the following:

Dôbutsuen e itte iroiro na omoshiroi dôbutsu o mimashita. Boku wa dôbutsu ga dai suki desu. Kyôto no uchi niwa neko ga sambiki imasu. Ichiban ôkina neko wa kurokute chiisai desu. Inu mo suki desu ga watakushitachi no neko wa inu ga kirai desu kara uchi niwa inu wa imasen.

Exercise 10

Translate the following:
1. If you open that window the room will get cold.
2. If you do not open that window the house will get warm.
3. If you make a mistake I will correct your Japanese.
4. If I do not study I will not become skilled.
5. If you study hard you will be able to read Japanese.

REVISION AND SELF-ASSESSMENT TESTS FOR CHAPTERS 11–15

Do the full test and mark it, using the mark scheme suggested. *If* you made any mistakes, make sure you go back and revise the relevant chapter(s) before proceeding with Chapter 16.

Section 1
Translate the following:
1. My friend fell ill.
2. The weather got cold.
3. I have a headache.
4. My wife has a fever.
5. I have caught a cold.

(Score: 15)

Section 2
What are these dates?
January 9
March 15
May 6
September 14
July 20

(Score: 10)

Section 3
Translate the following:
1. I loathe saké.
2. I want some water.
3. I like Tokyo.
4. I have a French car.
5. I like watching television.

(Score: 10)

Section 4
Nani o shinakereba narimasen ka?
1. Hataraku.
2. Mado o akeru.
3. Uchi e kuru.
4. Tomodachi ni au.
5. Matsu.

(Score: 10)

Section 5
Translate the following:
1. Please don't eat that apple.
2. Please don't drink that water.
3. Please don't wait.
4. Please don't speak English.
5. Please don't come to-morrow.

(Score: 10)

Section 6
What do you say in the following circumstances?
1. When you are taking your first mouthful.
2. When you greet someone first thing in the morning.
3. When you have just finished a meal prepared for you.
4. When you want to know what is wrong with someone.
5. When someone has told you he is ill.

(Score: 5)

Section 7
Put in the numbers:
1. Neko ga (2) imasu.
2. Nihonjin ga (2) imasu.
3. Tegami o (2) kakimashita.
4. Tabako o (2) nomimashita.
5. Isu ga (2) arimasu.

(Score: 5)

Section 8
Translate the following:
1. If you study you will get skilled.
2. If you go to Japan you will be able to see Mt Fuji.
3. If you take this medicine you will get better.
4. If you wait ten minutes that will be all right.

5. If you meet Mr Itô please go to the bank with him.

(Score: 15)

Section 9

Translate the following:
1. Terebi o minagara okashi o mittsu tabemashita.
2. Nodo ga itai node tabetaku wa arimasen.
3. Ebi o tama ni shika tabemasen.
4. Atarashii hon wa takasugimasu kara kaimasen.
5. Oishasan no hanashi dewa kanai wa sampo suru koto ga dekimasu.

(Score: 15)

Section 10

Read the following conversation or listen to it on your cassette. If you have the cassette, do *not* read the text. Then answer the questions underneath.

Mr Satô: Nani o suru tsumori desu ka?

Mr Jones: Yûrakuchô e itte eiga o mimasu.

Mr Satô: Sô desu ka. Nani o mitai desu ka?

Mr Jones: Nihon no eiga o mitai desu yo. Anata mo ikitai desu ka?

Mr Satô: Ikitai desu yo. Futari de ikimashô.

Mr Jones: Moshi watakushi ga Nihongo ga wakaranakereba setsumei shite kudasai.

Mr Satô: Mochiron.

Mr Jones: Arigatô.

Mr Satô: Densha de ikimashô ka?

Mr Jones: Iie, jikan ga arimasen kara takushii de ikimashô.

Mr Satô: Takai deshô.

Mr Jones: Sô desu ne. Sen-en deshô.

Mr Satô: Kinô anata wa onaka ga sukoshi itaku narimashita ne. Kyô wa ikaga desu ka?

Mr Jones: Kusuri o nomimashita kara mô naorimashita. Arigatô.

Mr Satô: Oisha-san e ikimashita ka?

Mr Jones: Iie, netsu ga demasen deshita kara dekakemasen deshita.

Mr Satô: Itsu Eikoku e kaerimasu ka?

Mr Jones: Raishû no kin'yôbi desu.

Mr Satô: Tôka desu ka?

166

Mr Jones: Chigaimasu. Kokonoka desu.
Mr Satô: Igirisu e iku nara nanjikan kakarimasu ka?
Mr Jones: Jûrokujikan kakarimasu.
Mr Satô: Watakushi wa rainen Eikoku e ikanakereba narimasen kara anata no kaisha o tazunetai desu.
Mr Jones: Itsu demo kekkô desu yo. Sore wa tanoshimi desu.

1. What is Mr Jones planning to do at Yûrakuchô?
2. If Mr Jones doesn't understand, what will Mr Satô do?
3. Are they going by train?
4. How much will the journey cost?
5. What was the matter with Mr Jones yesterday?
6. Why didn't he go to the doctor?
7. When is he going back to England?
8. Is it the tenth?
9. How long will the flight take?
10. What will Mr Satô do next year?

(**Score: 10**)

Self-assessment grades:
Maximum total score = 105.
Over 85:   Excellent
50–85:   Satisfactory
Under 50:   More revision needed

THE JAPANESE FAMILY

16.1 DIALOGUES 📼

Dialogue 1
How old are the children?
Mr Itô: Botchan wa ima nansai desu ka?
Mr Foster: Ima jûrokusai desu.
Mr Itô: Ojôsan no tanjôbi wa itsu desu ka?
Mr Foster: Musuko wa shichigatsu tôka ni umaremashita ga
musume wa jûnigatsu nijûgonichi desu.
Mr Itô: Kurisumasu desu nê!
Mr Foster: Sô desu nê! Musume dake de naku minna okuri-
mono o moraimasu.
Mr Itô: Kawaisô desu nê!

Dialogue 2 📼
The photographs of Mr Itô's parents.
Mr Itô: Kono shashin o mite kudasai. Chichi desu.
Mr Foster: Otôsan desu ka? Tôkyô ni sunde imasu ka?
Mr Itô: Mô imasen keredomo. Jûnen mae ni nakunarimashita.
Mr Foster: Osabishii deshô.
Mr Itô: Haha wa itsumo Matsumoto ni sunde imasu. Ima
hachijûnisai desu. Kore wa haha no shashin desu.
Kyonen no Shôgatsu ni torimashita.
Mr Foster: Okaasama no kimono wa subarashii desu ne. Hige
no aru kata wa donata desu ka?
Mr Itô: Ani desu.
Mr Foster: Oniisan mo Matsumoto ni sunde imasu ka?
Mr Itô: Sô desu. Furusato desu. Boku wa soko de
umaremashita.
Mr Foster: Okusan mo Matsumoto desu ka?
Mr Itô: Iie, chigaimasu. Kanai wa Edokko desu!

Dialogue 3 📼
Mr Itô's brothers and sisters.
Mr Foster: Itô-san wa oniisan ga hitori imasu ka?
Mr Itô: Sô desu. Ichirô to iu ani wa sûgaku no sensei desu.
Otôto ga futari imasu. Mite kudasai. Kore wa
kyôdai no shashin desu. Megane o kakete iru otôto
wa ima Amerika ni sunde imasu ga rainen kikoku
suru deshô.
Mr Foster: Sono onna no kata wa otôtosan no okusama desu
ka?
Mr Itô: Iie, imôto desu.

Mr Foster: Kyôdai ga ôi desu nê!

Mr Itô: Sô desu nê! Ani wa gojussai desu, ane wa yonjûhassai desu, mo hitori no ane wa yonjûgosai desu, boku wa yonjûissai desu, otôto wa sanjûkyûsai desu, imôto wa sanjûrokusai desu, mo hitori no otôto wa sanjûyonsai desu.

Dialogue 4 🎴

Visiting grandparents.

Mr Foster: Mainen Matsumoto e kaerimasu ka?

Mr Itô: Futsû O-Bon no toki ni kaerimasu. Kodomotachi wa obaasan o tazuneru koto ga dai suki desu yo.

Mr Foster: Ryôshin wa Rondon ni sunde imasu kara Simon to Jenny wa ojiisan to obaasan ni shibashiba aimasu. Mite kudasai. Kore wa ane no shashin desu.

Mr Itô: Oneesan mo Rondon ni sunde imasu ka?

Mr Foster: Sô desu. Boku wa ane ga hitori imasu.

Mr Itô: Oneesan wa goshujin ga imasu ka?

Mr Foster: Hai. Gonen mae ni kekkon shimashita.

Mr Itô: Kodomosantachi ga imasu ka?

Mr Foster: Ee, imasu yo. Boku to kanai wa oji to oba ni narimashita!

Mr Itô: Omedetô gozaimasu!

16.2 VOCABULARY

botchan	your son
nansai	what age
-sai	suffix to express age
jûrokusai	sixteen years old
ojôsan	your daughter
tanjôbi	birthday
umaremashita	was born (from **umareru**)
musuko	my son
musume	my daughter
dake de naku	not only
kurisumasu	Christmas
okurimono	present
moraimasu	receive (from **morau**)
kawaisô	what a pity! poor thing!
shashin	photograph
chichi	my father

otôsan	your father
sunde imasu	is living (from sumu) (in the sense of 'dwelling')
mô imasen	is dead (literally 'is no more')
nakunarimashita	died (from nakunaru)
(o)sabishii (deshô)	(now you must be) lonely
haha	my mother
Shôgatsu	New Year
torimashita	took (a photograph) (from toru)
okaasama	your mother
hige	beard
ani	my elder brother
oniisan	your elder brother
furusato	native place, birthplace, home-town
Edokko	native of Tokyo (Edo is the old name for the city)
sûgaku	maths
sensei	teacher
otôto	my younger brother
kyôdai	brothers and sisters
megane	spectacles
kakete iru	is wearing (glasses) (from kakeru)
kikoku suru	return to one's native land
otôtosan	your younger brother
imôto	my younger sister
ôi	many, numerous, plenty of
O-Bon	Buddhist Festival of the Dead (August 15th)
ryôshin	both parents
ojiisan	respectful term for grandfather
obaasan	respectful term for grand-mother
shibashiba	frequently
oneesan	your elder sister
kekkon shimashita	got married
kodomosantachi	kodomo, child plus honorific and plural ending
oji	uncle
oba	aunt

16.3 EXPLANATIONS

(a) More about honorifics
The difference between shujin, my husband, kanai, my wife, and goshujin, your husband, okusan, your wife, occurs with all members of the family. In the following list, the honorific form is on the *right*:

chichi	otôsan	father
haha	okaasan	mother
ani	oniisan	elder brother
ane	oneesan	elder sister
otôto	otôtosan	younger brother
imôto	imôtosan	younger sister
sofu	ojiisan	grandfather
sobo	obaasan	grandmother
oji	ojisan	uncle
oba	obasan	aunt
musuko	botchan, musukosan	son
musume	ojôsan	daughter

In all cases -sama can be substituted for -san to show *extra politeness*.

In practice, as grandparents are automatically revered, the honorific form is generally used for one's own grandmother and grandfather. Also, in some families, the terms otôsan and okaasan are used to show *respect*. In addressing one's *own parent* directly, the honorific form is used. -chan is a charming suffix, used particularly after young girl's names and within the family otôchan and okaachan are equivalents for daddy and mummy.

(b) Religion and festivals
In Japanese life, rituals attending birth and death tend to be Buddhist whereas the wedding ceremony would be Shintô. Individual prayers before a shrine are preceded by the ringing of a bell or the double clapping of hands to, as it were, call the god's attention. In some places written replies are given by priests and, if these are unfavourable, the recipient ties them to the fence or a tree – you often see what appear to be white flowers around a shrine but which are in fact rejected oracles.

Each local shrine has an *annual festival* when young men carry round the parish a palanquin containing sacred symbols. These are colourful and jolly occasions and everyone turns out to watch.

At *New Year* the sacred emblems of bamboo and pine-branches are placed before every home. **Shôgatsu** is very much a family affair and visits are exchanged with presents offered, time-honoured games played and special food eaten. At **O-Bon**, a kind of All Souls' Day, lanterns are lit in the gardens to guide friendly souls of the departed back home.

There are thirteen *national holidays* each year when banks and offices – though not shops! – are closed:

January 1	shôgatsu
January 15	Coming of Age Day
February 11	National Foundation Day
March 20	Spring Equinox
April 29	Greenery Day
May 3	Constitution Day
May 5	Boys' Day
September 15	Respect for the Aged Day
September 23	Autumn Equinox
October 10	Sports Day
November 3	Culture Day
November 23	Thanksgiving for Labour Day
December 23	Birthday of the Emperor

The three early summer holidays coming close together are called *Golden Week*.

There are three yearly festivals associated with *children*. On March 3 **Hina matsuri** (the Dolls' Festival), girls arrange court-effigies in splendid costumes. On May 5, households with boy-children fly flags with carp on them to signify energy and long life. On November 15 those families with children of three, five and seven years old go to the shrines – the so-called **shichi-go-san** festival. Women wear a bright kimono and men one of a sombre blue. You still see people going out for the evening in traditional costume and most people change from Western clothes at home into a comfortable flowing **yukata**.

(c) How old are you?

Kodomo wa gosai desu. The child is 5 years old.

The suffix **-sai** is added to all numbers except 1, 8 and 20:

issai 1
nisai 2
sansai 3
yonsai 4
gosai 5
rokusai 6
shichisai *or* nanasai 7
hassai 8
kyûsai 9

10s are slightly different:

jissai *or* jussai 10
hatachi 20
sanjissai *or* sanjussai 30

(d)   Verb and noun
Certain verbs go automatically with certain nouns:

Shashin o torimashita.   I took a photograph.
Megane o kakemashita.   I wore (*or* put on) spectacles.

(e)   Relative clauses in the present tense
To make relative clauses in the present tense, you use the *infinitive form* of the verb and put the clause *before* the relevant word:

Otôto wa megane o kakete imasu.
My younger brother is wearing spectacles.
Megane o kakete iru hito wa otôto desu.
The man who is wearing spectacles is my younger brother.

Ani wa hige ga arimasu.
My elder brother has a beard.
Hige ga (*or* no) aru hito wa ani desu.
The chap wearing a beard is my elder brother.

Compare: Ano hitotachi wa Matsumoto e itte imasu.
                    Those people are going to Matsumoto.
                    Matsumoto e itte iru hito wa okurimono o
                    motte imasu
                    People going to Matsumoto are holding presents.
                    Sakana o taberu hito wa itsumo genki desu.
                    Those who eat fish are always healthy.

Amerika ni sunde iru tomodachi wa kikoku shimasu.

My friend who is living in America is coming back to Japan.

(f) nakunaru

nakunaru means to die when referring to a *loved one*. Otherwise, used impersonally, the verb is shinu:

Shakespeare wa 1616 ni shinimashita. Shakespeare died in 1616.

16.4 EXERCISES

Section A
Exercise 1
Answer the following questions, converting the honorific titles to members of your own imaginary family:
1. Otôsan wa nansai desu ka? He's 61.
2. Okaasan wa? She's 58.
3. Botchan wa? He's 13.
4. Ojôsan wa? She's 11.
5. Okusan wa/Goshujin wa? She's/He's 38.
6. Oniisan ga imasu ka? I have two.
7. Imôtosan ga imasu ka? I have one.

Exercise 2
Tell us about yourself:
1. Anata no tanjôbi wa itsu desu ka?
2. Doko de umaremashita ka?
3. Ima doko ni sunde imasu ka?
4. Anata no furusato wa doko desu ka?
5. Ima nansai desu ka?
6. Shôwa jûnen ni umaremashita ka?
7. Hontô desu ka?
8. Kekkon shimashita ka? (Itsu?)
9. Goshujin wa/Okusama wa nansai desu ka?

Exercise 3
Make relative clauses: (**Example**: Ano hito wa megane o kakete imasu. Ani desu. – Megane o kakete iru hito wa ani desu.):
1. Ano hito wa hon o yonde imasu. Otôto desu.

2. Ano otoko no kata wa mainichi eki e kimasu. Otomo-dachi desu ka?
3. Ano hito wa osake o takusan nomimasu. Itsumo byôki desu.
4. Ano onna no hito wa utsukushii kimono ga arimasu. Ane desu.

Exercise 4
Answer changing to the honorific form (**Example:** Kore wa chichi no shashin desu. – Otôsan desu ka?):
1. Kore wa haha no shashin desu.
2. Kore wa musume no shashin desu.
3. Kore wa oba no shashin desu.
4. Kore wa kanai no shashin desu.
5. Kore wa ani no shashin desu.
6. Kore wa kodomotachi no shashin desu.
7. Kore wa imôto no shashin desu.
8. Kore wa musuko no shashin desu.

Exercise 5
Put in the correct counters (**Example:** Amerikajin ga (2) imasu – Futari):
1. Neko ga (2) imasu.
2. Otôto ga (1) imasu.
3. Nihonjin ga (3) imasu.
4. Inu ga (3) imasu.
5. Shashin ga (5) arimasu.
6. Okurimono o (2) moraimashita.
7. Naganegi o (6) kaimashita.
8. Kasa o (1) kaimashita.

Section B

Exercise 6
Translate:
1. My son is five years old.
2. Does your mother live in Yokohama?
3. My grandfather died in 1973.
4. My elder brother has a black beard.
5. Did your son get many presents on his birthday?
6. When did your daughter get married?
7. When is your father coming back to this country?

8. My younger sister wears glasses.
9. I took this photograph on New Year's Day.
10. My friend's mother is a French teacher.

Exercise 7
Translate:
1. Nihongo o hanashite iru hito wa Eigo no sensei desu.
2. Kanji o kaku koto ga dekiru gaikokujin wa ojôzu desu ne.
3. Tabako o takusan nomu hito wa oishasan e ikanakereba narimasen.
4. Mainichi kaisha de hataraku hito wa doyôbi ni inaka e ikitai desu.

Exercise 8
Answer the following questions:
1. Eigakan de nani o suru koto ga dekimasu ka?
2. Dôbutsuen de nani o miru koto ga dekimasu ka?
3. Yûbinkyoku de nani o kau koto ga dekimasu ka?
4. Jinja no mae de nani o miru koto ga dekimasu ka?

Exercise 9
Translate:
1. People who live in Hakone can see Mt Fuji every day.
2. The man who teaches maths in this university is my younger brother.
3. Those who take a walk every day are healthy.
4. The man who is driving that red Japanese car is my father.

Exercise 10 📼
Play the part of the foreign visitor in the following dialogue:
Mr Jones: Anata no tanjôbi wa itsu desu ka?
Mr Satô: .... (March 9th.)
Mr Jones: Okurimono o takusan moraimashita ka?
Mr Satô: ... (Yes, I got a Japanese dictionary, a beautiful kimono and a new pen.)
Mr Jones: Subarashii desu nê!
Mr Satô: .... (Yes but now I must write lots of letters!)
Mr Jones: Otôsan wa Amerika kara kaerimashita ka?
Mr Satô: .... (Not yet. He'll be returning home next month probably.)
Mr Jones: Amerika de nani o shite imasu ka?
Mr Satô: .... (He's working in an office.)

Mr Jones: Okaasan wa ogenki desu ka?
Mr Satô: .... (No, she's caught a cold.)
Mr Jones: Oishasan e ikimashita ka?
Mr Satô: .... (No, but she's taken some medicine.)
Mr Jones: Ki o tsukete kudasai. Samuku narimashita ne.
Mr Satô: ..... (Yes, and it rained yesterday. My younger brother visited us but he'd forgotten his umbrella!)
Mr Jones: Otôsan wa ima nansai desu ka?
Mr Satô: .... (28.)
Mr Jones: Sô desu ka. Imôtosan wa?
Mr Satô: .... (21.)
Mr Jones: Nani o shite imasu ka?
Mr Satô: .... (She's working in the museum.)
Mr Jones: Goshujin ga imasu ka?
Mr Satô: .... (Yes, she got married last month. Look. This is a photograph of her husband.)
Mr Jones: Ureshisô desu nê!
Mr Satô: .... (They seem both very happy.)
Mr Jones: Hige no aru hito wa donata desu ka?
Mr Satô: .... (It's my sister's husband's elder brother.)
Mr Jones: Tôkyô ni sunde imasu ka?
Mr Satô: .... (No, he works in Matsumoto.)

EATING OUT

17.1 DIALOGUES 📼

Dialogue 1
The Sushi Bar. すし屋

Mr Itô: Komban wa!
Mr Foster: Komban wa!
Mr Itô: Osushi o tabe ni ikimashô ka?
Mr Foster: So shimashô. Sore wa tanoshimi desu ne.

Mr Itô: Kauntaa ni suwarimashô. Osushiya-san ga osushi o tsukuru tokoro ga yoku wakarimasu yo. Mite kudasai. Kabe ni sakana no namae ga kaite arimasu.

Mr Foster: Yominikui desu nê!

Mr Itô: (addressing the owner) Kyô wa nani ga oishii desu ka?

Owner: Iki no ii ebi ga arimasu yo.

Mr Itô: Foster-san. Nani ga ii desu ka?

Mr Foster: Ebi o kudasai.

Mr Itô: Watakushi mo ebi ni shimasu.

Owner: Tsugi wa nani ni shimasu ka?

Mr Foster: Watakushi wa tako o tabeta koto ga arimasen kara tsugi wa tako ni shimasu.

Mr Itô: Zehi tabete mite kudasai. Watakushi niwa maguro o kudasai.

Owner: Onomimono wa nani ni shimasu ka?

Mr Itô: Biiru o kudasai.

Dialogue 2 📼
The Tempura Restaurant. てんぷら屋

Mr Itô: Kore wa yûmei na tempuraya desu. Hairimashô ka?

Mr Foster: Ee, demo takasô desu kara sukoshi hairinikui desu ne.

Mr Itô: Watakushi wa koko e kita koto ga arimasu. Sonna ni takaku wa arimasen yo.

Mr Foster: Sore dewa hairimashô. Okane wa tappuri arimasu!

Mr Itô: Mado no soba no teeburu e ikimashô ka?

Mr Foster: Menyu wa rômaji de kaite arimasu kara kondo wa yomiyasui desu ne! Demo, matsu, take, ume to wa nan desu ka?

Mr Itô: Teishoku desu. Matsu ga ichiban takai desu. Matsu niwa ebi to ika to nasu to shiitake ga haitte imasu.

Dialogue 3 📼
The Sukiyaki Restaurant. すきやき屋

Mr Itô: Anata wa gaikoku no kata desu kara mochiron niku ga suki deshô.

Mr Foster: Watakushi wa Nippon no tabemono ga dai suki desu keredomo kyô wa hisashiburi ni gyûniku o tabetai desu nê.

Mr Itô: Sukiyaki o tabeta koto ga arimasu ka?

Mr Foster: Arimasu yo. Ah . . . Saifu o wasurete shimaimashita! Uchi e kaeranakereba narimasen.

Mr Itô:　Iie Foster-san. Watakushi ga gochisô shimasu!
Mr Foster:　Arigatô. Dewa tsugi wa watakushi ga Itô-san to okusama o oyobi shimasu yo.

Mr Foster:　Kono tôfu wa oishii desu ne.
Mr Itô:　Takenoko wa suki desu ka?
Mr Foster:　Ammari suki ja arimasen.
Mr Itô:　Gyûniku o mô sukoshi ikaga desu ka?
Mr Foster:　Mô onaka ga ippai ni natte shimaimashita!
Mr Itô:　Okanjô o onegai shimasu.

17.2 VOCABULARY

komban wa	good evening! (said after sunset)
(o)sushi	slices of raw fish, cooked egg or caviare on cold rice-cakes
kauntaa	counter, bar
suwarimashô	let's take a seat (from **suwaru**)
tsukuru	prepare
kabe	wall
yominikui	difficult to read
tokoro	place
iki no ii	fresh
tabeta	ate, eaten (past plain form of **taberu**)
zehi	by all means
maguro	tuna fish
yûmei	famous
tempuraya	restaurant for deep-fried food
hairimashô ka	shall we go in (from **hairu**, to enter) (strong verb)
ee	well, yes
hairinikui	'we'd best not go in' (literally, troublesome to enter)
kita	came (past plain form of **kuru**)
tappuri	ample, 'loaded', 'flush'
menyu	menu
kondo	this time

yomiyasui	easy to read
matsu	pine-tree (the most expensive *table-d'hôte*)
take	bamboo (the next most expensive *table-d'hôte*)
ume	plum (the cheapest *table-d'hôte*)
teishoku	the set menu, *prix fixe*, *table-d'hôte*
ika	cuttlefish
nasu	egg-plant, aubergine
shiitake	mushroom
niku	meat
tabemono	food
hisashiburi ni	after a long abstinence
sukiyaki	beef and vegetables simmered in soya sauce and saké
saifu	purse, wallet, pocket-book
shimaimashita	I've ended up by (from shimau, a terminal verb)
gochisô suru	treat
yobu	take out, invite
oyobi suru	polite form of yobu
oyobi shimasu	polite form of yobimasu
tôfu	bean-curd
takenoko	bamboo shoot
ammari (with negative)	not too much
gyûniku	beef
ippai	full
(o)kanjô	bill
onegai shimasu	polite form of negaimasu (see yobu above): I'm asking for

17.3 EXPLANATIONS

(a) Restaurants
In the large cities in Japan there are French, Italian, American, Chinese, German and Korean restaurants – but, when in Rome . . . The visitor should experiment with the variety of Ja-

panese ways of eating. *Noodle-stalls* are to be found everywhere with customers standing, devouring delicious cheap bowls of soba (noodles made from buckwheat) with hashi or chopsticks (shorter than the Chinese variety). But for more elaborate meals there are sushi bars where experts slice raw tunafish, octopus, cuttlefish, or place prawns, red caviare or cooked egg on carefully moulded cakes of rice, binding them with strips of seaweed (nori). There are tables, but it is better (and more expensive) to sit at the bar and watch the expert at work – also, at a table you get a 'set-tray' in which the food may not be quite so fresh as that which you see prepared before your very eyes! Tempura is said to have been introduced to Japan by Portuguese missionaries and consists of deep-fried slices of white fish and vegetables. Sukiyaki means 'cooked on the blade of a plough', and is traditional hunter's or farmer's fare, though now prepared in rather more sophisticated ways.

Japanese restaurants are specialist places and you go to a certain one for a certain kind of food. Great care is taken over the 'look' of the food and, in the more expensive restaurants, the china will be very beautiful and be changed in order to match its colour with the season.

(b) Street-sellers

In the winter *sweet-potato sellers* ply their hot wares in the street calling out yaki-imo (baked potatoes) as the fragrant smoke rises from their stalls. And all the year round, men on bicycles blowing plaintive horns tow trailers filled with water in which cubes of fresh bean-curd are kept.

(c) The past plain form

To form this you merely alter the last letter of the -te form to -ta:

kuru	to come	kite	kita
taberu	to eat	tabete	tabeta

The past plain form is really a simpler form of the *past tense* – and, indeed (as we shall see in Chapter 18) especially men use it instead of the -mashita form. Its main use, however, is in the construction -ta koto ga arimasu, meaning 'have already done such a thing':

Watakushi wa koko e kita koto ga arimasu.
I have been here before.
Tako o tabeta koto ga arimasen.
I've never eaten octopus before.

Compare:

> Kyôto e itta koto ga arimasu ka?
> Have you ever been to Kyoto?

Its other use, as we shall see later, is in *relative clauses* (see Grammar summary 13(b.).

(d) Coming and going
With ni iku, kuru *or* kaeru you can use the stem of any verb to give the idea of *going, coming or returning* somewhere to do something. Merely cut the -masu of the present tense:

> Osushi o tabe (masu) ni ikimashô ka?
> Shall we go and eat some sushi?
> Furansu no eiga o mi (masu) ni ikimashita.
> I went and saw a French film.
> Koko e shimbun o yomi (masu) ni kimasu.
> He comes here to read the paper.

(e) -te form with arimasu

> sakana no namae ga kaite arimasu
> the names of the fish are written

(f) -te form with mite kudasai

Tabete mite kudasai	Try it – i.e., Eat and see
Yonde mite kudasai	Read it and see

(g) Easy, hard and troublesome
-yasui and -nikui, tacked on to the sterm of the verb as in (d) above mean, respectively, 'easy to' and 'hard to' or 'troublesome to':

ano kanji wa yominikui desu	those kanji are hard to read
kondo wa yomiyasui desu	this time they're easy to read

(h) -te form with shimau
This means something has been *thoroughly and completely done:*

> Saifu o wasurete shimaimashita.
> I've gone and forgotten my wallet!

Neko wa sakana o tabete shimaimashita.
The cat's eaten up all the fish.

(i) More polite forms

As touched on in Chapter 8, there are other politer ways of using verbs: instead of yobimasu

(watakushi ga) oyobi shimasu
I call
(anata ga) oyobi ni narimasu
you call

instead of dekekemasu

(watakushi ga) odekake shimasu
I go out
(anata ga) odekake ni narimasu
you go out

One hears these forms all the time, and there are certainly occasions when it would strike the Japanese ear as odd to hear anything else; but basically for a foreigner the straightforward verb-form is always acceptable.

The set-phrase onegai shimasu, however, should be *learnt by heart*, as this is the standard way of attracting attention.

(j) -mono

The suffix -mono makes a *noun* (mono means thing):

nomimono drink(s)
tabemono food
kaimono purchase(s)

(k) -niku

The suffix -niku means 'meat':

gyûniku beef
butaniku pork

17.4 EXERCISES

Section A
Exercise 1

Show definitely complete actions (**Example:** Saifu o wasurema-shita. – Saifu o wasurete shimaimashita.):

1. Anata no hon o yomimashita.
2. Tomodachi wa ikimashita.
3. Amerika kara kaerimashita.

4. Tempuraya e hairimashita.
5. Benkyô shimashita.

Exercise 2
Have you ever . . . ? Alter the question (**Example:** Rondon e ikimashita ka? – Rondon e itta koto ga arimasu ka?):
1. Kono hon o yomimashita ka?
2. Kanji o kakimashita ka?
3. Kimono o kaimashita ka?
4. Shashin o torimashita ka?
5. Yamada-san o tazunemashita ka?
6. Unten shimashita ka?

Exercise 3
Just for practice, change the verb-form to a politer style (**Example:** Shimbun o yomimasu. – (Watakushi ga) shimbun o oyomi shimasu.):
1. Itô-san ni aimashita.
2. Itô-san to hanashimashita.
(**Example:** shimbun o yomimasu ka? – (Anata ga) shimbun o oyomi ni narimasu ka?):
3. Eigo de hanashimasu ka?
4. Atarashii pen de kakimasu ka?

Exercise 4
Suggest a friend should have a go (**Example:** Tako o tabete mite kudasai.):
1. Try and write this kanji.
2. Try this saké.
3. Try going in to this tempura restaurant.
4. Have a go at speaking Japanese.
5. Try opening this window.

Exercise 5
Vocabulary-test. What do words in italics mean?
1. *Otôto* wa osake o nonde imasu.
2. *Subarashii* desu nê!
3. *Ongaku* ga suki desu.
4. *Nasu* o tabemashita.
5. *Otôsan* wa Yokohama ni sunde imasu.
6. Tokidoki *sabishii* desu.
7. *Daigaku* e ikimashita.
8. *Natsu* wa mushiatsui desu.

SECTION B
Exercise 6
Use the -ni iku/kuru/kaeru form:
1. Let's go and see a film.
2. He came back to hear the music.
3. I'll come and learn some Japanese.
4. He went to write a postcard.

Exercise 7
Translate:
1. Anata wa Nihonjin desu kara mochiron sakana ga suki deshô.
2. Doitsu no shimbun o katta koto ga arimasu ka?
3. Tsugi wa maguro ni shimasu.
4. Ame ga futte shimaimashita.
5. Ane wa Shôwa yonjûgonen ni umaremashita.

Exercise 8
Translate:
1. This letter is hard to read.
2. Japanese is hard to write!
3. That music is easy to hear (listen to).
4. Those kanji are easy to forget!
5. That tôfu is easy to eat.
6. Those words are hard to remember.

Exercise 9
Revision of adjectives: Takai desu.
Takaku wa arimasen.
Takasô desu.
Takakute mezurashii desu.

Now conceal the above example, and do the following sentences:
1. It's cheap.
2. It's not cheap.
3. It looks cheap.
4. It's cheap and tasty.
5. It's new.
6. It's not new.
7. It looks new.
8. It's new and beautiful.

Exercise 10 📼

Play the part of the foreigner in the following dialogue:

Mr Satô: Kyô wa tempura o tabe ni ikimashô ka?

MrJones: .... (That'd be delightful. I've never eaten tempura before.)

Mr Satô: Oishii desu yo. Kore wa yûmei na tempuraya desu. Hairimashô ka?

MrJones: .... (It looks expensive.)

Mr Satô: Sonna ni takaku wa arimasen yo.

MrJones: .... (Is it crowded?)

Mr Satô: Sô desu keredomo mado no soba ni teeburu ga arimasu.

MrJones: .... (Shall we sit over there then?)

Mr Satô: Menyu o yomu koto ga dekimasu ka?

MrJones: .... (No! It's written in Japanese!)

Mr Satô: Kono menyu wa rômaji de kaite arimasu kara yomi-yasui deshô.

MrJones: .... (It's easy to read but please teach me some kanji.)

Mr Satô: Ano . . kono kanji no yomikata wa matsu desu.

MrJones: .... (I do not understand.)

Mr Satô: Matsu wa pine-tree desu ga koko dewa ichiban takai teishoku to iu imi desu.

MrJones: .... (What is included?)

Mr Satô: Ebi to ika to nasu to shiitake ga haitte imasu.

MrJones: .... (How many prawns are put in?)

Mr Satô: Futsû sambon.

MrJones: .... (It sounds delicious.)

Mr Satô: Ikaga desu ka?

Mr Jones: .... (These mushrooms are delicious.)

Mr Satô: Nasu wa suki desu ka?

MrJones: .... (Not a lot.)

Mr Satô: Ebi o mô sukoshi ikaga desu ka?

MrJones: .... (I'm full to bursting!)

Mr Satô: Ah . . . saifu o wasurete shimaimashita.

MrJones: .... (I am treating you. Bill, please!)

LANGUAGE FOR MEN AND WOMEN

18.1 DIALOGUES 📼

Dialogue 1
Mr Itô and his brother arrange a visit to a baseball match.

Mr Itô: Kondo no nichiyô yakyû o mi ni ikô ka?
Toshio: Chotto matte kure. Techô o miru kara. Dame da yo.
Doyô nara ii yo. Goji ni kyûjô no mae de aô.
Mr Itô: Wakatta.
Toshio: Dotchi ga katsu ka na?
Mr Itô: Mochiron Kyojin da ze.
Toshio: Baka yarô! Hanshin ni kimattera.
Mr Itô: Chikatetsu de kuru kai?
Toshio: Ore wa kuruma da kara tochû de hirotte yaru yo.

Mr Itô: Kondo no nichiyôbi ni yakyû o mi ni ikimashô ka?
Toshio: Chotto matte kudasai. Techô o mimasu kara. Dame
desu yo. Doyôbi nara ii desu keredomo. Goji ni
kyûjô no mae de aimashô.
Mr Itô: Wakarimashita.
Toshio: Dochira ga katsu to omoimasu ka?
Mr Itô: Mochiron Kyojin desu yo.
Toshio: Chigaimasu! Hanshin ga katsu ni kimatte imasu.
Mr Itô: Chikatetsu de kimasu ka?
Toshio: Watakushi wa kuruma ga arimasu kara tochû de anata
o hiroimashô.

Dialogue 2 📼
Mrs Itô and Mrs Yamada discuss flower arranging.

Mrs Itô: Raishû no nichiyô ni tomodachi no kekkonshiki ga aru
no. Atashi wa hana o ikenakereba naranai kara
hana o erabu no o tetsudatte kurenai?
Mrs Yamada: Mochiron ii wa. Donna hana ga ii kashira?
Mrs Itô: Sô ne. Akarui hana ga ii wa nê.
Mrs Yamada: Sore ja bara wa dô?
Mrs Itô: Ii wa ne. Sore ni kiku to yuri mo iremashô yo. Sô
sureba aka, kiiro, momoiro de totemo utsuku-
shiku naru wa.
Mrs Yamada: Sô nê. Utsukushii wa nê.
Mrs Itô: Demo umaku dekiru kashira.
Mrs Yamada: Imôtosan no kekkon no toki ni anata ga iketa
hana wa subarashikatta ja nai?
Mrs Itô: Ah . . . kinô katta osaifu o mô miseta kashira?
Mrs Yamada: Totemo kirei da wa.

Mrs Itô: Raishû no nichiyôbi ni tomodachi no kekkonshiki ga arimasu. Watakushi wa hana o ikenakereba narimasen kara hana o erabu koto o tetsudatte kudasaimasen ka?

Mrs Yamada: Mochiron ii desu yo. Donna hana ga ii deshô ka?

Mrs Itô: Sô desu ne. Akarui hana ga ii deshô nê.

Mrs Yamada: Sore dewa bara wa dô deshô ka?

Mrs Itô: Sore wa ii desu nê. Sore ni kiku to yuri mo iremashô yo. Sô sureba aka, kiiro, momoiro de totemo utsukushiku narimasu nê.

Mrs Yamada: Sô desu nê. Utsukushii desu nê.

Mrs Itô: Demo jôzu ni dekiru deshô ka?

Mrs Yamada: Imôtosan no kekkon no toki ni anata ga iketa hana wa subarashikatta desu.

Mrs Itô: Ah . . . kinô katta osaifu o mô misemashita ka?

Mrs Yamada: Totemo kirei desu nê.

18.2 VOCABULARY

yakyû	baseball
ikô	'male' language for ikimashô
kure	'male' language for kudasai
techô	notebook, memorandum-book
dame	no good
da	plain form of desu
kyûjô	baseball-park
aô	'male' language for aimashô
wakatta	past plain form of wakaru
dotchi	which (same as dochira)
katsu	win
na	d'you think
Kyojin	Giants
ze	emphatic particle (like yo)
baka yarô!	idiot!
Hanshin 阪神	the Osaka–Kobe baseball team
kimattera	are sure to = kimatte imasu (from kimaru, to be certain, to be bound to)

kuru kai	= kimasu ka
ore	'male' language for 'I'
tochû de	on the way
hirotte yaru	I'll make sure I pick you up
hirotte	from hirou, to pick up (by car)
yaru	familiar verb equalling suru
to omoimasu ka	do you think
shiki	ceremony
no	'female' particle used for emphasis or query
atashi	'female' language for 'I'
hana	flower
ikeru	arrange (hence ikebana, flower-arranging) (a weak verb)
erabu	choose
tetsudau	give a hand, help
kurenai	= kudasai
wa	'female' language for yo
kashira	I wonder
akarui	light-coloured
ja	= dewa
bara	rose
kiku	chrysanthemum
yuri	lily
iremashô	let's put in (from ireru) (a weak verb)
aka	red (the noun)
kiiro	yellow
momoiro	pink (literally, peach-coloured)
umaku	skilfully (from umai)
dekiru	do, be able to do, be capable of doing (a weak verb)
iketa	past plain form of ikeru
subarashikatta	was splendid, past form of subarashii
katta	past plain form of kau
mô	already
miseta	past plain form of miseru, to show

18.3 EXPLANATIONS

(a) Men and Women speaking

In this chapter, we see the striking differences in the way men and women talk Japanese. It is not recommended that foreigners adopt these forms of speaking – and as modern life is gradually altering the relationship between the sexes, these differences are becoming less marked – but, as they are a very important feature of spoken Japanese, they are included here.

Basically 'male' speech is gruffer, more brusque; 'female' speech gentler, more gracious. The *plain form* of the verb is preferred by men – aru for arimasu, wakatta for wakarimashita, aô for ai-mashô. And, as you have seen, the *final particles* differ considerably.

(b) Ikebana

Flower-arranging is very much an art in Japan. There must never be an even number of flowers in any ikebana composition, and especially not 4 as the sound shi (4) is the same as shi (death). This is why you never give four of anything to a Japanese. In stores, saké-cups or tea-cups are always sold in sets of *five*.

(c) The past plain form in relative clauses

Whereas as in Chapter 16.3(e), the *infinitive* replaces the *present tense* in sentences like:

Megane o kakete iru hito wa otôto desu.
The man who is wearing spectacles is my younger brother.

the *past tense* is replaced by the *past plain form*:

anata ga iketa (ikemashita) hana
the flowers you arranged
kinô katta (kaimashita) osaifu o misemashita ka?
Have I shown you the purse I bought yesterday?

Almost always in the relative clause, the *subject* is signalled by ga:

Watakushi ga eranda kuruma wa akai desu.
The car I chose is red.
Satô-san ga kaita hon o yomimashita ka?
Have you read the book Mr Satô wrote?

(d) The past plain form of adjectives
Adjectives, too, have a past plain form. You cut off the final -i of any true adjective and add -katta:

    ano Nihon no eiga wa   that Japanese film was
    muzukashikatta   difficult

For ii the old form yoi is used:

    yokatta   it was good

In conversation, no desu is sometimes added:

    warukatta no desu   it was bad

(e) To think that . . .
. . . to omoimasu after the plain form means 'think that . . . ':

    Dochira ga katsu to omoimasu ka?
    Who do you think will win?
    Kôbe e itta to omoimasu.
    I think he has gone to Kôbe.

(f) To be certain to, to be bound to
. . . ni kimaru means 'to be certain to', 'to be bound to':

    Kyojin ga katsu ni kimatte imasu.
    The Giants are bound to win.
    Itô-san ga ikeru hana wa utsukushii ni kimatte imasu.
    The flowers which Mr Itô arranges are bound to be splendid.

(g) To make a verb into a noun
To make a verb into a noun you can either add koto as in **14.3 (o)** or no to the infinitive:

    hana o erabu koto o tetsudatte kudasai
    hana o erabu no o tetsudatte kudasai
    please help me to choose some flowers

(h) How do you find . . . ?
. . . dô desu ka? How do you find . . . ?

    atarashii kaisha wa dô desu ka? how is your new firm?

18.4 EXERCISES

Section A
Exercise 1
You prefer something else (**Example:** Shiroi hana? (Red ones) – Iie, akai hana no hô ga ii desu.):

1. Takushii? (Underground)
2. Kiku? (Lilies)
3. Naganegi? (Aubergine)
4. Futsuka? (The third)
5. Ashita? (The day after to-morrow)
6. Pan? (Rice)
7. Jûsu? (Water)
8. Momo? (Japanese pear)
9. Gogo? (a.m.)
10. Ocha? (Indian tea)
11. Keisu? (Despatch-case)
12. Shimbun? (Magazine)

Exercise 2
Doko de aimashô ka? Where shall we meet?

1. In front of the museum.
2. Behind the bank.
3. Next to Mr Satô's house.
4. At the station.
5. In front of the baseball-park.

Exercise 3
Nani o erabimashita ka? What did you choose?

1. 5 red roses.
2. 7 big chrysanthemums.
3. 3 white lilies.
4. 6 small eggs.
5. 20 cigarettes.
6. 3 100 yen stamps.

Exercise 4
Change the plain form (**Example:** Wakatta. – Wakarimashita):

1. Hon o yonda.
2. Ringo o katta.
3. Ongaku o kiita.
4. Gaikokujin ni atta.

5. Ehagaki o kaita.
6. Sushi o tabeta.

Exercise 5
Change the verb in brackets to the past plain form (**Example:** Kinô (kau) osaifu o mimashita ka? – Kinô katta osaifu o mimashita ka?):
1. Kinô (yomu) hon wa omoshirokatta no desu.
2. Tôkyô e (kuru) sensei ni aimashita ka?
3. Motte (iku) tamago o tabemashita ka?
4. Kyonen (toru) shashin o mô misemashita ka?
5. (Wasureru) tegami o motte kimashita ka?
6. (Narau) kanji o oboete imasu ka?
7. (Morau) ehagaki o mitsukemasu.
8. (Ikeru) hana wa kirei desu nê.

Section B
Exercise 6
Make verb-nouns (**Example**: I hate reading books. – Hon o yomu koto ga kirai desu.):
1. I like eating sushi.
2. I hate studying.
3. I like walking.
4. I hate drinking saké.
5. I like going to the cinema.
6. I hate listening to music.

Exercise 7
Translate:
1. I think I shall go to Yokohama tomorrow.
2. I think he went to Kobe yesterday.
3. Do you think he will come to the office today?
4. Do you think he bought a dictionary at the bookshop?

Exercise 8
Translate:
1. Momoiro no kiku o nambon kau tsumori desu ka?
2. Mainichi Nihongo o kiku no wa benri desu.
3. Tomodachi no kuru no o matsu koto wa omoshiroku wa arimasen.
4. Takai yama no soba ni matsu ga takusan arimasu.

5. Eigo o oboetai desu kara yoku benkyô suru tsumori desu.
6. Eiga o mite kara osushi o tabe ni ikimashô ka?

Exercise 9
Translate:
1. The dictionary I bought yesterday is not good.
2. The medicine I took last Friday was not very nice.
3. The flowers your mother arranged are lovely.
4. Where are the photographs you took in America?
5. The book I chose this morning is uninteresting.

Exercise 10 📼
Play the part of Mr Satô in the following dialogue:
Mr Itô: Kondo no suiyôbi ni Yokohama e ikimashô ka?
Mr Satô: (Hold on a minute. I'll look in my diary. Sorry, that's no good. Thursday would be all right. How about you?)
Mr Itô: Kekkô desu. Doko de aimashô ka?
MrSatô: .... (Shall we meet in front of your house?)
Mr Itô: Sô shimashô. Nanji ni?
MrSatô: .... (At eight-thirty.)
Mr Itô: Densha de ikimashô ka?
MrSatô: ... (No, I'll have the car so I'll pick you up on the way.)
Mr Itô: Arigatô.
MrSatô: ... (Oh . . . have you seen the flowers my sister brought from the country?)
Mr Itô: Totemo kirei desu ne.
MrSatô: .... (I love chrysanthemums.)
Mr Itô: Bara no hô ga utsukushii to omoimasu.
MrSatô: .... (I like red roses but I don't like white ones.)
Mr Itô: Oneesan no kekkonshiki wa itsu desu ka?
MrSatô: .... (On the 24th. Here's a photo of her new house. Look.)
Mr Itô: Subarashii desu nê.
MrSatô: .... (Now she's living in Matsumoto but she intends coming to Tôkyô on the 15th.)
Mr Itô: Sô desu ka. Tôkyô de hatarakitai desu ka?
MrSatô: .... (Yes. As she's an English teacher she'll teach in a middle school.)
Mr Itô: Oneesan wa Igirisu e itta koto ga arimasu ka?
MrSatô: (Yes, she went to London last July and two years ago she went to America.)

AT THE BANK
AND AT THE GARAGE

19.1 DIALOGUES 📼

Dialogue 1

Mr Foster asks where the bank is.

Mr Foster: Nanji ni ginkô wa akimasu ka?
Mr Itô: Kuji han desu.
Mr Foster: Nanji ni shimarimasu ka?
Mr Itô: Yoji han desu.
Mr Foster: Ichiban chikai ginkô wa doko ni arimasu ka?
Mr Itô: Kôban wa shitte imasu ka?
Mr Foster: Shitte imasu yo.
Mr Itô: Kôban no soba ni supaa ga arimasu ne.
Mr Foster: Ee. Kinô supaa e itte sekken o kaimashita.
Mr Itô: Ano . . . Sono supaa no ushiro ni ôkina tatemono ga arimasu.
Mr Foster: Sore ga ginkô deshô.
Mr Itô: Chigaimasu. Sore wa apaato desu ga sono tatemono no yoko ni ginkô ga arimasu.

Dialogue 2 📼

Mr Foster opens an account.

Mr Foster: Sumimasen ga . . . Ano . . . kôza o hirakitai no desu ga dô sureba ii no deshô ka?
Clerk: Kantan desu yo. Kochira ni onamae o kaite itadakereba sugu ni kôza o hiraku koto ga dekimasu.
Mr Foster: Pondo o en ni kaete kudasaimasu ka?
Clerk: Hai.
Mr Foster: Kyô wa ichipondo wa nan-en desu ka?
Clerk: Chotto matte kudasai. Ima shirabete kimasu kara . . . . Kyô wa nihyakuhachijûnana-en desu.
Mr Foster: Kinô yori yasui desu nê.
Clerk: Sô desu ne. Mainichi kawarimasu kara.
Mr Foster: En wa kawariyasui desu nê!
Clerk: Iie! Pondo desu yo!
Mr Foster: Hyakupondo o en ni kaete itadakemasen ka?
Clerk: Kashikomarimashita. Tesûryô o itadakimasu ga yoroshii desu ka?
Mr Foster: Sore wa shirimasen deshita. Nampaasento deshô ka?
Clerk: Gopaasento desu. Sumimasen.
Mr Foster: Iie, kamaimasen.

Dialogue 3 🔲

At a filling-station.

Mr Foster: Gasorin o irenakereba narimasen. Asoko ni gasorinsutando ga arimasu kara tomarimashô.
Mantan ni shite kudasai.

Attendant: Hai.
Okyakusan! Enjinoiru wa daijôbu desu ka?

Mr Foster: Chotto shirabete kudasai.

Attendant: Ah . . . kore wa daibu furui desu nê. Makkuro desu
yo. Hora!

Mr Foster: Kore wa rentakaa desu ga . . .

Attendant: Hidoi kaisha da nâ! Oiru o sukoshi iremashô ka?

Mr Foster: Irete kudasai.

Attendant: Ichirittoru iremashô.

Mr Foster: Taiya mo chiekku shite kudasai.

Attendant: Wakarimashita. Sore dewa kuruma o chotto achira
e ugokashite kudasai. Furonto garasu o
araimashô ka?

Mr Foster: Iie, arawanakute mo ii desu. Kirei desu kara. Mada
ato hyakkiro mo unten shinakereba narimasen.

Attendant: Kôsokudôro wa konde imasu kara ki o tsukete
kudasai. Mata dôzo!

19.2 VOCABULARY

akimasu	from aku, to open up, be opened
shimarimasu	from shimaru, to shut up, close up, be closed
kôban	police-box
shitte	-te form of shiru, to know (a strong verb)
supaa	supermarket
sekken	soap
ushiro	behind
apaato	block of flats
kôza	account
hiraku	open, start, establish
kantan	simple
sugu ni	straightaway
pondo	pound sterling

kaete	-te form of **kaeru**, to change, convert (a weak verb)
shirabete	-te form of **shiraberu**, to check, look into, examine (a weak verb)
kawarimasu	from **kawaru**, to change, alter
kawariyasui	changeable, fickle
kashikomarimashita	certainly, sir
tesûryô	commission, charge, fee
yoroshii	all right, fine, OK
paasento	per cent
kamaimasen	that doesn't matter, never mind (from **kamau**, to care about)
gasorin	petrol
gasorinsutando	filling-station
tomarimashô	from **tomaru**, to stop
mantan ni suru	fill up
(o)kyaku(san)!	sir! (literally, honoured guest)
enjinoiru	oil
daibu	considerably
furui	old
makkuro	black as pitch
hora!	just look!
rentakaa	hired car
hidoi	awful, dreadful
nâ!	I'd say!
-rittoru	litre
taiya	tyre
chiekku suru	check
achira	over there
ugokasu	move
furonto garasu	windscreen
araimashô	from **arau**, to wash
-nakute mo ii desu	there is no need to
kirei	clean
ato	after
-kiro	kilometre
kôsokudôro	motorway
mata dôzo!	until the next time! hope to see you again!

19.3 EXPLANATIONS

(a) The police

The main police-station in each area is the keisatsusho. Keisatsu means the police-force *as a whole*. An *individual policeman* is technically junsa, though the term generally used is omawarisan (adapted from mawaru, to make one's rounds, to patrol).

Supplementary to the keisatsusho are many small *police-boxes* or kôban. These are especially useful as Japanese streets are not named and so, very often, the only way of finding one's way is to 'ask a policeman'. There will usually be a map of the area by the kôban to enable one to thread the impenetrable maze of Japanese streets.

(b) Buildings

Because of the frequent *earthquakes*, Japanese buildings used to be low and chiefly made of wood. Modern techniques have encouraged the construction of many high concrete buildings which are all supposed to be earthquake-proof.

(c) Pairs of transitive/intransitive verbs

There are several pairs of verbs in Japanese (aku/akeru; shimaru/ shimeru; tomaru/tomeru). The *weak* verbs are *transitive* – that is, they *take an object*. The *strong* verbs are *intransitive* – that is, they can *stand on their own*:

mado o akemashita	I opened the window
mado o shimemashita	I closed the window
kuruma o tomemashita	I stopped the car

Compare:

Nanji ni ginkô wa akimasu ka?	What time do the banks open?
Nanji ni shimarimasu ka?	What time do they close?
tomarimashô	let's stop

(d) shiru

shiru, to know, is usually used in the continuous form because it is assumed if you knew it once, *you still do!*:

Kôban wa shitte imasu ka?	Do you know the police-box?

The *past negative* is straightforward:

> Sore wa shirimasen   I didn't know that.
> deshita.

(e) The potential form

The potential form is another way of expressing 'to be able to'. We actually came across this in Chapter 6, with the verb **itadakeru**. Basically, you can take any strong verb and replace the final -u by -eru, thus making it into a *weak verb*:

hanas-u	hanas-e	hanaseru	hanasemasu
yom-u	yom-e	yomeru	yomemasu
itadak-u	itadak-e	itadakeru	itadakemasu

This form means exactly the same as the construction **koto ga dekimasu** but, as it can be done only with *strong* verbs, it is not as 'universal' as the **koto ga dekimasu** form:

> Samman-en de otsuri o itadakemasu ka?
> Samman-en de otsuri o itadaku koto ga dekimasu ka?
> May I please have the change from 30 000 yen?
> (Literally, can I ask you for the change from 30, 000 yen?)
> Hyakupondo o en ni kaete itadakemasen ka?
>   itadaku koto ga
>   dekimasen ka?
> Would you be so kind as to change 100 pounds into yen?
> (Literally, can't I ask you to change 100 pounds into yen?)

A slight complication with the potential form is that usually it requires **ga** rather than **o**.

> Nihongo o hanasu koto ga dekimasu ka?
> Nihongo ga hanasemasu ka?
>   Can you speak Japanese?
>
> Sono hon o yomu koto ga dekimasu ka?
> Sono hon ga yomemasu ka?
>   Can you read that book?

Especially as you can only use the **koto ga dekimasu** form with *weak verbs*, it is probably safer to stick with the form we have learnt – but the potential form is a very useful 'short cut', and is very common in colloquial Japanese. It is as well to be able to recognise it, at least.

(f) I'll just go and see
Shirabete kimasu (literally, 'having checked, I'll return' – i.e., I'll just go and see).

(g) Japanese roads
Kôsokudôro: kô = high, soku = speed, dôro = roadway

Japanese roads tend to use one kanji from each of the cities they are linking, thus altering the reading. For instance, the roads linking Tokyo (東 京) and Yokohama (横 浜) are called the dai-ichi or dai-ni Kei-hin (京 浜) (no. 1 or no. 2 with the on or Chinese reading of kyô (京) and hama (浜)). In Chapter 18 we met Han-shin (阪 神) – han is the on reading of saka (阪) and shin the on reading of Kô (神), hence Osaka (大 阪) and Kobe (神 戸). Once more, you can see how important it is to start reading place-names!

Note that when driving on the motorway, you must not exceed the 105 kph speed limit – each car must have a bell or 'bleeper' that tells you when you have touched 106 kph.

(h) -nakute mo ii desu
The opposite of -nakereba narimasen is -nakute mo ii desu. This really means 'even not doing something is all right'. You take the *negative infinitive form* (see Chapter **11.3 (f)** if you need to refresh your memory), cut off the final -i and add -kute mo ii desu:

Nihongo de hanasanai.
    hanasanakute mo ii desu. You don't need to
    speak Japanese.
Osashimi o tabenakute mo ii desu.
You don't have to eat that raw fish.

(i) Expressions with suru
In current Japanese there are several expressions borrowed from the English and used with suru:

chiekku shite kudasai	please check
purinto shite kudasai	please print it
koppii shimashô ka	shall I make a copy?

(j) no desu/n desu

As we saw in Chapter **18.3(d)**, no desu (or sometimes n desu) is used to *complete an idea*:

> Kôza o hirakitai no desu.   I wish to open an account.
> Kôbe e ikitai n desu.   I want to go to Kobe.

It has no special meaning, but seems to soften the 'rawness' of the expression.

19.4 EXERCISES

Section A
Exercise 1
Which verb should we use? aku/akeru; shimaru/shimeru; tomaru/tomeru?

1. Kuruma o .... (tomarimashita? tomemashita?)
2. Kuruma wa .... (tomarimashita? tomemashita?)
3. Hako o .... (akimashita? akemashita?)
4. Hon'ya wa rokuji ni .... (shimarimasu? shimemasu?)

Exercise 2
Change the reply (**Example**:
Nihongo de hanasanakereba narimasen ka? – Iie, Nihongo de hanasanakute mo ii desu.):

1. Tabako o nomanakereba narimasen ka?
2. Mado o akenakereba narimasen ka?
3. Shashin o toranakereba narimasen ka?
4. Tegami o kakanakereba narimasen ka?
5. Momo o kawanakereba narimasen ka?
6. Ashita konakereba narimasen ka?

Exercise 3
Give instructions – and be as polite as you like!

1. Mado o arau.
2. En o pondo ni kaeru.
3. Onamae o kaku.
4. Kuruma o ugokasu.
5. Shiraberu.
6. Mantan ni suru.

Exercise 4
Link the following sentences putting the first verb in brackets into the
-te form and the second verb into the past tense:
1. Ginkô ni (hairu) kôza o (hiraku).
2. Kôza o (hiraku) pondo o en ni (kaeru).
3. Pondo o (kaeru) ginkô kara (kaeru).
4. Ginkô kara (kaeru) denwa o (kakeru).
5. Denwa o (kakeru) tomodachi o kuruma de (hirou).
6. Tomodachi o kuruma de (hirou) tempura o (taberu).
7. Tempura o (taberu) yûbinkyoku e (iku).
8. Yûbinkyoku e (iku) kitte o (kau).
9. Kitte o (kau) ehagaki o (kaku).
10. Ehagaki o (kaku) shimbun o (yomu).

Exercise 5
Translate the following:
1. Gasorin wa irimasu.
2. Gasorin o irete kudasai.
3. Osatô wa irimasu ka?
4. Osatô o iremashita.

Section B
Exercise 6
Translate:
1. Do you know Mr. Satô?
2. I didn't know that.
3. Do you know the police-box by the saké shop?
4. You must know that word!

Exercise 7
What do the following expressions mean?
1. Okyakusan!
2. Kashikomarimashita.
3. Kamaimasen.
4. Sumimasen.
5. Ki o tsukete kudasai.
6. Onegai shimasu.
7. Gomen kudasai.
8. Gochisô shimasu.

Exercise 8
Translate:
1. Shall I move the car over there a bit?
2. There's a lot of traffic on the motorway.
3. Please check the tyres.
4. I've got another eighty kilometres to do.

Exercise 9
Transpose the following into the -koto ga dekimasu form (**Example**: Asahi Shimbun ga yomemasu – Asahi Shimbun o yomu koto ga dekimasu.):
1. Furansugo ga hanasemasen.
2. Nemuremashita.
3. Hatarakemasen.
4. Itadakemasu ka?

Exercise 10
Play the part of Mr Smith in the following dialogues:

Dialogue 1
Mr Satô: Nanji ni jimusho wa akimasu ka?
MrSmith: .... (8:15)
Mr Satô: Nanji ni otaku e kaerimasu ka?
MrSmith: .... (About 7 p.m.)
Mr Satô: Ichiban chikai tabakoya wa doko ni arimasu ka?
MrSmith: .... (How many cigarettes do you smoke a day?)
Mr Satô: Nijippon gurai.
MrSmith: .... (Really! Anyway . . . you know the bank?)
Mr Satô: Hai.
MrSmith: .... (There's a filling-station next to the bank isn't there.)
Mr Satô: Sô desu.
MrSmith: .... (Well, behind the filling-station there's a tobacconist's)

Dialogue 2
MrSmith: ... (Excuse me. I'd like to open an account. How do I do it?)
Clerk: Kantan desu yo. Kochira ni onamae o kaite kudasai.
MrSmith: .... (I understand.)
Clerk: Amerika no kata de gozaimasu ka?
MrSmith: .... (No, I'm English.)
Clerk: Nihongo ga ojôzu desu nê!

MrSmith: .... (How many yen to the pound to-day?)
Clerk: Kyô wa sambyaku-en desu.
MrSmith: .... (Really? It's higher than yesterday. Could you change £50 please?)

A JAPANESE INN

20.1 DIALOGUES

Dialogue 1 📼
Mr Foster books a room by telephone.
Mr Foster: Moshi moshi.
Clerk: Hakutsuru ryokan de gozaimasu.
Mr Foster: Chotto okiki shitai no desu ga jûgatsu muika no ban heya wa aite imasu ka?
Clerk: Shôshô o machi kudasai ... Nanninsama de irasshaimasu ka?
Mr Foster: Futari desu.
Clerk: Nannichi otomari desu ka?
Mr Foster: Mikkakan desu.
Clerk: Chôdo keshiki no yoi heya ga aite imasu ga ikaga desu ka?
Mr Foster: Oikura deshô ka?
Clerk: Hitoban de nishoku tsuki ichiman-en ni narimasu.
Mr Foster: Igirisu yori yasui desu nê! Ima yoyaku dekimasu ka?
Clerk: Mochiron kekkô de gozaimasu. Nanji ni otsuki deshô ka?
Mr Foster: Tôkyô kara kisha de ikimasu kara tabun rokuji gurai ni tsuku to omoimasu.
Clerk: Hai. Wakarimashita. Okoshi o omachi shite orimasu.
Mr Foster: Gomen kudasai.

Dialogue 2 📼
Mr Foster writes to Mr Itô from Kyoto.

Sakuban rokujihan ni buji ni tsukimashita. Watakushitachi no heya wa totemo subarashii desu. Mado kara Higashiyama o miru koto ga dekimasu. Yûhan no mae ni ofuro e ikimashita ga hajimete deshita no de sukoshi hazukashikatta n desu. Tonikaku daijôbu deshita! Ofuro kara kaette yukata o kite mimashita. Yûhan o motte kita jôchûsan wa watakushitachi o mite bikkuri shimashita! Ryokan niwa hoka ni gaikokujin wa imasen kara. Osake o nomanai kanai wa ocha o nomimashita.

Tôkyô de awanakatta imôtosan wa Matsumoto e kaerimashita ka?

Kisha de atta Doitsujin wa anata no kaisha o shitte imashita. Yononaka semai mono desu ne!

Watakushitachi wa getsuyôbi niwa Tôkyô e kaerimasu kara kyô denkigaisha e tegami o kakanakute mo ii desu. Watakushi ga kaette kara kakimasu.

Sora ga kuraku natte kimashita kara ame ga furu kamo shiremasen. Sampo shitakatta no desu ga zannen desu!

Kesa anata ga kaita ehagaki o moraimashita. Kono tegami ga watakushitachi ga Tôkyô ni kaeru mae ni todoku to ii no desu ga . . .

Okusama ni yoroshiku

Jim Foster

東京都大田区
長原2丁目39-4
伊藤二郎様

Tôkyô-to Ôta-ku
Nagahara 2 Chôme 39–4
Mr Itô Jirô

20.2 VOCABULARY

moshi moshi!	Hallo! (on the telephone)
hakutsuru	white crane
ryokan	traditional Japanese inn
ban	evening (see p. 302)
aite imasu	(from aku) free, unoccupied, vacant
shôshô	a little while (like chotto)
(o)tomari	staying, stopping
chôdo	just, exactly, precisely
keshiki	scenery
keshiki no ii/yoi	with a beautiful view
hitoban	one evening
shoku	meal
tsuki	including
yoyaku	reservation, booking
(o)tsuki	arrival (from tsuku, to arrive)
(o)koshi	coming
orimasu	(here) a politer form of imasu
sakuban	yesterday evening
buji ni	safely

higashi	east
yama	mountain
(o)furo	bath
tonikaku	anyway
yukata	Japanese dressing-gown
kite	-te form of kiru, put on (kimono, a thing you put on), (a weak verb)
kite mimashita	tried on
jôchû(san)	maid
bikkuri suru	be surprised
hoka ni	apart from, otherwise
nomanai	negative of nomu
awanakatta	past negative of au
yononaka	the world
semai	narrow
mon(o)	thing
denki	electricity
denkigaisha	electric company
sora	sky
kurai	dark
kamo shiremasen	may, might
zannen	pity, shame
todoku	reach, get to
to	if (after infinitive)
to ii	it would be nice if – i.e., I hope that
ni yoroshiku	best wishes to

20.3 EXPLANATIONS

(a) The ryokan

Accommodation in a traditional Japanese inn consists of a room floored in tatami with a kotatsu, a kind of sunken heated area beneath a table so you can sit snugly in winter (even though your back can still be chilly!). All meals are served in the room.

There will be two huge *bathrooms*, one for men and one for women. Families can book smaller bathrooms. If the hotel is at a hot spring or spa the bath will be a great feature of the place.

Washing in Japan takes place *outside* the bath. You sluice yourself with hot water (and the unwary foreigner should be warned that Japanese baths are *very* hot!), soap yourself, get yourself nice and clean, sluice all the soap off and when you are spick and span from top to toe you enter the big bath and wallow luxuriously.

Yukata, cotton gowns are provided by the hotel and people wear them inside the hotel.

(b) The 'Bullet' train

The first high-speed train in the world running on welded rails was constructed in Japan in the 1960s and ran from Tokyo to Ôsaka via Kyôto. It is called the **shinkansen**, the new main line.

(c) Addresses

Japan is divided administratively into prefectures, ken – Aomori-ken, Chiba-ken. Cities carry the suffix -shi – Yokohama-shi, Kôbe-shi. Tôkyô, the metropolis, alone carries the suffix -to and is subdivided into -ku – Ôta-ku Shinjuku-ku, Chiyoda-ku, etc. Small towns or suburbs are divided into chôme. Mr Itô (who, being the second son, is called Jirô) lives in the second house built in the thirty-ninth plot of no. 2 chôme. It is by no means likely that his neighbours on each side are numbered consecutively, as numbering depends on *when* the house was built, not where. He could live in 39–2 and be flanked by 39–11 on one side and 39–4 on the other.

(d) Another proverb

Yononaka semai mono desu ne.
It's a small world.

Japanese proverbs, as you will recall from Chapter 4.3, *dispense with particles*.

(e) Making an enquiry

kiku, to hear, means also to enquire:

Chotto kikitai desu (or, more politely, chotto o kiki shitai no desu) I'd like to enquire

(f) aku

The verb **aku** is used to express the idea of something being *free*, *vacant* or *unoccupied*:

heya wa aite imasu ka?	Have you a room available?
asoko ni teeburu ga aite imasu.	there's a table free over there.

(g) The plain form in the negative

You use the plain form in the negative to make *relative clauses*:

Kanai wa osake o nomi-masen	My wife does not drink saké.
Osake o nomanai kanai wa mizu o nomimashita	My wife who does not drink saké drank water.
Yokohama e ikanai hito wa koko e kite kudasai.	Those not going to Yokohama come over here please (see Grammar Summary 13(b) and (c)).

(h) The past negative plain forms

The past negative plain forms are made as in Chapter **18.3(d)** because the negative infinitives are in fact *adjectives*. Take off the -i and put -katta in its place:

au, to meet	awanai	awanakatta
taberu, to eat	tabenai	tabenakatta

This form is used in *relative clauses*:

Awanakatta imôtosan wa kaerimashita ka?
Has your sister whom I didn't meet gone back?
neko wa watakushi ga tabenakatta sakana o tabete shimaimashita.
The cat ate up the fish I didn't eat.

So the four tenses of each verb have *alternative plain forms*:

mimasu	(I) see	miru
mimasen	don't see	minai
mimashita	saw	mita
mimasen deshita	didn't see	minakatta
hanashimasu	(I) speak	hanasu
hanashimasen	don't speak	hanasanai
hanashimashita	spoke	hanashita

hanashimasen deshita	didn't speak	hanasanakatta
shimasu	(I) do	suru
shimasen	don't	shinai
shimashita	did	shita
shimasen deshita	didn't	shinakatta

(i) Expressions of time

In Chapter **15.3(f)**, we met jikan:

Sanjikan kakarimasu.	It takes three hours.

The suffix -kan can also be used after other *expressions of time*:

mikkakan desu	it'll be three days
sanshûkan desu	it'll be for three weeks

but note:

isshûkan	1 week
hasshûkan	8 weeks
jisshûkan	10 weeks
rokunenkan	for six years

For *numbers of months*, the suffix -kagetsu is used:

nikagetsu	2 months

but note:

ikkagetsu	1 month
rokkagetsu	6 months
jikkagetsu	10 months

(j) kamo shiremasen

After the plain form, this means 'may', or 'may possibly':

ame ga furu kamo shiremasen	it may rain
imôto ga konai kamo shiremasen	my sister may not come

(k) sora ga kuraku natte kimashita.

The sky has clouded over, has come over dark.

(l) to after the infinitive
to after the infinitive means 'if':

Yokohama e iku to otôto ni au koto ga dekimasu.

    If you should go to Yokohama you can meet my brother.

This construction is often used with ii desu, and this is the best way of expressing the ideas of 'hoping to':

    Kono tegami ga ashita todoku to ii desu.
    I hope this letter will arrive to-morrow.
    (literally, if this letter arrives to-morrow good!)
    kono tegami ga watakushi ga Tôkyô ni kaeru mae ni todoku to ii desu.
    I hope this letter will arrive before I return to Tôkyô.

20.4 EXERCISES

Section A
Exercise 1
Put in the appropriate particles (ga, ka, ni, o, to, wa):
1. Ashita kuru ——— kimatte imasu.
2. Sensei ——— kaita hon ——— yomimashita ———?
3. Sukiyaki ——— tabe ——— ikimashô ———?
4. Maguro ——— shimasu.
5. Sore ——— shirimasen deshita.
6. Biiru ——— nihon kudasai.
7. Mado ——— akemashita.
8. Dochira ——— katsu ——— omoimasu ———?
9. Nanji ——— jimusho ——— akimasu ———?
10. En ——— pondo ——— kaemashita.

Exercise 2
Say it may occur (**Example:** Ame ga furimasu. – Ame ga furu kamo shiremasen.):
1. Tôkyô e ikimasu.
2. Bikkuri shimasu.
3. Kanji o naraimasu.
4. Hairimasu.

Exercise 3

Convert to the past negative plain form (**Example**: aimasen deshita – awanakatta):
1. Yomimasen deshita.
2. Todokimasen deshita.
3. Akemasen deshita.
4. Koko e kimasen deshita.
5. Yukata o kimasen deshita.
6. Shirimasen deshita.
7. Purinto shimasen deshita.
8. Tomarimasen deshita.
9. Kuruma o ugokashimasen deshita.
10. Ikimasen deshita.

Exercise 4

Say what you want and wanted to do (**Example**: Sampo suru. – Sampo shitai no desu. Sampo shitakatta no desu.):
1. Shimbun o yomu.
2. Eiga o miru.
3. Yûbinkyoku e iku.
4. Asoko ni tomaru.
5. Nihongo de hanasu.

Exercise 5

You are telephoning a ryokan. Ask if there is a room free on:
1. January 25.
2. March 4.
3. July 8.
4. August 13.
5. September 2.
6. Next Wednesday.
7. Next Saturday.
8. On Friday the week after next.

Exercise 6

The clerk asks you how many people are involved:
Nanninsama de irasshaimasu ka?
You reply:
1. One.
2. Two.
3. Three.
4. Four.

5. Myself and my son.
6. My wife and my daughter.

Exercise 7
The clerk asks you how long you are intending to stay: Nannichi otomari desu ka? *you reply*:
1. One night.
2. Two nights.
3. Four nights.
4. Five nights.
5. Six nights.
6. One week.
7. Two weeks.
8. One month.
9. Six months.
10. Seven months.

Exercise 8
The clerk tells you how much. You turn to your friend and say how much it comes to per night with two meals included:
1. 9500 yen.
2. 11 000 yen.
3. 14 000 yen.
4. 20 000 yen.

Section B
Exercise 9
Translate:
1. The book I didn't read.
2. The man who didn't write that letter.
3. The man who didn't come to the office yesterday.
4. The purse you didn't buy.

Exercise 10
What sort of a person is it? (**Example:** A woman who doesn't drink saké. – Osake o nomanai onna no kata desu.)
1. A man who does not speak Japanese.
2. A child who does not study.
3. A man who does not smoke.
4. A Japanese who does not eat raw fish.
5. A friend who does not return to his home-town.

Exercise 11

Translate:

1. When we got back to Tokyo we used the phone.
2. When we reached Kyoto we met your friend.
3. If we stop the car over there we'll be able to see Mt Fuji.
4. I hope we arrive at the inn before 6.
5. I hope he'll come before dinner.

REVISION AND
SELF-ASSESSMENT TESTS
FOR CHAPTERS 15–20

Do this test and mark it, using the mark-scheme suggested. *If* you made any mistakes make sure you go back and revise the relevant chapter(s).

Section 1
1. Ask where the toilet is.
2. Ask where the police-station is.
3. Ask where the doctor's house is.
4. Ask where the Japanese inn is.
5. Ask where the nearest police-box is.

(Score: 5)

Section 2
Put in the appropriate particles (de, ga, na, ni, no, o, to, wa)
1. Eigo —— wakarimasu.
2. Yûmei —— tokoro desu.
3. Tôkyô —— umaremashita.
4. Oji —— kaita tegami —— yomimashita.
5. Jirô —— iu tomodachi —— shitte imasu ka?
6. Biiru —— shimasu.
7. Itsu tsuku —— omoimasu ka?
8. Supaa —— soba —— ginkô —— arimasu.
9. Takushii —— kimashita.
10. Raishû kaeru —— kimatte imasu.
11. Kauntaa —— suwarimashô.

(Score: 15)

Section 3

Reply converting the name (**Example:** Okusan wa itsu Nihon e kimashita ka? (Yesterday) – Kanai wa kinô Nihon e kimashita.):

1. Ojôsan no tanjôbi wa itsu desu ka? (April 1st)
2. Botchan wa nansai desu ka? (8)
3. Okaasan wa itsu kaerimasu ka? (July 10th)
4. Oniisan wa nani o shite imasu ka? (He's working in an office)
5. Imôtosan wa nannen ni umaremashita ka? (1956)

(Score: 10)

Section 4

What is the Japanese for these words?

1. To open (something).
2. To close (something).
3. Light-coloured.
4. Dark.
5. Last year.
6. This year.
7. The day before yesterday.
8. The day after tomorrow.
9. Happy.
10. Lonely.

(Score: 10)

Section 5

What do the following set-phrases mean?

1. Sore wa ikemasen ne.
2. Zannen desu ga.
3. Go yukkuri.
4. Ki o tsukete kudasai.
5. Okanjô o onegai shimasu.
6. Dame desu.
7. Omedetô gozaimasu.
8. Kashikomarimashita.

(Score: 8)

Section 6

Translate the following:

1. I like eating.
2. I dislike going to the cinema.

3. I like driving.
4. I dislike arranging flowers.

(Score: 4)

Section 7
Answer the following questions:
1. Byôki ni naru to nani o shinakereba narimasen ka?
2. Kitte o kaitai hito wa doko e ikimasu ka?
3. Tempuraya e iku to nani o taberu koto ga dekimasu ka?
4. Hamigaki o kaitakereba doko e ikanakereba narimasen ka?

(Score: 12)

Section 8

Translate the following:
1. Those kanji are easy to read.
2. That book is hard to read.
3. The weather is changeable.
4. Your name is easy to write.

(Score: 4)

Section 9
Who are these people and what are they doing?
1. Shashin o totte iru hito wa asoko ni sunde imasu.
2. Megane o kakete iru kata wa sûgaku no sensei desu.
3. Aruite kaette iru hito wa ane desu.
4. Tabako o sutte iru otoko wa gaikokujin desu.

(Score: 8)

Section 10
Translate:
1. Ongaku o kikinagara zasshi o yomimashita.
2. Kono jibiki wa ii desu kara otomodachi no tame ni narimasu.
3. Gekijô e itta koto ga arimasu ka?
4. Hazukashigaranaide yûgohan o taberu mae ni ofuro e itte kudasai.
5. Kanai ga kawanakatta saifu wa chiisakute akakatta n desu.

(Score: 15)

Section 11
Express the following in Japanese:
1. It may snow.
2. He may arrive before lunch.
3. You don't have to wash my car.
4. You don't have to change your pounds into yen.

(Score: 8)

Section 12
Translate:
1. Satô-san no okusan ga tsukutta nasu to shiitake wa oishii desu.
2. Senshû hairanakatta hon'ya e itte kimi ga kaita hon o kaimashita.
3. Otomodachi ga eranda heya wa totemo subarashikatta n desu.
4. Watakushi ga shiranakatta kanji o oshiete kudasaimasen ka?

(Score: 12)

Section 13
What shall we do?
1. Let's take a seat.
2. Let's open an account.
3. Let's pick up Nobuo on the way.
4. Let's go in.

(Score: 4)

Section 14 🖭
Read the following conversation or listen to it on your cassette. If you have the cassette, do *not* read the text. Then answer the questions underneath.

A. : Eiga o mi ni ikimashô ka?
B. : Sô shimashô. Sore wa tanoshimi desu ne. Itsu deshô ka?
A. : Kondo no kin'yôbi wa ikaga desu ka?
B. : Chotto matte kudasai. Techô o mimasu kara. Ah . . . dame desu yo. Imôto ga Yokohama kara kuru sô desu kara. Raishû no getsuyôbi nara ii desu keredomo.
A. : Raishû no getsuyôbi desu ka? Doko de aimashô ka?
B. : Watakushi wa kuruma ga arimasu kara tochû de anata o hiroimashô.

A. : Arigatô gozaimasu. Demo futsû kuruma ga konde imasu kara chikatetsu de iku hô ga ii to omoimasu. Desu kara eki no mae de aimashô ne.

B. : Nan no eiga o mimashô ka?

A. : Atarashii Igirisu no eiga o mitai desu keredomo.

B. : Eigakan wa nanji ni akimasu ka?

A. : Shimbun ga arimasu ka?

B. : Arimasu yo . . . Eeto . . . Doko ni arimasu ka? Omoi-dashimashita! Daidokoro ni arimasu. Chotto matte kudasai. Shimbun o mitsukete kimasu . . . Ano, sono eigakan wa niji ni akimasu.

A. : Yoru wa?

B. : Shichijihan desu.

A. : Watakushi wa getsuyôbi hirugohan no ato ni Yamada to iu tomodachi ni awanakereba narimasen kara yoru ni shimashô ka?

B. : Kekkô desu. Eiga o mite kara doko de yûgohan o tabemashô ka?

A. : Tempuraya wa dô deshô ka?

B. : Ii desu yo.

1. What does the first speaker suggest they do?
2. When does he suggest?
3. Why cannot the second speaker make it?
4. When does the second speaker prefer?
5. How does the second speaker suggest they get there?
6. Why is this a bad idea?
7. What does the first speaker propose?
8. Where will they meet?
9. What would he like to see?
10. Where is the newspaper?
11. What time does the place open?
12. Why cannot the first speaker make it in the afternoon?
13. When will they in fact go?
14. When will they have dinner?
15. Where will they have it?

(Score: 15)

Self-assessment grades: Maximum total = 130.
Over 100: Excellent
75–100: Satisfactory
Under 75: More revision needed

II REFERENCE MATERIAL

A NOTE ON
WRITTEN JAPANESE

The aim of everyone who wishes to master Japanese should be to *read* and *write* the language as well as *speak* it. This is difficult, of course, because English and Japanese have no common alphabet or convention of writing it down. It must be stressed that this book is a *first stage.* Japanese transcribed into Western script (rômaji, or Roman letters) is an *entirely artificial* invention, created so as to make the initial approach to the language for the average enthusiast an easy one. But, in fact, many of the difficulties encountered in the language as written in rômaji melt away when you have mastered the written Japanese language. And it does not take long to make a start!

Hiragana consists of 45 symbols (a, i, u, e, o, ka, ki, etc.) with accents to *alter the sound* from k to g, s to z, t to d, and h to b or p. These are used to write the *sound* of Japanese down.

Katakana consists of 45 different symbols for the same sounds and is used to transcribed *foreign words* that have entered the language (basu, terebi, takushii: bus, television, taxi); to give *emphasis* much in the same way as we use italics: I *said* so!; and for *writing telegrams.*

The written Japanese language itself derived from Chinese, and one has to learn many Chinese characters or kanji. The minimum laid down by the Japanese government is 1850 plus 92 which are authorised for names, but in practice one's own interests dictate, after a certain point, which kanji one knows . . . or does not know.

The sentence Watakushi wa Tôkyô e basu de ikimashita would be written like this: Watakushi (one Chinese character); wa (hiragana); Tôkyô (two Chinese characters); e (hiragana); basu (two katakana); de (hiragana); i (Chinese character); kimashita (four hiragana). Thus:

私は東京へバスで行きました

No-one is saying it is easy . . . but it *is* fascinating *and* the proper way to 'see' the written language. There is very little rômaji around in Japan, and the foreigner needs to be able to recognise the Japanese way of indicating *Gents*, *Ladies*, *Entrance*, *Exit*, etc. Some examples of the written language have been introduced in the later chapters of this book – which, we hope, will have whetted the reader's appetite for more. Hiragana and katakana are listed on pp. 330–7, together with those kanji one is most likely to need at first.

Gambatte kudasai! (Keep at it!)

TRANSLATION OF DIALOGUES

IN

CHAPTERS 1–20

Chapter 1: Greetings and introductions
Dialogue 1
Mr Foster: Mr Itô?
Mr Itô: Yes, I'm Itô.
Mr Foster: I'm Foster.
Mr Itô: Is that right? Are you Mr Foster? How do you do?
Mr Foster: How do you do. This is my wife, Mary.
Mr Itô: This is your wife? 'Mary'? Is that right?
Mrs Foster: That's right. I'm Mary. How do you do?
Mr Itô: How are you? Well?
Mrs Foster: Yes, thank you. Very well. And you too I hope?
Mr Itô: Yes, thank you. I'm fine. Now . . . Where are your cases?
Mr Foster: Here. These are our cases. Those by you are not our
            cases.

Dialogue 2
Mrs Foster: My case is a red one.
Mr Itô: Is it big or small?
Mrs Foster: It's a big one. My husband's case also.
Mr Foster: Mine's a big case but it isn't red. It's black.
Mr Itô: Is this it?
Mr Foster: That's it. That's my case.
Mrs Foster: The red case is mine. Thank you.
Mr Foster: Where's my briefcase?
Mrs Foster: Mr Itô! Where's my husband's briefcase?
Mr Itô: Is your husband's briefcase big?
Mrs Foster: No, not big. It's small.
Mr Itô: Is it red? Black?
Mrs Foster: Black.

Mr Itô: Is this your husband's briefcase?
Mrs Foster: That's it.
Mr Foster: That's it. That's my briefcase. Thank you.

Chapter 2:   The family car
Dialogue 1
Mr Foster: Where is your car?
Mr Itô: Over there. It's that red one over there.
Mr Foster: An English car?
Mr Itô: No! It's not an English car. It's a Japanese one.
Mr Foster: Is it! A Japanese car? A Honda?
Mr Itô: No, not a Honda. It's a Mitsubishi.
Mr Foster: My car's a Honda – not an English car!
Mrs Foster: My husband's car is a Honda but my little car is an English car.
Mr Foster.   Yes, indeed. My wife's car is an Austin.

Dialogue 2
Mr Itô: Ah! This is an English car, isn't it.
Mr Foster: It is indeed. This car is a Hillman.
Mr Itô: 'Hi-ru-man'! English names *are* difficult aren't they!
Mr Foster: Difficult?
Mr Itô: Yes. Very difficult.
Mrs Foster: Japanese names are difficult too. 'Yokohama.' 'Yamashita.' 'Kawasaki.' The pronunciation is hard.
Mr Itô: Really? 'Itô' isn't hard! It's easy!
Mrs Foster: It's easy but difficult for English people and Americans.
Mr Itô: That's true. Japanese names are easy for Japanese but they are difficult for foreigners.
Mr Foster: English names are easy for us.
Mr Itô: That's right! They are easy for you.
   Well . . . Here it is. This is my car. Small isn't it!
Mrs Foster: No, it's not small. It's a big one.
Mr Itô: It isn't big.

Chapter 3:   Eating at home
Dialogue 1
Mrs Foster: What do Japanese people eat?
Mrs Itô: A lot of rice. Fish too. Do the English eat rice?
Mr Foster: Yes.
Mrs Foster: Yes, they do.
Mr Itô: They eat rice but they don't eat raw fish!

Mr Foster: Usually they don't but I've eaten raw fish.
Mrs Itô: Have you? In England?
Mr Foster: No. In Japan.
Mrs Itô: And your wife. Has she ever eaten raw fish?
Mrs Foster: No, I haven't.
Mr Itô: Well . . . what are we having for dinner?
Mrs Itô: Rice and fish and leeks.
Mr Itô: What are we drinking?
Mrs Itô: Saké or beer.
Mr Foster: My wife doesn't drink beer. Is there water?
Mrs Itô: Do you drink 'ocha'?
Mrs Foster: What is that?
Mr Foster: Ocha is a Japanese drink. It is good for you!
Mrs Itô: It certainly is!

Dialogue 2:
Mrs Itô: Those are shrimps.
Mrs Foster: Aren't they huge!
Mr Itô: Japanese shrimps are big.
Mr Foster: How do you like them?
Mrs Foster: Mmmm! They're delicious.
Mrs Itô: Aren't English shrimps large?
Mr Foster: No. They aren't big. They're small.
Mrs Foster: American shrimps are big too.
Mr Itô: Yes, they are, aren't they?. Did you eat shrimps in America?
Mrs Foster: Yes.

Dialogue 3
Mr Itô: Mr Foster, will you have some saké?
Mr Foster: Thank you.
Mr Itô: Mrs Foster doesn't drink beer?
Mrs Foster: No, I don't.
Mrs Itô: Will you have some ocha?
Mrs Foster: Thank you. It's delicious.
Mrs Itô: These are leeks. Do you have leeks in England?
Mr Foster: Yes indeed.
Mr Itô: I've eaten leeks in England.
Mr Foster: Japanese leeks are small but English ones are large.
Mr Itô: That's right. They're large, aren't they.
Mrs Itô: Now . . . there's some fruit. What will you have? An apple? A peach?
Mrs Foster: A peach, please.

Mrs Itô: Mr Foster. What will you have?
Mr Foster: I'll have a peach too. Thank you.

Chapter 4:   After dinner
Dialogue 1
Mr Itô: Mr Foster. When did you come to Japan before?
Mr Foster: 1976.
Mrs Itô: 1976 . . . That was Shôwa 51, wasn't it.
Mr Itô: That's right. Shôwa 1 was 1926. Therefore Shôwa 10 was 1935.
Mrs Itô: It's difficult, isn't it!
Mr Itô: It's easy! Shôwa 20 was 1945.
Mr Foster: Shôwa 30 . . .
Mrs Foster: Was 1955!
Mr Itô: You're clever, Mrs Foster!
Mrs Foster: No, I'm not!

Dialogue 2
Mrs Itô: Did you come to Japan too in Shôwa 51, Mary-san?
Mrs Foster: No. I didn't come. My husband came here alone.
Mr Itô: Did you come in the autumn?
Mr Foster: No. In the summer.
Mr Itô: Tokyo summers are hot aren't they!
Mr Foster: They certainly are! They're hot.
Mrs Itô: They're hot and humid.
Mrs Foster   That word mushiatsui? What is it? I don't understand.
Mrs Itô: It is hot. It rains. There is no wind.
Mr Itô: It's bad weather.

Dialogue 3
Mrs Foster: Now it isn't mushiatsui! It's lovely weather.
Mrs Itô: Cool, isn't it?
Mrs Foster: It certainly is.
Mrs Itô: Another cup of tea?
Mrs Foster: No. Thank you very much. That's fine.
Mr Foster: That was an excellent meal!
Mrs Itô: Mr Foster speaks Japanese very well, doesn't he?
Mr Foster: No, I don't.
Mrs Itô: You both speak well. Is Japanese difficult for foreigners?
Mr Foster: Yes! Very difficult!
Mrs Foster: Mr Itô. Is English easy or difficult?
Mr Itô: Very difficult!

Mr Foster: English is easy for the English but Japanese is difficult for them.

Mr Itô: That's true! Japanese is not difficult for Japanese but it is for foreigners.

Chapter 5: The next morning
Dialogue 1

Mrs Itô: Good morning!
Mrs Foster: Good morning!
Mrs Itô: Did you sleep well?
Mrs Foster: Yes, thank you. Very well.
Mrs Itô: A lovely day, isn't it?
Mrs Foster: Oh yes. It's not 'hot and humid'!
Mrs Itô: Now it's September so it's not hot. Is the weather good in England in the autumn?
Mrs Foster: Sometimes but sometimes it rains a lot.
Mrs Itô: In Japan it rains a lot in June and July but usually in autumn it doesn't.
Mrs Foster: Does it snow in winter?
Mrs Itô: In the north and west of Japan but not in Tokyo. Tokyo winters are very cold.
Mrs Foster: Are they? Usually London winters aren't cold. It rains a lot but it doesn't snow.
Mrs Itô: In September there are typhoons. Take care!
Mrs Foster: Every year?
Mrs Itô: No, of course not every year but last year there was a big one.

Dialogue 2:
Mr Itô: Today is Saturday so I'm not going to the office. In England as well is Saturday a holiday?
Mr Foster: Yes. Now it is but ten years ago I went to the office every day - of course not on Sunday!
Mr Itô: The same in Japan but now it's from Monday to Friday.
Mr Foster: Do the children go to school?
Mr Itô: Yes. They go on Saturdays as well. How about England?
Mr Foster: Ten years ago they did but not now. What time do Japanese children go to school?
Mr Itô: 8 in the morning.
Mr Foster: Really! In England it's 9. They come back home at 4.
Mr Itô: In Japan it's 5.

Mr Foster:　When do they have breakfast?
Mr Itô:　7.
Mr Foster:　And lunch?
Mr Itô:　Usually at 12.15.

Dialogue 3
Mr Itô:　What shall we do today?
Mr Foster:　What's the time?
Mr Itô:　10.
Mr Foster:　No! ten past!
Mr Itô:　Is it? Well . . . when did you come yesterday? Half past six, wasn't it?
Mr Foster:　That's right. At 6.30.
Mrs Itô:　It's a lovely day.
Mr Itô:　Beautiful. Shall we drive out into the country?
Mrs Itô:　Let's lunch at 1. Then go for a walk. How about that?
Mr Foster:　A lovely idea! Let's do that!

Chapter 6:　Shopping – 1 Going to the bookshop
Dialogue 1
Mrs Foster:　I'd like to go shopping.
Mrs Itô:　Would you? Where would you like to go?
Mrs Foster:　I'd like to go to the bookshop if that's all right.
Mrs Itô:　Fine. I want to buy a dictionary at the bookshop.
Mrs Foster:　Where is the bookshop?
Mrs Itô:　In front of the Post-Office.
Mrs Foster:　Really? Well, that's good. As I want to get some stamps shall we go together to the Post-Office?
Mrs Itô:　Let's walk. It's only ten minutes.
Mrs Foster:　As it's fine I'd like a walk.
Mrs Itô:　So would I. Shall we be off?
Mrs Foster:　Right. I'd like to see a Japanese bookshop.
Mrs Itô:　It'll be interesting.
Mrs Foster:　Yes, very interesting. What time will you get back to your house?
Mrs Itô:　At half past eleven.

Dialogue 2
Mrs Itô　The bookshop is next to the fruit shop.
Mrs Foster:　Do you want to buy some fruit?
Mrs Itô:　No. I don't want to get any fruit but the fruit do look beautiful don't they?

Mrs Foster: Indeed they do. They are beautiful. The colours of the peaches and the Japanese pears and the apples are really beautiful.

Mrs Itô: Here's the bookshop. Let's go on in. Anyone there?

Shopkeeper: Come on in!

Mrs Itô: My friend is English.

Shopkeeper: Is she really? Has she come over from England?

Mrs Foster: Yes. I arrived in Japan yesterday.

Shopkeeper: Ah! You understand Japanese? You speak it well!

Mrs Foster: No, I'm not at all good at it.

Dialogue 3

Mrs Itô: I want to buy an English–Japanese dictionary. Have you got one?

Shopkeeper: I have indeed. This is a good dictionary

Mrs Itô: Is it expensive?

Shopkeeper: It's a little expensive but it is a very useful dictionary.

Mrs Itô: How much is it?

Shopkeeper: 25 800 yen.

Mrs Itô: Is it? 25 800 yen! It is dear. However as I want to read English books a dictionary is necessary. English words are very hard for me. Here's 30 000 yen.

Shopkeeper: Many thanks. And here's 4200 yen change.

Mrs Itô: Thank you.

Chapter 7: Shopping – 2 At the post office
Dialogue

Mrs Itô: What do you want to get, Mary?

Mrs Foster: Some stamps. As I wrote some letters this morning I want to send them to England.

Mrs Itô: How many did you write?

Mrs Foster: Five.

Mrs Foster: Excuse me. Do you understand English?

Employee: No.

Mrs Foster: Mrs Itô! Would you be so kind as to buy my stamps for me?

Mrs Itô: No! Since you speak Japanese so well, speak it now!

Mrs Foster: Well . . . I'd like to send these letters to England. How much would that be?

Employee: To England? Just a moment.

Mrs Itô: How much are they?

Mrs Foster: I don't know yet.
Employee: Let's see . . . If they're for England it's 350 yen.
Mrs Foster: Five 350 yen stamps please.
Employee: That comes to 1750 yen.
Mrs Foster: Oh I've remembered. My husband wrote two post-cards. How much are they?
Employee: To England?
Mrs Foster: Yes. England.
Employee: Just a moment.
Mrs Itô: Are the stamps expensive?
Mrs Foster: No, not expensive. They're cheap.
Mrs Itô: Are the postcards cheap too?
Mrs Foster: I don't know yet.
Employee: For postcards it's 150 yen.
Mrs Foster: Two, please.
Employee: 300 yen then. So . . . 1750 and 300 makes 2050 yen.
Mrs Foster: I'm sorry. I've only got a 10 000 yen note. Is that all right?
Employee: No problem. There's 7950 yen change. Thank you. Next please.
Mrs Itô: Ten 150 yen stamps, please.
Employee: 1500 yen.
Mrs Itô: Yes. Here's 2000 yen.
Employee: Thank you. So . . . 500 yen change.
Mrs Itô: Many thanks.

Chapter 8:   At Mr Maeda's office
Dialogue 1

Mr Itô: I'd like to speak to Mr Maeda. Is he busy now?
Secretary: He's on the 'phone.
Mr Itô: Is he? My friend who's called Foster would like to speak to him. He's come from England. He arrived in Japan the day before yesterday.
Secretary: Would you please write your name on this piece of paper?
Mr Foster: I'm sorry. I haven't got a pen. I mean to buy one today but I haven't yet.
Secretary: Mr. Foster speaks excellent Japanese, doesn't he?
Mr Foster: I can speak a little but not very well.
Mr Itô: Yesterday you were speaking it very well with that Japanese fellow!
Mr Foster: As I was drinking beer I could speak Japanese!
Mr Itô: How many bottles did you drink?

Mr Foster: Only two.
Mr Itô: Only two? Is that true?
Mr Foster: I've forgotten!

Dialogue 2

Mr Itô: Have you got a newspaper?
Secretary: We have, yes, but Mr Yamamoto is reading it at the moment.
Mr Itô: Is it the **Asahi Shimbun**?
Secretary: Yes.
Mr Itô: Ah well, I read that this morning. Have you got a magazine?
Mr Foster: Yes! Look here! There are some magazines behind this chair.
Secretary: Would you like some ocha or would you prefer some Indian tea?
Mr Foster: I'd like a cup of Indian. Thank you.
Mr Itô: Me too. Ah. Have you got a spoon?
Mr Foster: Yes! There are five spoons on the table.
Mr Itô: Five? Thanks! One will do!
Mr Foster: About how long will we have to wait?
Secretary: Probably only about ten minutes. Another cup of tea? How about that?
Mr Foster: No, that's fine, thank you.

Dialogue 3

Mr Foster: What's the date to-day?
Mr Itô: The 17th.
Mr Foster: So the day after to-morrow will be the 19th. Shall we come back then? Mr Maeda is probably busy now. He is working whereas I'm not.
Mr Itô: I'm free today all morning but the day after tomorrow I'll be working.
Mr Foster: I see. Well, how about next Tuesday? That'll be the 25th.
Mr Itô: Wednesday's the 26th so I won't be busy.
Mr Foster: Let's do that then. Let's come back next Wednesday.

Chapter 9: On the Ginza
Dialogue 1

Mr Itô: What is your wife doing now?

Mr Foster: She's shopping. What's the time?

Mr Itô: It's half past eleven.

Mr Foster: At this moment she is drinking coffee and eating cakes.

Mr Itô: Really? Does she drink coffee and eat cakes every day?

Mr Foster: She drinks coffee every day but sometimes doesn't eat cakes.

Mr Itô: Would you like a beer?

Mr Foster: Yes! As I'm not working today I'd like to have a bottle of beer. How about you?

Mr Itô: No! I'm not working now but as I'm going to the office at two I won't have a beer. A pity but there it is.

Mr Foster: When you get to the office what will you do?

Mr Itô: I'll write cards and read letters and speak on the phone. What will you do after you've had lunch?

Mr Foster: I'll go to the Ginza and meet my wife.

Mr Itô: After meeting your wife will you go shopping?

Mr Foster: Probably! My wife likes shopping every day.

Dialogue 2

Mr Foster: Good day!

Mr Itô: Good day!

Mr Foster: What did you do this morning?

Mrs Foster: After coming into town Mrs Itô and I saw all sorts of interesting things.

Mrs Itô: We really did. We went to Asakusa and saw the temple. It's splendid. Japanese temples are truly beautiful.

Mr Foster: They certainly are. Two years ago I went to Kyôto and saw a temple called Kiyomizu Temple.

Mrs Itô: Ah that's a beautiful one, isn't it.?

Mrs Foster: I'd like to go to Kyôto.

Mr Foster: Let's go there the week after next.

Mrs Foster: Yes, let's. You will be working next week but the week after you're free, aren't you?

Mr Foster: Well, are you off to Yûrakuchô now? Have you an umbrella?

Mrs Foster: Yes, I have.

Dialogue 3

Mrs Itô: Just a minute. I want to phone my husband. Is there a phone?

Mr Foster: Yes, over there. There are two in front of the chemist's.

Mrs Foster: Oh I've remembered. I want to get some toothpaste.

Mr Foster: There's a tobacconist's next to the chemist's so could you buy me some cigarettes?

Mrs Foster: One packet?

Mr Foster: Two, please.

Mrs Itô: How many do you smoke a day?

Mrs Foster: He smokes a lot.

Mr Foster: No, I don't! Only five or six.

Mrs Itô: My husband smokes about thirty. He's certainly smoking now at the office.

Mrs Foster: It's bad for the health, isn't it?

Mrs Itô: Indeed it is.

Chapter 10: By taxi and by train

Dialogue 1

Mrs Itô: As it's raining shall we take a taxi?

Mrs Foster: What time does the train leave?

Mrs Itô: Every ten minutes. Look! There's a taxi in front of that store.

Mrs Itô: Yûrakuchô please. You go straight ahead and turn right at that big building. Then take the third turning on the left.

Taxi driver: Got it!

Mr Foster: Mary, have you got all your parcels?

Mrs Foster: One, two, three, four, five, six, yes. I've got them all.

Mr Foster: Here's one more.

Mrs Foster: Ah, bring that one too please. Thank you.

Mr Foster: 'Bye then. Take care.

Mrs Itô: Of course the underground is quicker but as you've got so many packages a taxi is useful.

Mrs Foster: Is Yûrakuchô far?

Mrs Itô: No, not very. It's close.

Mrs Foster: About how long will it take?

Mrs Itô: Driver? About how long?

Taxi driver: As there's a lot of traffic it'll probably take about twenty minutes.

Mrs Itô: How much was that?

Taxi driver: 700 yen.

Mrs. Itô: Here's 1000 yen.

Taxi driver: 300 change. Thanks.

Mrs Foster: About how much would the tube have been?

Mrs Itô: 120.

Mrs Foster: Really? Not very expensive.

Mrs Itô: No, it's cheap isn't it. A taxi's more expensive than the underground but as it's very crowded now a taxi's preferable.

Dialogue 2

Mrs Itô: Two to Nagahara please.

Clerk: 540 yen.

Mrs Itô: Here's 600.

Clerk: Thank you. Here's sixty change.

Mrs Itô: Thank you.

Mrs Itô: We change at Gotanda.

Mrs Foster: How many stops between Yûrakuchô and Gotanda?

Mrs Itô: Let's see . . . Shimbashi, Hamamatsuchô, Tamachi, Shinagawa, Ôsaki, Gotanda. Six.

Mrs Foster: And from Gotanda to Nagahara?

Mrs Itô: Five.

Mrs Foster: I saw the name of the station! It was in English!

Mrs Itô: That's right. You can read the names of the stations. And listen! Before we arrive at a station the conductor calls out the name. So even foreigners can understand.

Mrs Foster: That's useful, isn't it?

Mrs Itô: Ah, look to your left. There are boats. That's Tokyo Bay. And on the right there's a small shrine. Can you see the red gateway? And those huge trees are called cryptomeria.

Mrs Foster: It is pretty. I'd like to go to a shrine.

Mrs Itô: Well, when we get home shall we go to our neighbouring shrine? It'll be interesting for you. Now the rain is stopping so after we get home let's go for a stroll, shall we?

Chapter 11: Feeling ill

Dialogue 1

Mrs Itô: Good morning, Mr. Foster. The rain's stopped and the weather has become fine, hasn't it?

Mr Foster: Yes, it has, hasn't it?

Mrs Itô: Yesterday you had a stomach-ache, didn't you? How are you today? Is it better?

Mr Foster: I'm better but my wife has a headache.

Mrs Itô: Really? I'm sorry to hear that. Has she a fever?

Mr Foster: A slight one. Her throat is sore too.

Mrs Itô: Perhaps she has caught a cold.

Mr Foster: Probably. On the 4th it rained a good deal but my wife wanted to go shopping and she walked to the shops.

Mrs Itô: Two days ago it got cold, didn't it? You must take care. The weather's got cold and nasty.

Mr Foster: On the 9th we want to go to Kyôto so my wife must get better.

Mrs Itô: Yes, she must, mustn't she?

Dialogue 2

Mr Foster: I'm sorry. My wife's throat hurts and she wants to drink a glass of water.

Mrs Itô: Does she? Well, I'll take it to her.

Mr Foster: No, I'll do it. I'll go to the kitchen and fetch some water.

Mrs Itô: You go and sit over there. I'll go and see your wife.

Mr Foster: You are kind. Thank you very much.

Dialogue 3

Mrs Itô: Good morning. According to your husband you don't feel too good. Is that the case?

Mrs Foster: Yes it really is. My throat hurts and I can't speak very easily.

Mrs Itô: Have you got a headache?

Mrs Foster: It's better than last night but still hurts.

Mrs Itô: You must go and see the doctor. Can you walk?

Mrs Foster: Oh yes. Is it far to the doctor's?

Mrs Itô: No, only five minutes walk. After you've had breakfast we'll go. Now . . . what do you want to eat? An egg? Bread?

Mrs Foster: Nothing thank you. Just something to drink.

Mrs Itô: What would you like to drink? Coffee? Tea?

Mrs Foster: I'd prefer some **ocha**. Is there any?

Mrs Itô: Indeed there is. Just wait a moment. I'll go to the kitchen and be back with the **ocha** in five minutes.

Mrs Foster: Thank you so much.

Chapter 12: At the Doctor's
Dialogue 1

Mrs Itô: This is a friend of mine called Mrs Foster. Ten days ago she came to Japan and now she's staying with us.

Doctor: Really? Is she English? Do you understand Japanese?

Mrs Foster: A little but if I cannot understand what you are saying, Mrs Itô has said she will be so kind as to translate.

Mrs Itô: I cannot speak English well but I'll explain anyway.

Mrs Foster: Thank you. So . . . please speak slowly.

Doctor: What seems to be the trouble?

Mrs Foster: I have a headache. I have a slight fever and my throat hurts.

Doctor: Your temperature is 38.3. It's not serious but you must go home and lie down.

Mrs Foster: On the day after tomorrow my husband and I are going to Kyôto. Will that be all right?

Doctor: If your temperature does not go back to normal then you cannot go to Kyôto but if you take this pale green medicine you'll soon be all right.

Dialogue 2

Mrs Foster: When should I take that green medicine?

Doctor: Take it before meals. Three times a day. Before breakfast, before lunch, before dinner. Do you understand?

Mrs Foster: Yes. What can I eat?

Doctor: Anything is all right but as it seems you have a sore throat, drink a lot.

Mrs Itô: What do you want, Mrs Foster?

Mrs Foster: Water.

Doctor: Do you like this medicine?

Mrs Foster: No! I do not like it at all! It's very unpleasant.

Doctor: It's a very good medicine but the taste is nasty. Sorry!

Mrs Foster: That's all right.

Dialogue 3

Mrs Itô: Come on! We must go back quickly. After you've eaten lunch you must go to bed. Would you like your lunch in bed?

Mrs Foster: No. I'll rest after lunch but I don't want to go to bed now.

Mrs Itô: Would you like to watch television?

Mrs Foster: Yes, I would.

Mrs Itô: Sit down and while you're drinking your ocha watch television. As it's in Japanese it'll be good for you.

Mrs Foster: Come off it, Mrs Itô! I'm ill. I don't want to study!

Mrs Itô: Please study every day. If you study you'll soon be good at Japanese!

Chapter 13: Shopping and business trips
Dialogue 1
Mrs Itô: If you take that medicine you'll get well.

Mrs Foster: But I *am* well! I really am much better.

Mrs Itô: If you don't go out to today you'll be able to go to Kyôto tomorrow.

Mrs Foster: Do you intend to go shopping today?

Mrs Itô: Yes. I'm going out at eleven o'clock.

Mrs Foster: Do you think you could get me some plums? If you're going to the fruiterer's could you get ten plums for me?

Mrs Itô: Of course. If I'm back at half past twelve, is that all right?

Mrs Foster: Fine. Please don't hurry. If the fruiterer hasn't any plums that's all right. As it's not important, you see.

Mrs Itô: If there aren't any plums I'll get some Japanese pears.

Mrs Foster: Thank you. I love those.

Mrs Itô: If you want some coffee there are eight cakes in the kitchen.

Mrs Foster: Eight! If I eat eight cakes I'll get fat!

Dialogue 2
Mr Itô: If I go to England next year by plane could I visit your firm?

Mr Foster: Any time you like. That would be a real pleasure. If you come to England we could see all sorts of interesting things together. When do you intend coming? Summer? Autumn?

Mr Itô: I'll be getting very busy in the spring so summer is probably preferable. How about July?

Mr Foster: Fine. I have to go to France in June but if I can't sell our products I'll be back in England pretty quickly. But if I can sell a lot I'll have to go to France again.

Mr Itô: Probably so. Do you usually manage to sell a lot?

Mr Foster: Sometimes seven, sometimes seventeen, at another time seven hundred. You never know. If the

French want to buy new things I can sell a lot. Last year I sold a lot but two years ago I couldn't sell one.

Mr Itô: Are you going out now?

Mr Foster: Yes, I am. I want to go to the bank. How about you?

Mr Itô: Yes. If we wait at the bank for ten minutes is that all right?

Mr Foster: Fine. Take your time!

Chapter 14: The young people arrive
Dialogue 1

Nobuo: Do you like music?

Simon: Yes. I like listening to records.

Nobuo: Have you a lot of records?

Simon: About a hundred but these days I only buy tapes.

Nobuo: Are they cheaper than records?

Simon: No, they're the same.

Nobuo: Do you like the cinema?

Simon: My elder sister likes films but I rarely go to a cinema. How about you?

Nobuo: I love them. If there's a samurai film on I rush to it!

Simon: Do you like television?

Nobuo: I hate television. It's too small. I prefer the big screen.

Simon: Do you like reading books?

Nobuo: I'm not keen. I have to read a lot at school so at home I rarely read.

Dialogue 2

Yoshiko: Would you like coffee or juice?

Jenny: Coffee please. Thank you.

Yoshiko: Do you need sugar and milk?

Jenny: I take both sugar and milk. How about you?

Yoshiko: I like coffee but I don't take sugar.

Jenny: How about milk?

Yoshiko: I take milk. I hate black coffee. Now . . . The milk . . . Ah, I've remembered. It's in the kitchen. Wait a minute.

Jenny: I'll come too.

Yoshiko: No, please don't. It's OK. I'll fetch the milk.

Yoshiko: Have another cake.

Jenny: Thank you, I will. I love Japanese cakes.

Yoshiko: Do you like English cakes as well?

Jenny: Yes, but they are a little different.

Yoshiko: What shall we do today? Shall we go to the cinema?
Jenny: Yes, I love films, but as I don't understand Japanese well, a
Japanese film will probably be a little difficult.

Dialogue 3
Jenny: Sorry. I'd like to go to the Ladies. Where would it be?
Yoshiko: Over there. Can you read the Chinese characters?
Jenny: No, I can't.
Yoshiko: Look. Those characters are danshi. That means *Men.*
Those characters are read as joshi. That's for
Women. Please don't forget!
Jenny: I'll certainly remember because now I've learnt them.
Yoshiko: If you learn the Chinese characters Japanese gradually
gets easier and easier. If you learn new characters
every day you'll soon get good at understanding
Japanese.
Jenny: I'm sure I will. If I do not forget the characters I can find a
Ladies to-morrow as well. It'll be useful.
Yoshiko: You must study!

Chapter 15: Planning a trip
Dialogue 1
Mr Itô: It seems the young people want to go to the cinema.
Mrs Itô: Nobuo looks so happy. It looks as if he really likes talking
to his English friend. He's got one or two friends at
school but sometimes he looks a little lonely.
Mr Itô: According to my wife Nobuo is lonely, but as far as I can
see Nobuo always looks cheerful. Of course he has to
study at school but every Sunday he goes to the cinema
in Tokyo with a friend.

Dialogue 2
Mr Itô: Take Simon with you. Go to Tokyo together. Before you go
to the cinema you've got some time, so Simon would
probably like to see all sorts of interesting things.
Simon: Yes, I would.
Nobuo: Where would you like to go – the zoo? a museum? a
theatre?
Simon: The zoo would be most interesting. I love animals. At
home in England we have one white cat and two dogs.
Nobuo: Really? But the dogs probably don't like the cat.
Simon: No, that's not the case. The three get on very well.

Dialogue 3
Simon: I want to speak Japanese but I am embarrassed.
Nobuo: Don't be shy! If you speak Japanese I'll correct your Japanese. Would that be OK?
Simon: Certainly. But do speak more slowly. Sometimes I understand your Japanese well but at other times I can't understand it at all!
Nobuo: Open the window!
Simon: Once more please. I didn't get that.
Nobuo: You're joking! I spoke clearly.
Simon: Please teach me. I do want to speak Japanese. If I make a mistake please correct me.
Nobuo: Well . . . what have you got to do?
Simon: Shut the window!

Chapter 16: The Japanese family
Dialogue 1
Mr Itô: How old is your son now?
Mr Foster: He's 16 now.
Mr Itô: When is your daughter's birthday?
Mr Foster: My son was born on July 10th but my daughter on December 25th.
Mr Itô: That's Christmas Day!
Mr Foster: That's right. Not only my daughter but everyone gets presents.
Mr Itô: Poor girl!

Dialogue 2
Mr Itô: Look at this photo. It's of my father.
Mr Foster: Is that your father? Does he live in Tokyo?
Mr Itô: No, he is dead. He died ten years ago.
Mr Foster: I'm sorry. You must miss him.
Mr Itô: My mother still lives in Matsumoto. She's 82. This is a photo of her. I took it last year at New Year.
Mr Foster: She has a splendid kimono on. Who is the man with the beard?
Mr Itô: That's my elder brother.
Mr Foster: Does he also live in Matsumoto?
Mr Itô: Yes, he does. That's our home town. I was born there.
Mr Foster: Is Mrs Itô also from Matsumoto?
Mr Itô: Oh no! She's a real Tokyoite born and bred!

Dialogue 3

Mr Foster: Have you only the one older brother?

Mr Itô: Yes. He's called Ichirô and he teaches maths. I've got two younger brothers. Look. Here's a photo of all the family. The man wearing spectacles is now living in America – he's my younger brother – but he's supposed to be coming back to Japan next year.

Mr Foster: Is that woman his wife?

Mr Itô: No, she's a younger sister of mine.

Mr Foster: What a large family!

Mr Itô: It is, isn't it! My older brother is 50, my elder sister 48, the next sister down is 45, I'm 41, the first younger brother is 39, my younger sister is 36 and the other brother is 34.

Dialogue 4

Mr Foster: Do you go back to Matsumoto every year?

Mr Itô: Usually at O-Bon. The children love visiting their grandmother.

Mr Foster: Both my parents live in London so Simon and Jenny see them frequently. Look. This is a photo of my elder sister.

Mr Itô: Does she too live in London?

Mr Foster: Yes. I've just got the one sister.

Mr Itô: Has she got a husband?

Mr Foster: Yes. She got married five years ago.

Mr Itô: Have they children?

Mr Foster: Yes! My wife and I have become aunt and uncle!

Mr Itô: Congratulations!

Chapter 17: Eating out

Dialogue 1

Mr Itô: Good evening!

Mr Foster: Good evening!

Mr Itô: Shall we go and eat some sushi?

Mr Foster: Let's do that. That'd be splendid.

Mr Itô: Let's sit at the bar. You can see the place where the owner prepares the sushi. And look. There are the names of the fish written up on the wall.

Mr Foster: It's not easy to read!

Mr Itô: What do you specially recommend to-day?

Owner: The prawns are fresh.

Mr Itô: Mr. Foster, what will you have?
Mr Foster: Prawns, please.
Mr Itô: Me too.
Owner: What can I give you next?
Mr Foster: I've never eaten octopus before so I'll have that.
Mr Itô: Yes, do try it. I'll have tuna.
Owner: What can I get you to drink?
Mr Itô: Beer, please.

Dialogue 2
Mr Itô: This is a famous tempura restaurant. Shall we go in here?
Mr Foster: Mmm yes, but it looks expensive. Perhaps we oughtn't to.
Mr Itô: I've been here before. It's not all that expensive.
Mr Foster: All right, let's go in. I'm flush today!
Mr Itô: Shall we go to that table near the window?
Mr Foster: As the menu's in Roman letters it's easy for me to read it! Now, 'pinetree', 'bamboo', 'plum-tree' – what's that mean?
Mr Itô: They are the set meals. 'Pine' is the dearest. With that you get prawn, cuttlefish, aubergine and mushrooms.

Dialogue 3
Mr Itô: You're a foreigner, so naturally you like meat.
Mr Foster: I do like Japanese food but today, as I haven't had it for a long time, I'd like to eat some beef.
Mr Itô: Have you ever had sukiyaki?
Mr Foster: Yes. Ah I've forgotten my wallet. I must go back to the house.
Mr Itô: No, I'll treat you.
Mr Foster: Thank you, but next time I'll take you and Mrs Itô out to a meal.
Mr Foster: This bean-curd is delicious.
Mr Itô: How do you like the bamboo-sprouts?
Mr Foster: Not a lot.
Mr Itô: How about a little more beef?
Mr Foster: No thank you! I'm full!
Mr Itô: Could we have the bill please.

Chapter 18: Language for men and women
Dialogue 1
Mr Itô: How about going to the baseball game this Sunday?
Toshio: Hold on a second. I'll look at my diary. No, it's no good. Saturday would be OK. Shall we meet in front of the stadium at five?
Mr Itô: Agreed.
Toshio: Who d'you think will win?
Mr Itô: No question! The Giants.
Toshio: Idiot! It'll be the Osaka/Kôbe team.
Mr Itô: Will you be coming by tube?
Toshio: I'll have the car so I'll pick you up on my way.

Dialogue 2
Mrs Itô: Next Sunday is the wedding of a friend of mine. I have to arrange the flowers so I wonder if you'd give me a hand in choosing them?
Mrs Yamada: Of course. I'd be delighted. What sort of flowers I wonder?
Mrs Itô: That's the question. Light-coloured ones would be good.
Mrs Yamada: In that case how about roses?
Mrs Itô: Yes. Good. Let's add chrysanthemums and lilies. If we do that, then with red, yellow and pink it'll become really beautiful.
Mrs Yamada: It will. It'll be a beautiful arrangement.
Mrs Itô: I just wonder if I'm up to it.
Mrs Yamada: The flowers you arranged at your sister's wedding were really lovely though, weren't they?
Mrs Itô: Oh by the way . . . have I already shown you the purse I bought yesterday?
Mrs Yamada: It's really lovely.

Chapter 19: At the bank and at the garage
Dialogue 1
Mr Foster: What time do the banks open?
Mr Itô: Half past nine.
Mr Foster: And what time do they close?
Mr Itô: Four thirty.
Mr Foster: Where's the nearest bank?
Mr Itô: Do you know where the police-box is?
Mr Foster: Yes.
Mr Itô: There's a supermarket near the kôban isn't there?
Mr Foster: Yes. I went there yesterday and bought some soap.

Mr Itô: Well . . . behind the supermarket there's a big building.

Mr Foster: That'll be the bank.

Mr Itô: No it won't. That's a block of flats but next to that building there is a bank.

Dialogue 2

Mr Foster: Excuse me. I want to open an account so what do I do?

Clerk: It's simple. I'll ask you to write your name here and then straightaway you can open an account.

Mr Foster: Would you please change these pounds into yen?

Clerk: Certainly.

Mr Foster: How many yen to the pound today?

Clerk: Just a moment, please. I'll go and check. It's 287.

Mr Foster: Lower than yesterday.

Clerk: Yes. It changes every day.

Mr Foster: The yen is changeable!

Clerk: No! It's the pound!

Mr Foster: Would you change a hundred pounds please?

Clerk: Certainly, sir. Is it all right if I deduct the commission?

Mr Foster: I didn't know anything about that. What percentage?

Clerk: I'm afraid it's five per cent.

Mr Foster: Oh well, it can't be helped.

Dialogue 3

Mr Foster: We need some petrol. There's a filling-station. Let's stop. Fill her up please.

Attendant: Right you are. Sir! Are you all right for oil?

Mr Foster: Would you check it please?

Attendant: It's very old-looking. Pitch black. Just take a look!

Mr Foster: This is a hired car actually . . .

Attendant: What an awful firm it must be! Shall I put some oil in?

Mr Foster: Yes.

Attendant: I'll put a litre in.

Mr Foster: Would you check the tyres too please.

Attendant: Certainly. But could you move the car over there please. Shall I clean the windscreen?

Mr Foster: No need, thank you. It's clean. We've got another hundred kilometres to do.

Attendant: The motorway is crowded so do take care. Hope to see you again!

Chapter 20: A Japanese inn

Dialogue 1

Mr Foster: Hallo!

Clerk: This is the White Crane Hotel.

Mr Foster: I'd like to know if you have a room free on October 6th.

Clerk: A moment please . . . For how many?

Mr Foster: Two.

Clerk: How many days will you be staying?

Mr Foster: Three.

Clerk: We have a room with a beautiful view free. How will that do?

Mr Foster: How much would that be?

Clerk: 10 000 yen a night including the two meals.

Mr Foster: That's cheaper than England! Can I reserve it now?

Clerk: Of course. What time will you be arriving?

Mr Foster: We're coming from Tokyo by train so I should think we'd be arriving at about six.

Clerk: Fine. We look forward to seeing you.

Mr Foster: Goodbye for now.

Dialogue 2

We arrived safely yesterday evening at 6.30. Our room is absolutely delightful. We can see the Eastern Mountains from our window. We went to the bath before dinner but as it was our first time we were a little embarrassed. However all went well! When we returned from the bath we tried on our yukata.

The maid who brought us our dinner was amazed to see us! We are the only foreigners in the ryokan. Mary, who doesn't drink saké, drank ocha.

Has your sister whom we didn't meet gone back to Matsumoto? A German we met on the train knows your firm. It's a small world! As we are getting back to Tokyo on Monday you don't have to write that letter to the electric company. I'll do it when I return.

The sky has got dark and it may rain. We wanted to go out for a stroll so that's a shame.

We got your card this morning. I hope this letter will arrive before we get back to Tokyo.

Please give my best wishes to Mrs Itô.

ANSWERS TO EXERCISES

Chapter 1: Greetings and introductions
Section A
Answers to Exercise 1
1. Watakushi wa Foster desu.
2. Anata wa Itô-san desu ka?
3. Keisu ja arimasen.
4. Kaban ja arimasen.
5. Kore wa keisu desu. Sore mo keisu desu ka?

Answers to Exercise 2
1. Watakushi no keisu desu.
2. Kore wa watakushi no keisu desu.
3. Anata no kaban wa ôkii desu ka?
4. Sore wa anata no keisu desu ka?
5. Shujin no keisu wa akai desu.
6. Anata no keisu wa chiisai desu ka?
7. Goshujin no kaban wa akaku wa arimasen.
8. Kanai no keisu wa kuroi desu. Chiisaku wa arimasen.
9. Watakushi no kaban wa ôkii desu. Kuroku wa arimasen.

Answers to Exercise 3
1. Kore wa kaban ja arimasen.
2. Kore wa keisu ja arimasen.
3. Kore wa chiisaku wa arimasen.
4. Kore wa akaku wa arimasen.
5. Kaban wa ôkiku wa arimasen.
6. Keisu wa ôkiku wa arimasen.
7. Watakushi wa Itô ja arimasen.
8. Watakushi wa Yamamoto ja arimasen.

Section B
Answers to Exercise 4
1. Anata no keisu wa (a) ôkii desu ka?
    (b) kuroi desu ka?
    (c) akai desu ka?
2. Goshujin no kaban wa (a) chiisai desu ka?
    (b) akai desu ka?
    (c) kuroi desu ka?
3. Kore wa anata no keisu desu ka?
4. Kore wa anata no kaban desu ka?
5. Kore wa goshujin no keisu desu ka?
6. Kore wa okusan no kaban desu ka?
7. Sore wa anata no keisu desu ka?
8. Sore wa anata no kaban desu ka?
9. Sore wa goshujin no kaban desu ka?
10. Sore wa okusan no keisu desu ka?

Answers to Exercise 5
1. Hajimemashite.
2. Arigatô gozaimasu.
3. Anata wa Itô-san desu ka? Hai, sô desu.
4. Ogenki desu ka? Hai, genki desu.
5. Sore wa anata no keisu desu ka? Hai, sô desu.

Answers to Exercise 6
Dialogue 1
(Hai. Watakushi wa Jones desu.)
(Sô desu ka? Anata wa Yamamoto-san desu ka? Haji-memashite.)
(Genki desu. Anata mo?)
Dialogue 2
(Koko desu.)
(Iie, sore wa watakushi no keisu ja arimasen.)
(Hai, sore wa watakushi no keisu desu. Arigatô.)
Dialogue 3
(Iie, ôkiku wa arimasen. Chiisai desu.)
(Hai, akai desu. Arigatô.)

Chapter 2: The family car
Section A
Answers to Exercise 1
1. Kono kuruma wa Honda desu.
2. Sono kuruma wa Mitsubishi desu.
3. Ano kuruma wa Toyota desu.
4. Watakushi no keisu wa doko desu ka? Koko desu.
5. Watakushi no kaban wa doko desu ka? Soko desu!

6. Anata no kuruma wa doko desu ka? Asoko desu.
7. Doitsu no kuruma wa akai desu.
8. Watakushi no Amerika no kuruma wa kuroi desu.
9. Nihon no namae wa muzukashii desu.
10. Igirisu (or Eikoku) no namae wa yasashii desu.

Answers to Exercise 2

1. Itarii no kuruma wa ôkii desu ga Furansu no kuruma wa chiisai desu.
2. Watakushi no keisu wa kuroi desu ga anata no keisu wa akai desu.
3. Kanai no kuruma wa chiisai desu ga akaku wa arimasen.
4. Shujin no kaban wa ôkii desu ga kuroku wa arimasen.

Answers to Exercise 3

1. Iie, Furansujin desu.
2. Iie, Itariijin desu.
3. Iie, kanai wa Nihonjin desu.
4. Iie, shujin wa Igirisujin desu.

Section B

Answers to Exercise 4

1. Untrue.
2. True.
3. Untrue.
4. Untrue.
5. True.
6. Untrue.
7. Untrue.

Answers to Exercises 5

(Hai, watakushi wa Satô desu.)
(Hajimemashite. Kore wa kanai desu.)
(Hai, kanai wa Furansujin desu.)
(Genki desu. Anata mo?)
(Asoko desu.)
(Iie, watakushi no keisu wa ôkiku wa arimasen.)
(Iie, sore wa kuroku wa arimasen. Watakushi no keisu wa kuroi desu.)
(Hai, sore wa watakushi no keisu desu. Arigatô.)
(Iie, kanai no keisu wa akai desu.)
(Hai, sore wa kanai no desu. Arigatô. Anata no kuruma wa asoko desu ka?)
(Nihon no kuruma desu ka?)
(Watakushi no kuruma wa Toyota desu.)
(Sô desu.)

Chapter 3: Eating at home
Section A
Answers to Exercise 1
1. Iie, Igirisujin desu.
2. Iie, kanai wa Furansujin desu.
3. Iie, Amerikajin desu.
4. Iie, Nihonjin desu.
5. Iie, Itariijin desu.

Answers to Exercise 2
1. Watakushi wa ringo o tabemashita.
2. Nihonjin wa sashimi o tabemasu.
3. Ebi matawa sakana ga arimasu.
4. Biiru to osake ga arimasu.
5. Ringo ya momo ga arimasu.
6. Nihon de osake o nomimashita.
7. Igirisu de (or no) biiru o nomimashita.
8. Igirisu no naganegi wa ôkii desu.
9. Watakushi no keisu wa kuruma ni arimasu.
10. Watakushi no kuruma wa akaku wa arimasen.
11. Sore wa kanai no keisu ja arimasen.

Answers to Exercise 3
1. ka.
2. ne.
3. nê.
4. yo.

Answers to Exercise 4
1. Kudamono o tabemasen.
2. Doitsujin wa osashimi o tabemasen.
3. Momo o tabemasen deshita.
4. Nihon de osashimi o tabemasen deshita.

Answers to Exercise 5
1. Nihonjin wa sakana ya gohan o tabemasu.
2. Doitsujin wa biiru o nomimasu.
3. Watakushi wa naganegi to ebi o tabemashita.
4. Nihon de osashimi o tabemasen deshita.
5. Kanai wa osake o nomimasen.

Section B
Answers to Exercise 6
    (Ebi/naganegi/gohan o tabemasu.)
    (Biiru/ocha/mizu o nomimasu.)
    (Hai, nomimasen.)

Answers to Exercise 7
1. Sore wa nan desu ka?
2. Kudamono o tabemasu ka?
3. Sore wa ocha desu ka?
4. Itô-san wa biiru o nomimasu ka?
5. Itô-san no okusan wa osake o nomimasen ka?
6. Igirisu no ringo wa akai desu ka?

Answers to Exercise 8
1. Mizu ga arimasu ka?
2. Ocha ga arimasu ka?
3. Osake ga arimasu ka?
4. Nihon de osake o nomimasu.
5. Oishii desu.

Answers to Exercise 9
1. Amerika no naganegi wa ôkii desu ga Nihon no wa chiisai desu.
2. Watakushi wa biiru o nomimasu ga kanai wa osake o nomimasu.
3. Shujin wa gohan o tabemashita keredomo Itô-san wa tabemasen deshita.
4. Nihonjin wa osake o nomimasu keredomo Igirisujin wa biiru o nomimasu.

Answers to Exercise 10
1. True.
2. Untrue.
3. Untrue.
4. Untrue.
5. True.
6. True.
7. Untrue.
8. True.

Chapter 4: After dinner
Section A
Answers to Exercise 1
1. Iie, yasashiku wa arimasen. Muzukashii desu.
2. Waruku wa arimasen. Ii desu.
3. Suzushiku wa arimasen. Atsui desu.
4. Muzukashiku wa arimasen. Yasashii desu.
5. Yoku wa arimasen. Warui desu.

Answers to Exercise 2
1. Nihongo o hanashimasu.

2. Doitsugo o hanashimasu.
3. Itariigo o hanashimasu.
4. Eigo o hanashimasu.

Answers to Exercise 3
    Senkyûkyaku nijûnen.   Senkyûhyaku hachijûgonen.
    Senkyûhyaku sanjûshichinen. Shôwa jûkyûnen.
    Senkyûhyaku gojûsannen.   Shôwa yonjûrokunen.

Answers to Exercise 4
Gojû, gojûichi, gojûni, gojûsan, gojûyon, gojûgo, gojûroku, gojûshichi (or -nana), gojûhachi, gojûkyû, rokujû, rokujûichi . . . shichijû, shichijûichi (or nanajû, nanajûichi).

Answers to Exercise 5
1. Satô-san wa Eigo o hanashimasen.
2. Okusama wa biiru o nomimasen.
3. Watakushi wa sashimi o tabemasen.
4. Kore wa watakushi no keisu ja arimasen.
5. Yamada-san wa Bonn de Doitsugo o hanashimasen deshita.
6. Anata wa osake o takusan nomimasen deshita.
7. Ano Nihonjin wa naganegi o tabemasen deshita.
8. Kuruma wa akaku wa arimasen.

Answers to Exercise 6
1. Shôwa sannen deshita.
2. Shôwa jûgonen deshita.
3. Shôwa sanjûshichinen deshita.
4. Shôwa gojûyonen deshita.

Section B
Answers to Exercise 7
    (Senkyûhyaku hachijûsannen no natsu ni kimashita.)
    (Iie, mushiatsui otenki deshita.)
    (Iie, kanai/shujin mo kimashita.)
    (Iie, heta desu yo!)

Answers to Exercise 8
1. Aki ni Nihon e kimasen deshita.
2. Shujin wa hitori de Tôkyô e kimashita.
3. Eigo wa Furansujin ni muzukashii desu.
4. Yamamoto-san no okusan wa Doitsugo o yoku hanashimasu.

Answers to Exercise 9
1. Untrue.
2. True.

3. Untrue.
4. Untrue.
5. True.
6. True(?).

Answers to Exercise 10

(Hai, arigatô. Genki desu. Anata mo?)
(Warui otenki desu ne.)
(Suzushii desu ne.)
(Ame ga takusan furimasu nê.)
(Biiru o nomimasu ka?)
(Ocha o nomimasu ka?)
(Oishii desu ka?)
(Mô ippai nomimasu ka?)

Chapter 5: The next morning

Section A

Answers to Exercise 1

gozen rokuji jûgofun.	kujihan.
asa hachiji	jûichiji gofun mae.
jûichiji gofun.	goji yonjippun
gogo ichiji nijippun.	yoji jûgofun mae
niji jippun.	yoji sanjûgofun.
shichiji (or nanaji) nijûgofun.	kuji jippun mae.

Answers to Exercise 2

1. Biiru o nomimashô.
2. Sakana o tabemashô.
3. Sampo o shimashô.
4. Uchi e kaerimashô.
5. Nihongo o hanashimashô.
6. Jimusho e ikimashô.

Answers to Exercise 3

1. Nichiyôbi ni Yokohama e kaerimashita.
2. Getsuyôbi ni jimusho e ikimashita.
3. Kayôbi ni hachiji ni uchi e kaerimashita.
4. Suiyôbi ni (o)sashimi o tabemashita.
5. Mokuyôbi ni Nihongo o hanashimashita.
6. Kin'yôbi ni jimusho e ikimasen deshita.
7. Doyôbi ni sampo shimashita.

Answers to Exercise 4

(Ohayô gozaimasu. Yoku nemurimashita ka?)
(Arigatô. Yoku nemurimashita. Warui otenki desu ne.)
(Kinô suzushii otenki deshita ne.)
(Ima nanji desu ka?)
(Doyôbi desu kara jimusho e ikimasen.)

(Tôkyô e ikimashô. Ikaga desu ka?)
(Shichiji jûgofun ni kaerimasu.)

Section B
Answers to Exercise 6
1. Hajimemashite.
2. Ohayô gozaimasu.
3. Ki o tsukete kudasai.
4. Omedetô gozaimasu.
5. Arigatô gozaimasu.
6. Sore wa oishii desu.
7. Kekkô desu.
8. Wakarimasen.

Answers to Exercise 7
1. Nigatsu desu kara samui desu.
2. Shichigatsu desu kara atsui desu.
3. Jûgatsu desu kara suzushii desu.
4. Rokugatsu desu kara mushiatsui desu.
5. Doyôbi desu kara inaka e ikimashô.
6. Nichiyôbi desu kara Itô-san wa jimusho e ikimasen.

Answers to Exercise 8
1. Nihon dewa kodomotachi wa shichiji ni asagohan o tabemasu.
2. Asa hachiji ni gakkô e ikimasu.
3. Futsû jûniji jûgofun ni hirugohan o tabemasu.
4. Gogo yoji ni uchi e kaerimasu.
5. Hai, doyôbi mo gakkô e ikimasu.

Answers to Exercise 9
1. Tokidoki ame ga furimasu.
2. Mochiron Itô-san wa gozen rokujihan ni jimusho e ikimasen.
3. Satô-san wa futsû goji jûgofun ni uchi e kaerimasu.
4. Kyonen Nihon e ikimashita.
5. Mainichi gohan o tabemasu.
6. Kayôbi kara Doyôbi made ii otenki deshita.
7. Asa kuji kara gogo yoji made atsui desu.

Chapter 6: Shopping – 1 Going to the bookshop
Section A
Answers to Exercise 1
1. Yûbinkyoku de kitte o kaimashita.
2. Hon o kaitaku wa arimasen.
3. Hon'ya wa gakkô no mae ni arimasu.
4. Issho ni Yokohama e ikimashô ka?
5. Ano hito wa Eigo ga wakarimasu ka?

6. Gaikokujin no hon wa omoshiroku wa arimasen.
7. Watakushi no tomodachi wa Eigo no hon o kaitai desu.

Answers to Exercise 2
1. Hon o yomimashita.
2. Sakana o tabemashita.
3. Osake o nomimashita.
4. Nihongo ga wakarimasu.
5. Nihongo o hanashimasu.
6. Ame ga furimashita.
7. Kinô Tôkyô e ikimashita.
8. Nigatsu ni Nihon e kimashita.
9. Nichiyôbi ni sampo o shimashita.
10. Kinô Igirisujin wa Eikoku e kaerimashita.

Answers to Exercise 3
1. Arukimashô.
2. Hairimashô.
3. Kaerimashô.
4. Kaimashô.

Answers to Exercise 4
1. Watakushi wa yûbinkyoku e ikitai desu.
   Tomodachi wa yûbinkyoku e ikitaku wa arimasen.
2. Nihon o mitai desu.
   Nihon o mitaku wa arimasen.
3. Sashimi o tabetai desu.
   Sashimi o tabetaku wa arimasen.
4. Ano hon o yomitai desu/yomitaku wa arimasen.
5. Momo o kaitai desu/kaitaku wa arimasen.
6. Yokohama e kaeritai desu/kaeritaku wa arimasen.

Answers to Exercise 5
1. (Iie, gakkô no yoko ni arimasu.)
2. (Hon'ya no mae ni arimasu.)
3. (Yûbinkyoku no yoko ni arimasu.)
4. (Momo no yoko ni arimasu.)

Answers to Exercise 6
1. Sambyaku-en desu.
2. Nisen happyaku-en desu.
3. Sanzen yonhyaku-en desu.
4. Gosen roppyaku-en desu.
5. Ichiman-en desu.
6. Niman yonsen nihyaku-en desu.
7. Samman hassen-en desu.
8. Samman kyûsen gohyaku-en desu.

Answers to Exercise 7
1. Ano kodomo wa Furansugo ga wakarimasu.
2. Okusama wa Doitsugo ga wakarimasu.
3. Shujin wa Nihongo ga wakarimasu.
4. Ano gaikokujin wa Itariigo ga wakarimasu.
5. Ano Nihonjin wa Eigo ga wakarimasu ka?

Section B
Answers to Exercise 8
1. Kudamonoya wa hon'ya no yoko ni arimasu.
2. Watakushi no kuruma wa uchi no mae ni arimasu.
3. Watakushi no keisu wa anata no kaban no yoko ni arimasu.
4. Momo wa ringo no yoko ni arimasu.
5. Gakkô wa watakushi no jimusho no mae ni arimasu.

Answers to Exercise 9
1. Arigatô gozaimasu. (Hyaku gojû-en no okaeshi desu.)
2. (Gohyaku-en no okaeshi desu.)
3. (Sen happyaku-en no okaeshi desu.)
4. (Sanzen-en no okaeshi desu.)
5. (Kyûsen roppyaku-en no okaeshi desu.)

Answers to Exercise 10
(Gomen kudasai!)
(Jibiki ga arimasu ka?)
(Ei-wa jiten o kaitai desu keredomo.)
(Takai desu ka?)
(Ikura desu ka?)
(Sô desu ka? Takai desu ga Nihon no hon o yomitai desu. Niman-en de otsuri o itadakemasu ka?)
(Dômo arigatô gozaimasu.)

Chapter 7: Shopping – 2 At the post office
Section A
Answers to Exercise 1
1. Chotto matte kudasai.
2. Eigo de hanashite kudasai.
3. Ehagaki o katte kudasai.
4. Omoidashite kudasai.

Answers to Exercise 2
1. Kitte o sammai kaitai desu.
2. Ehagaki o gomai kaitai desu.
3. Kitte o hachimai kaitai desu.

4. Ehagaki o jûmai kaitai desu.
5. Kitte o jûichimai kaitai desu.

Answers to Exercise 3
1. Iie, mada kaimasen.
2.   kaerimasen.
3.   nomimasen.
4.   furimasen.

Answers to Exercise 4
1. Igirisu e ikitai desu.
2. Furansu e kono ehagaki o okuritai desu.
3. Benri na jibiki desu ka?
4. Hyaku-en no kitte o kaitai desu.
5. Kanai wa Itariigo ga wakarimasu.
6. Hon'ya wa uchi no mae ni arimasu.
7. Kudamonya de ringo o kaimashita.

Answers to Exercise 5
1. Sen-en.
2. Sambyaku-en.
3. Ichiman gojû-en.
4. Sanzen nanajûgo-en.
5. Happyaku-en
6. Roppyaku-en.
7. Hyaku hachijû-en.

Answers to Exercise 6
1. Yûbinkyoku de.
2. Kudamonoya de.
3. Hon'ya de.
4. Sakaya de.
5. Kudamonoya de.
6. Sakanaya de.
7. Kudamonoya de.
8. Hon'ya de.

Section B
Answers to Exercise 7
1. Iie, ame ga furimashita.
2. Iie, kitte o rokumai kaimashita.
3. Iie, kuji ni kaerimashita.
4. Iie, Doyôbi Tôkyô e ikimashita.
5. Iie, watakushi no kaban wa akai desu.
6. Iie, kinô nashi o kaimashita.
7. Iie, yûbinkyoku e ikitai desu.
8. Iie, shujin wa ehagaki o nimai kakimashita.

Answers to Exercise 8
1. Kinô tegami o sammai kakimashita.
2. Kesa ocha o nihai nomimashita.
3. Kin'yôbi Nihonjin o futari mimashita.
4. Sanji nijippun ni ehagaki o gomai kaimashita.
5. Shichiji ni tegami o yommai kakimashita.

Answers to Exercise 9
(Yûbinkyoku e ikitai desu.)
(Iie, arukimashô.)
(Kesa ehagaki o kakimashita kara Amerika e okuritai desu.)
(Sammai kakimashita.)
(Sumimasen. Eigo o hanashimasu ka? *or* Eigo ga wakarimasu ka?)
(Ano . . . Amerika e ehagaki o sammai okuritai desu. Ikura desu ka?)
(Hyaku gojû-en no kitte o sammai kudasai.)
(Gosen-en satsu shika arimasen ga ii desu ka?)
(Arigatô gozaimasu.)

Chapter 8: At Mr Maeda's office
Section A
Answers to Exercise 1
1. Katte imasu.
2. Kaite imasu.
3. Yonde imasu.
4. Hanashite imasu.
5. Matte imasu.
6. Nonde imasu.
7. Hataraite imasu.

Answers to Exercise 2
1. Suiyôbi desu.
2. Mokuyôbi desu.
3. Getsuyôbi deshita.
4. Nichiyôbi deshita.

Answers to Exercise 3
1. Sangatsu sanjûnichi desu.
2. Sangatsu sanjûichinichi desu.
3. Sangatsu nijûhachinichi deshita.
4. Sangatsu nijûshichinichi deshita.

Answers to Exercise 4
1. Jûgatsu nijûninichi desu.
2. Jûgatsu nijûsannichi desu.

3. Jûgatsu nijûgonichi desu.
4. Jûgatsu nijûrokunichi desu.

Answers to Exercise 5
1. Mite kudasai.
2. Hanashite kudasai.
3. Tabete kudasai.
4. Katte kudasai.
5. Kaite kudasai.
6. Nonde kudasai.

Answers to Exercise 6
1. Nichiyôbi ni shimashô.
2. Biiru ni shimasu.
3. Rokugatsu jûsannichi ni shimashô.
4. Ocha ni shimasu.
5. Doyôbi ni shimashô.

Answers to Exercise 7
1. Biiru o nihon kaimashita.
2. Ebi o jippon kaimashita.
3. Naganegi o sambon kaimashita.
4. Supuun o gohon kaimashita.
5. Pen o roppon kaimashita.
6. Kasa o ippon kaimashita.

Answers to Exercise 8
1. Gofun
2. Jippun
3. Jûgofun.
4. Nijippun.
5. Sanjippun.

Answers to Exercise 9
1. Eigo de (*or* o) hanashimasu.
2. Satô-san to hanashimashita.
3. Teeburu no ue ni nani ga arimasu ka?
4. Mô ippai?
5. Kôcha ni shimasu.
6. Itô to iu tomodachi desu.
7. Sono hon wa omoshiroku wa arimasen.
8. Hon'ya de jibiki o kaimashita.

Section B
Answers to Exercise 11
1. Iie, hataraite imasu.
2. Iie, ocha o nonde imasu.
3. Iie, ebi o tabete imasu.
4. Iie, shimbun o yonde imasu.

5. Iie, tegami o kaite imasu.
6. Iie, ehagaki o katte imasu.
7. Iie, zasshi o yonde imasu.

Answers to Exercise 12
1. Denwa no mae ni pen ga sambon arimasu.
2. Hon no ushiro ni kitte ga nimai arimasu.
3. Isu no ue ni kami ga gomai arimasu.
4. Teeburu no ue ni biiru ga roppon arimasu.
5. Ringo no yoko ni naganegi ga gohon arimasu.

Answers to Exercise 13
(Iie, isogashiku wa arimasen.)
(Wasuremashita.)
(Arimasu keredomo ima Itô-san ga sore o yonde imasu.)
(Hai, teeburu no ue ni arimasu.)
(Kôcha ni shimasu. Arigatô.)
(Ah! Supuun wa arimasu ka?)

Chapter 9: On the Ginza
Section A
Answers to Exercise 1
1. Tôkyô e itte . . .
2. Kaimono o shite . . .
3. Kôhii o nonde . . .
4. Yokohama e kite . . .
5. Tomodachi ni atte . . .
6. Tegami o kaite . . .
7. Otera o mite . . .

Answers to Exercise 2
(a) Zannen desu ga.
(b) Gomen kudasai.
(c) Dôzo.
(d) Chotto matte kudasai.
(e) Irasshaimase.
(f) Sumimasen.

Answers to Exercise 3
1. shikashi.
2. sukoshi.
3. tokidoki.
4. matawa.
5. soretomo.
6. futsû.
7. mochiron.
8. mada.

9. mata.
10. shika.
11. ikaga.
12. ikura.

Answers to Exercise 4
1. Ano akai otera wa utsukushii desu.
2. Ano kuroi hon wa omoshiroi desu.
3. Nihongo wa yasashii desu ga Eigo wa muzukashii desu.
4. Ano chiisai jibiki wa yasui desu.
5. Kyô mushiatsui desu. Kinô suzushii otenki deshita.

Section B
Answers to Exercise 6
1. Gozenchû yasunde imasu.
2. Denwa de hanashite imasu.
3. Nannichi ni shimashô ka?
4. Asatte mata kimashô.
5. Ototoi Kimura-san ni aimashita.

Answers to Exercise 7
(Ima jûjihan desu.)
(Jimusho de hataraite imasu.)
(Ginza e itte kaimono o shitai desu.)
(Hamigaki o kaitai desu. Kusuriya ga arimasu ka?)
(Ah! omoidashimashita! Tabako o kaitai desu.)
(Hito hako?)
(Mainichi nambon suimasu ka?)
(Jûgohon gurai. Karada ni warui desu nê!)

Chapter 10: By taxi and train
Section A
Answers to Exercise 1
1. Depaato wa yûbinkyoku yori tôi desu.
2. Nihongo wa Eigo yori omoshiroi desu.
3. Furansugo wa Doitsugo yori yasashii desu.
4. Natsu wa aki yori atsui desu.
5. Shimbun wa zasshi yori yasui desu.

Answers to Exercise 2
1. tabete.
2. kaite.
3. atte.
4. magatte.
5. yonde.

Answers to Exercise 3
1. Nihongo o yomu koto ga dekimasu.

2. Doitsugo o hanasu koto ga dekimasu.
3. Osake o nomu koto ga dekimasu.
4. Ashita Tôkyô e iku koto ga dekimasu.
5. Takai jibiki o kau koto ga dekimasu.

Answers to Exercise 4
1. nimai.
2. roppon.
3. itsutsu.
4. gohon.
5. shichinin.
6. sammai.
7. sambon.
8. mittsu.
9. yottsu.
10. ippon.

Answers to Exercise 5
1. suru deshô.
2. kakaru deshô.
3. iku deshô.
4. kaku deshô.
5. hanasu deshô.

Answers to Exercise 6
1. Amari chiisaku wa arimasen. Ôkii desu.
2. Amari yasashiku wa arimasen. Muzukashii desu.
3. Amari takaku wa arimasen. Yasui desu.
4. Amari muzukashiku wa arimasen. Yasashii desu.
5. Amari yoku wa arimasen. Warui desu.

Answers to Exercise 7
1. gofun gurai.
2. jûgofun gurai.
3. nijippun gurai.
4. sanjippun gurai.
5. yonjippun gurai.
6. gojippun gurai kakarimasu.

Section B
Answers to Exercise 8
1. Nijihan ni demasu.
2. Sanji gofun mae ni demasu.
3. Shichiji jûgofun ni demasu.
4. Gofun oki ni demasu.
5. Sanjûgofun oki ni demasu.

Answers to Exercise 9
1. After drinking some saké I ate some fish.

2. As the saké is good let's drink some.
3. After I went to Tokyo I did some shopping.
4. As I'm going to Tokyo I can meet Mr Satô.
5. As it is snowing let's go home.
6. As the snow is stopping I'd like to go for a walk.
7. After I spoke on the phone I got to work.
8. As there's a good deal of traffic let's go by underground.

Answers to Exercise 10
1. Massugu itte kudasai.
2. Hidari e magatte kudasai.
3. Futatsume no kado o migi e magatte kudasai.
4. Ano ôkina yûbinkyoku no tokoro o hidari e magatte kudasai.
5. Tabakoya no tokoro o migi e magatte kudasai.

Answers to Exercise 11
1. Watakushi wa eki e takushii de ikimashita.
2. Watakushi wa Nihon e fune de kimashita.
3. Yûrakuchô e chikatetsu de kaerimashita.
4. Kyôto e kisha de ikitai desu.
5. Depaato e kuruma de ikimashita.

Chapter 11: Feeling ill
Section A
Answers to Exercise 1
1. Shichigatsu tsuitachi.
2. Jûgatsu muika.
3. Ichigatsu (or Shôgatsu) jûyokka.
4. Gogatsu kokonoka.
5. Rokugatsu mikka.
6. Nigatsu futsuka.
7. Sangatsu nanoka.
8. Shigatsu tôka.
9. Hachigatsu itsuka.
10. Kugatsu hatsuka.

Answers to Exercise 2
1. Kuruma wa ôkikute akai desu.
2. Hon wa chiisakute kuroi desu.
3. Nihongo wa yasashikute omoshiroi desu.
4. Nodo ga itakute akai desu.

Answers to Exercise 3
1. Atsuku narimashita.
2. Muzukashiku narimashita.
3. Ôkiku narimashita.

4. Itaku narimashita.
5. Waruku narimashita.

Answers to Exercise 4
1. Itô-san wa kuruma ga arimasu.
2. Watakushi wa kitte ga arimasu.
3. Yamada-san wa nodo ga itai desu.
4. Satô-san no okusan wa atama ga itai desu.
5. Ano kata wa ôkina ie ga arimasu.

Answers to Exercise 5
1. Nomanakereba narimasen.
2. Minakereba narimasen.
3. Kaeranakereba narimasen.
4. Hanasanakereba narimasen.
5. Tsukenakereba narimasen.
6. Yasumanakereba narimasen.
7. Naranakereba narimasen.
8. Tabenakereba narimasen.
9. Norikaenakereba narimasen.
10. Mitsukenakereba narimasen.

Answers to Exercise 6
1. Stomach-ache.
2. Headache as well.
3. Caught a cold.
4. Got a fever.
5. Sore throat.

Section B
Answers to Exercise 7
1. Kinô.
2. Yokka mae ni.
3. Senkyûhyaku nanajûnananen (*or* Shôwa gojûninen) ni.
4. Jûichigatsu yôka ni.
5. Tôka mae ni.
6. Jûnigatsu nijûyokka ni.
7. Gozen kujihan ni.
8. Ototoi.
9. Sakuban.
10. Kesa.

Answers to Exercise 8
(Iie, yamimashita.)
(Iie, samuku narimashita.)
(Kaze o hikimashita.)

(Netsu ga demashita.)
(Mada ikimasen.)
(Iie, tôku wa arimasen. Chikai desu.)
(Watakushi wa atama ga itai desu.)
(Hontô desu.)
(Sumimasen. Hai, uchi e kaeranakereba narimasen.)
(Arigatô gozaimasu.)

Answers to Exercise 9

1. Tamago o tabete kôcha o nomitai desu.
2. Yokohama e itte kaban o kaitai desu.
3. Itô-san no okusan wa daidokoro e itte okashi o motte kimashita.
4. Kanai wa sampo shite kaimono o shitai desu.
5. Nihonjin ni atte Nihongo o hanashimashita.

Chapter 12: At the doctor's

Section A

Answers to Exercise 1

1. Watakushi wa biiru ga suki desu.
2. Anata wa mizu ga hoshii desu ka?
3. Shujin wa ocha ga dai kirai desu.
4. Kodomo wa atama ga itai desu.
5. Itô-san wa okane ga arimasu yo.

Answers to Exercise 2

1. Nominagara.
2. Minagara.
3. Tabenagara.
4. Ikinagara.
5. Shinagara.

Answers to Exercise 3

1. (nomeba) If you drink this medicine you will get better.
2. (ikeba) If you go to Kyôto you can see some splendid temples.
3. (hanaseba) If one speaks Japanese one will get good at it.
4. (tabereba) If you eat rice you'll grow tall.
5. (kureba) If you come here you can see Mt Fuji.

Answers to Exercise 4

1. Mâ.
2. Ano.
3. Ano nê.
4. Eeto.
5. Sâ.

Answers to Exercise 5
1. Hayaku hanashimashita.
2. Mazui desu.
3. Kirai desu.
4. Igirisu e ikitaku wa arimasen.
5. Yasashii desu.

Answers to Exercise 6
(Iie, mada ikimasen.)
(Iie, kinô deshita.)
(Mikka desu.)
(Iie, kin'yôbi desu.)
(Iie, hitori de ikimasu.)
(Hatsuka ni kaerimasu.)
(Nan demo kekkô desu.)
(Ocha no hô ga ii desu.)

Section B
Answers to Exercise 7
1. Genki ni nareba Nikkô e iku koto ga dekimasu.
2. Genki ni naranakereba Kyôto e iku koto ga dekimasen.
3. Yokohama e ikeba Doitsu no jibiki o kau koto ga dekimasu.
4. Nihon e ikanakereba Fuji-san o miru koto ga dekimasen.
5. Kono kusuri o nomeba genki ni narimasu.
6. Benkyô shinakereba ojôzu ni narimasen.
7. Depaato e ikeba isu o kau koto ga dekimasu.

Answers to Exercise 9
1. Setsumei shite kudasaimasu.
2. Depaato e itte kudasaimasu.
3. Ehagaki o kaite kudasaimasu.
4. Koko e kite kudasaimasu.
5. Jibiki o katte kudasaimasu.

Answers to Exercise 10
(Atama ga itakute nodo mo itai desu.)
(Sukoshi demashita. Taion ga sanjû shichido kyûbu arimasu.)
(Iie. Kinô wa itaku narimashita ga kyô wa daijôbu desu).
(Ebi to gohan o tabemashita.)
(Hai. Nodo ga itai desu kara mizu o takusan nomimasu.)
(Sakuban yori ii desu keredomo itai desu.)
(Hidoi desu ka?)

(Tôka ni Matsushima e ikimasu. Daijôbu desu ka?)
(Itsu sono kusuri o nomanakereba narimasen ka?)
(Arigatô gozaimasu. Sayonara.)

Answers to Exercise 11

1. Anyway.
2. Kind.
3. Egg.
4. Kitchen.
5. Too bad.
6. 9th day *or* nine days.
7. Fetch, look for, find.
8. Taste.
9. Utterly.
10. Explanation.

Answers to Exercise 12

1. That is a shame.
2. Anything will do.
3. It's only ten minutes on foot.
4. Excuse me!
5. You are probably busy.
6. Turn left please.
7. You must study.
8. Do sit down.
9. Good morning.
10. What seems to be the trouble?

Chapter 13: Shopping and business trips
Section A
Answers to Exercise 1

1. naganegi.
2. jibiki.
3. ringo.
4. tamago.
5. kitte.

Answers to Exercise 2

1. benkyô suru.
2. eki e iku.
3. kaimono o suru.
4. zasshi o yomu.
5. Itô-san no kaisha o tazuneru.

Answers to Exercise 3

1. tabenaide kudasai.
2. kakanaide kudasai.
3. nomanaide kudasai.

4. hanasanaide kudasai.
5. kawanaide kudasai.
6. matanaide kudasai.
7. ikanaide kudasai.
8. tazunenaide kudasai.

Answers to Exercise 4
1. Shôwa gojûichi-nen desu.
2. Shôwa gojûninen desu.
3. Shôwa rokujûyonen deshita.
4. Senkyûhyaku hachijûgonen deshita.

Answers to Exercise 5
1. ringo o tô.
2. okashi o nanatsu.
3. tamago o itsutsu.
4. momo o kokonotsu.
5. teeburu o yattsu.
6. denwa o jûichi.

Answers to Exercise 6
1. ikanakereba . . . aimasen.
2. nomanakereba . . . narimasen.
3. tabenakereba . . . futorimasen.
4. yomanakereba . . wakarimasen.
5. kakanakereba . . . ikimasen.
6. isoganakereba . . . tsukimasen.

Answers to Exercise 7
1. Ginkô e ikitai desu.
2. Dekaketai desu.
3. Sampo shitai desu.
4. Uchi e kaeritai desu.
5. Tegami o kakitai desu.
6. Tomodachi ni aitai desu.

Section B
Answers to Exercise 8
1. hon/jibiki/Ei-wa jiten
2. kippu
3. sakana/ebi
4. hagaki/kitte
5. osake

Answers to Exercise 9
(Mô naorimashita yo. Ima totemo genki desu.)
(Hai, jûjihan ni dekakemasu.)
(Ginkô e iku tsumori desu.)
(Ginkô e itte kara yûbinkyoku e ikimasu.)

(Mochiron katte kimasu yo. Nammai deshô?)

(Anata wa kyô Tôkyô e iku tsumori desu ka?)

(Sukoshi isogashii desu kara watakushi no kaisha o tazunete kudasaimasen ka?)

(Moshi kaisha e ikeba watakushi no tegami o motte kite kudasaimasen ka?)

(Moshi tegami ga nakereba ii desu yo. Sore hodo jûyô ja arimasen kara.)

Answers to Exercise 10

1. Sore wa tanoshimi desu ne.
2. Zenzen wakarimasen.
3. Shichigatsu no hô ga ii deshô.
4. Niji ni dekakereba, ii desu ka?
5. Mô ichido Doitsu e ikanakereba narimasen.
6. Go yukkuri!

Chapter 14: The young people arrive

Section A

Answers to Exercise 1

1. Yasunde imasu.
2. Mite imasu.
3. Matte imasu.
4. Tazunete imasu.
5. Naotte imasu.
6. Kiite imasu.
7. Naratte imasu.
8. Hanashite imasu.
9. Itte imasu.
10. Kite imasu.

Answers to Exercise 2

1. Oboenakereba narimasen.
2. Matanakereba narimasen.
3. Ikanakereba narimasen.
4. Konakereba narimasen.
5. Arawanakereba narimasen.
6. Magaranakereba narimasen.
7. Nomanakereba narimasen.
8. Hanasanakereba narimasen.

Answers to Exercise 3

1. Arukitai desu. Arukitaku wa arimasen.
2. Tabetai desu. Tabetaku wa arimasen.
3. Yomitai desu. Yomitaku wa arimasen.
4. Kitai desu. Kitaku wa arimasen.

Answers to Exercise 4
1. Tama ni shika ikimasen.
2. Tama ni shika kimasen.
3. Tama ni shika hanashimasen.
4. Tama ni shika nomimasen.
5. Tama ni shika tabemasen.
6. Tama ni shika mimasen.

Answers to Exercise 5
1. Nomu deshô.
2. Oboeru deshô.
3. Kiku deshô.
4. Suru deshô.
5. Kaeru deshô.
6. Wakaru deshô.
7. Kuru deshô.
8. Konde iru deshô.

Section B
Answers to Exercise 6
1. Aruku koto ga suki desu.
2. Oishasan e ikimasu.
3. Iie, takushii de ikanakereba narimasen.
4. Biiru no hô ga ii desu. Arigatô.
5. Nani o suru koto ga kirai desu ka?
6. Ha ga itaku nareba nani o shimasu ka?
7. Rondon made kisha de iku koto ga dekimasu ka?
8. Kôcha to kôhii to dochira ga ii desu ka?

Answers to Exercise 7
1. Sono naganegi wa takasugimasu.
2. Ano kanji wa muzukashisugimasu.
3. Okashi o tabesugimashita.
4. Jûgofun hayaku kisugimashita.

Answers to Exercise 8
1. Can you read those kanji?
2. The reading of those kanji is hon'ya.
3. I can remember those kanji.
4. Those kanji are read as isha.

Answers to Exercise 9
1. zenzen.
2. dandan.
3. onna.
4. rainen.
5. kyonen.
6. otoko.

Answers to Exercise 10

1. Eki no ushiro ni arimasu.
2. Depaato no mae ni arimasu.
3. Asoko desu. Ginkô no yoko ni arimasu.
4. Massugu itte, hitotsume no kado o migi e magatte kudasai. Ôkina tatemono desu. Eki no yoko ni arimasu.

Answers to Exercise 11

1. Kyô atarashii kanji o naraimashita.
2. Eigakan e itte Nihon no eiga o mimashita.
3. Kono chiisakute akai hon wa yasashisugimasu.
4. Satô to iu tomodachi wa eki e tonde ikanakereba narimasen.

Answers to Exercise 12

(Kôcha no hô ga ii desu. Arigatô.)
(Miruku wa irimasu ga osatô wa irimasen.)
(Iie! Okashi o tabesugireba byôki ni narimasu yo!)
(Arigatô, itadakimasu.)
(Atama ga itai desu kara dekakemasen.)
(Kaze o hikimashita.)
(Kekkô desu. Arigatô.)

Chapter 15: Planning a trip

Section A

Answers to Exercise 1

1. omoshirosô desu.
2. hanashitasô desu.
3. hoshisô desu.
4. sabishisô desu.
5. hazukashisô desu.

Answers to Exercise 2

1. Ane to issho ni eiga o mi ni ikimashô.
2. Momo to (or ka) ringo to (or ka) dochira ga suki desu ka?
3. Gakkô ni tomodachi ga futari imasu.
4. Kusuri o nonde kara kanai wa naorimashita.
5. Gakkô de Eigo o naraimasu.
6. Kusuri wa watakushi no tomodachi o naoshimashita.
7. Okusama wa genki ni narimashita.

Answers to Exercise 3

1. Chittomo wakarimasen.
2. Heta desu.
3. Sukoshi wakarimasu.
4. Yoku wakarimasu.
5. Hanasu koto ga dekimasu ga kaku koto wa dekimasen.

Answers to Exercise 5
1. Okusama o tsurete kudasai.
2. Yukkuri hanashite kudasai.
3. Mado o shimete kudasai.
4. Kono kusuri o nonde kudasai.
5. Wasurenaide kudasai.
6. Sono tegami o akenaide kudasai.
7. Mô ichido itte kudasai.

Answers to Exercise 6
1. Sengetsu.
2. Rokugatsu nijûyokka.
3. Igirisu/Eikoku kara.
4. Hikôki de.
5. Jûgatsu tôka.

Section B
Answers to Exercise 7
1. Mr Itô has to go to Tôkyô every week.
2. Peaches are dearer than Japanese pears but apples are the dearest.
3. My friend taught me Japanese.
4. Have you got the time to do it?
5. Which do you like, dogs or cats?

Answers to Exercise 8
(Kanai wa Nihon ga dai suki desu.)
(Mada hanashimasen keredomo naraitai desu.)
(Iie, heta desu ga hanashitai desu yo.)
(Ii desu yo. Shikashi sukoshi hazukashii desu.)
(Muzukashii desu ga dandan yasashiku natte imasu.)
(Mada yomimasen ga ano kanji o naraimashita.)
(Ano kanji wa Nihon to yomimasu.)
(Sono kanji wa wakarimasen.)

Answers to Exercise 9
I went to the zoo and saw all sorts of interesting animals. I love animals.
In our home in Kyôto we have three cats. The biggest is small and black.
I like dogs too but as our cats hate dogs we don't have any dogs in the house.

Answers to Exercise 10
1. Moshi sono mado o akereba heya wa samuku narimasu.
2. Sono mado o akenakereba uchi wa atsuku narimasu.

3. Machigaeba watakushi wa anata no Nihongo o naoshimasu.
4. Benkyô shinakereba jôzu ni narimasen.
5. Yoku benkyô sureba Nihongo o yomu koto ga dekimasu.

Chapter 16: The Japanese family
Section A
Answers to Exercise 1
1. Chichi wa rokujûissai desu.
2. Haha wa gojûhassai desu.
3. Musuko wa jûsansai desu.
4. Musume wa jûissai desu.
5. Kanai/Shujin wa sanjûhassai desu.
6. Ani ga futari imasu.
7. Imôto ga hitori imasu.

Answers to Exercise 3
1. Hon o yonde iru hito wa otôto desu.
2. Mainichi eki e kuru otoko no kata wa otomodachi desu ka?
3. Osake o takusan nomu hito wa itsumo byôki desu.
4. Utsukushii kimono ga aru onna no hito wa ane desu.

Answers to Exercise 4
1. Okaasan desu ka?
2. Ojôsan desu ka?
3. Obasan desu ka?
4. Okusan desu ka?
5. Oniisan desu ka?
6. Kodomosantachi desu ka?
7. Imôtosan desu ka?
8. Botchan (or) musukosan desu ka?

Answers to Exercise 5
1. nihiki.
2. hitori.
3. sannin.
4. sambiki.
5. gomai.
6. futatsu.
7. roppon.
8. ippon.

Section B
Answers to Exercise 6
1. Musuko wa gosai desu.
2. Okaasan wa Yokohama ni sunde imasu ka?

3. Ojiisan wa sen kyûhyaku shichijûsannen ni nakunari-mashita.
4. Ani wa kuroi hige ga arimasu.
5. Botchan (or musukosan) wa tanjôbi ni okurimono o takusan moraimashita ka?
6. Ojôsan wa itsu kekkon shimashita ka?
7. Otôsan wa itsu kikoku shimasu ka?
8. Imôto wa megane o kakete imasu.
9. Kono shashin o Shôgatsu ni torimashita.
10. Tomodachi no okaasan wa Furansugo no sensei desu.

Answers to Exercise 7

1. The man speaking Japanese is an English teacher.
2. Foreigners who can write kanji are clever, aren't they!
3. People who smoke a lot have to go and see the doctor.
4. People who work for a company every day like to go to the country on Saturdays.

Answers to Exercise 8

1. Eiga o miru koto ga dekimasu.
2. Dôbutsu o miru koto ga dekimasu.
3. Kitte o kau koto ga dekimasu.
4. Torii o miru koto ga dekimasu.

Answers to Exercise 9

1. Hakone ni sunde iru hito wa Fuji-san o mainichi miru koto ga dekimasu.
2. Kono daigaku de sûgaku o oshieru hito wa otôto desu.
3. Mainichi sampo suru hito wa genki desu.
4. Ano akai Nihon no kuruma o unten shite iru hito wa chichi desu.

Answers to Exercise 10

(Sangatsu kokonoka desu.)
(Hai, Nihongo no jibiki to utsukushii kimono to ata-rashii pen o moraimashita.)
(Sô desu keredomo ima tegami o takusan kakanake-reba narimasen!)
(Mada kaerimasen. Raigetsu kikoku suru deshô.)
(Jimusho de hataraite imasu.)
(Iie, kaze o hikimashita.)
(Mada ikimasen keredomo kusuri o nomimashita.)
(Sô desu nê! Kinô ame ga takusan furimashita. Otôto wa watakushitachi o tazunemashita ga kasa o wasure-mashita!)
(Ima nijûhassai desu.)
(Nijûissai desu.)
(Hakubutsukan de hataraite imasu.)

(Hai, sengetsu kekkon shimashita. Mite kudasai. Kore wa imôto no shujin no shashin desu.)
(Futaritomo ureshisô desu.)
(Imôto no shujin no ani desu.)
(Iie, Matsumoto de hataraite imasu.)

Chapter 17: Eating out
Section A
Answers to Exercise 1
1. Yonde shimaimashita.
2. Itte shimaimashita.
3. Kaette shimaimashita.
4. Haitte shimaimashita.
5. Shite shimaimashita.

Answers to Exercise 2
1. Yonda koto ga arimasu ka?
2. Kaita koto ga arimasu ka?
3. Katta koto ga arimasu ka?
4. Totta koto ga arimasu ka?
5. Tazuneta koto ga arimasu ka?
6. Unten shita koto ga arimasu ka?

Answers to Exercise 3
1. Itô-san ni o ai shimashita.
2. Itô-san to o hanashi shimashita.
3. Eigo de o hanashi ni narimasu ka?
4. Atarashii pen de o kaki ni narimasu ka?

Answers to Exercise 4
1. Kono kanji o kaite mite kudasai.
2. Kono osake o nonde mite kudasai.
3. Kono tempuraya ni haitte mite kudasai.
4. Nihongo de hanashite mite kudasai.
5. Mado o akete mite kudasai.

Answers to Exercise 5
1. My younger brother.
2. Splendid.
3. Music.
4. Aubergine.
5. Your father.
6. Lonely.
7. University.
8. Summer.

Section B
Answers to Exercise 6
1. Eiga o mi ni ikimashô.

2. Ongaku o kiki ni kaerimashita.
3. Nihongo o narai ni kimasu.
4. Ehagaki o kaki ni ikimashita.

Answers to Exercise 7
1. As you're Japanese of course you must like fish.
2. Have you ever bought a German newspaper?
3. I'll have tunafish next.
4. It's finally stopped raining.
5. My elder sister was born in 1970.

Answers to Exercise 8
1. Kono tegami wa yominikui desu.
2. Nihongo wa kakinikui desu!
3. Ano ongaku wa kikiyasui desu.
4. Ano kanji wa wasureyasui desu!
5. Ano tôfu wa tabeyasui desu.
6. Ano kotoba wa oboenikui desu.

Answers to Exercise 9
1. Yasui desu.
2. Yasuku wa arimasen.
3. Yasusô desu.
4. Yasukute oishii desu.
5. Atarashii desu.
6. Atarashiku wa arimasen.
7. Atarashisô desu.
8. Atarashikute utsukushii desu.

Answers to Exercise 10
(Sore wa tanoshimi desu ne. Tempura o tabeta koto ga arimasen.)
(Takasô desu.)
(Konde imasu ka?)
(Desu kara asoko ni suwarimashô ka?)
(Iie! Nihongo de kaite arimasu!)
(Yomiyasui desu ga kanji o watakushi ni oshiete kudasai.)
(Wakarimasen.)
(Nani ga haitte imasu ka?)
(Ebi ga nambon haitte imasu ka?)
(Oishisô desu ne.)
(Kono shiitake wa oishii desu.)
(Ammari suki ja arimasen.)
(Mô onaka ga ippai ni natte shimaimashita!)
(Iie. Watakushi ga gochisô shimasu yo. Okanjô o onegai shimasu.)

Chapter 18: Language for men and women
Section A
Answers to Exercise 1
1. Iie, chikatetsu no hô ga ii desu.
2. Yuri.
3. Nasu.
4. Mikka.
5. Asatte.
6. Gohan.
7. Mizu.
8. Nashi.
9. Gozen.
10. Kôcha.
11. Kaban.
12. Zasshi.

Answers to Exercise 2
1. Hakubutsukan no mae de.
2. Ginkô no ushiro de.
3. Satô-san no otaku no yoko de.
4. Eki de.
5. Kyûjô no mae de.

Answers to Exercise 3
1. Akai bara o gohon.
2. Ôkina kiku o nanahon.
3. Shiroi yuri o sambon.
4. Chiisana tamago o muttsu.
5. Tabako o nijippon.
6. Hyaku-en no kitte o sammai.

Answers to Exercise 4
1. Yomimashita.
2. Kaimashita.
3. Kikimashita.
4. Aimashita.
5. Kakimashita.
6. Tabemashita.

Answers to Exercise 5
1. yonda.
2. kita.
3. itta.
4. totta.
5. wasureta.
6. naratta.

7. moratta.
8. iketa.

Section B

Answers to Exercise 6
1. Sushi o taberu koto ga suki desu.
2. Benkyô suru koto ga kirai desu.
3. Aruku koto ga suki desu.
4. Osake o nomu koto ga dai kirai desu.
5. Eigakan e iku koto ga suki desu.
6. Ongaku o kiku koto ga kirai desu.

Answers to Exercise 7
1. Ashita Yokohama e iku to omoimasu.
2. Ano hito wa kinô Kôbe e itta to omoimasu.
3. Ano hito wa kyô jimusho e kuru to omoimasu ka?
4. Hon'ya de jibiki o katta to omoimasu ka?

Answers to Exercise 8
1. How many pink chrysanthemums do you intend to buy?
2. It's useful to hear Japanese every day.
3. It's not much fun waiting for a friend to come.
4. There are many pine-trees near a high mountain.
5. As I want to remember English I intend to study hard.
6. After we've seen the film shall we go and eat some sushi?

Answers to Exercise 9
1. Kinô katta jibiki wa warui desu/yoku wa arimasen.
2. Senshû no kin'yôbi ni nonda kusuri wa mazukatta no desu.
3. Okaasan ga iketa hana wa utsukushii desu.
4. Amerika de totta shashin wa doko desu ka?
5. Kesa eranda hon wa omoshiroku wa arimasen.

Answers to Exercise 10
(Chotto matte kudasai. Techô o mimasu. Dame desu yo. Mokuyôbi nara ii desu keredomo. Anata wa?)
(Otaku no mae de aimashô ka?)
(Hachijihan.)
(Iie, watakushi wa kuruma ga arimasu kara tochû de anata o hiroimashô.)
(Ah ... ane ga inaka kara motte kita hana o mimashita ka?)
(Watakashi wa kiku ga dai suki desu.)
(Akai bara ga suki desu ga shiroi no wa kirai desu.)
(Nijûyokka ni. Ane no atarashii uchi no shashin desu. Mite kudasai.)

(Ima Matsumoto ni sunde imasu ga jûgonichi ni Tôkyô
e kuru tsumori desu.)

(Hai, Eigo no sensei desu kara chûgakkô de oshie-
masu.)

(Hai, kyonen no shichigatsu ni Rondon e itte ototoshi
Amerika e ikimashita.)

Chapter 19: At the bank and at the garage
Section A
Answers to Exercise 1
1. Kuruma o tomemashita.
2. Kuruma wa tomarimashita.
3. Hako o akemashita.
4. Hon'ya wa rokuji ni shimarimasu.

Answers to Exercise 2
1. Tabako o nomanakute mo ii desu.
2. Mado o akenakute mo ii desu.
3. Shashin o toranakute mo ii desu.
4. Tegami o kakanakute mo ii desu.
5. Momo o kawanakute mo ii desu.
6. Ashita konakute mo ii desu.

Answers to Exercise 3
1. Mado o aratte kudasaimasen ka?
2. En o pondo ni kaete kudasai.
3. Onamae o kaite kudasaimasen ka?
4. Kuruma o ugokashite kudasai.
5. Shirabete kudasai.
6. Mantan ni shite kudasai.

Answers to Exercise 4
1. haitte . . . hirakimashita.
2. hiraite . . . kaemashita.
3. kaete . . . kaerimashita.
4. kaette . . . kakemashita.
5. kakete . . . hiroimashita.
6. hirotte . . . tabemashita.
7. tabete . . . ikimashita.
8. itte . . . kaimashita.
9. katte . . . kakimashita.
10. kaite . . . yomimashita.

Answers to Exercise 5
1. We need petrol.
2. Please put some petrol in.
3. Do you take sugar?
4. I've put some sugar in.

Section B
Answers to Exercise 6
1. Satô-san wa shitte imasu ka?
2. Sore wa shirimasen deshita.
3. Sakaya no soba ni aru kôban wa shitte imasu ka?
4. Ano kotoba wa shiranakereba narimasen.

Answers to Exercise 7
1. Sir!/Madam!
2. Certainly, sir/madam.
3. It makes no odds.
4. I'm sorry.
5. Do take care.
6. Please!
7. Excuse me.
8. I'm treating. (It's on me.)

Answers to Exercise 8
1. Kuruma o chotto achira e ugokashimashô ka?
2. Kôsokudôro wa konde imasu.
3. Taiya o shirabete kudasai. (*or* chiekki shite kudasai.)
4. Mada ato hachijûkiro mo unten shinakereba narimasen.

Answers to Exercise 9
1. Furansugo o hanasu koto ga dekimasen.
2. Nemuru koto ga dekimashita.
3. Hataraku koto ga dekimasen.
4. Itadaku koto ga dekimasu ka?

Answers to Exercise 10
(Hachiji jûgofun desu.)
(Gogo shichiji gurai.)
(Mainichi nambon nomimasu/suimasu ka?)
(Hontô desu ka! Ano . . . ginkô wa shitte imasu ka?)
(Ginkô no soba ni gasorinsutando ga arimasu ne.)
(Ano . . . gasorinsutando no ushiro ni tabakoya ga arimasu.)
(Sumimasen ga . . . Kôza o hirakitai n desu ga dô sureba ii no deshô ka?)
(Wakarimashita.)
(Chigaimasu. Watakushi wa Igirisujin desu.)
(Kyô wa ichipondo wa nan-en desu ka?)
(Sô desu ka? Kinô yori takai desu nê. Gojûpondo o en ni kaete itadakemasen ka?)

Chapter 20: A Japanese inn
Section A
Answers to Exercise 1
1. Ashita kuru ni kimatte imasu.
2. Sensei ga kaita hon o yomimashita ka?
3. Sukiyaki o tabe ni ikimashô ka?
4. Maguro ni shimasu.
5. Sore wa shirimasen deshita.
6. Biiru o nihon kudasai.
7. Mado o akemashita.
8. Dochira ga katsu to omoimasu ka?
9. Nanji ni jimusho wa akimasu ka?
10. En o pondo ni kaemashita.

Answers to Exercise 2
1. Tôkyô e iku kamo shiremasen.
2. Bikkuri suru kamo shiremasen.
3. Kanji o narau kamo shiremasen.
4. Hairu kamo shiremasen.

Answers to Exercise 3
1. yomanakatta.
2. todokanakatta.
3. akenakatta.
4. konakatta.
5. kinakatta.
6. shiranakatta.
7. shinakatta.
8. tomaranakatta.
9. ugokasanakatta.
10. ikanakatta.

Answers to Exercise 4
1. Shimbun o yomitai no desu. Shimbun o yomitakatta no desu.
2. Eiga o mitai no desu. Eiga o mitakatta no desu.
3. Yûbinkyoku e ikitai no desu. Yûbinkyoku e ikitakatta no desu.
4. Asoko ni tomaritai no desu. Asoko ni tomaritakatta no desu.
5. Nihongo de hanashitai no desu. Nihongo de hanashi-takatta no desu.

Answers to Exercise 5
1. Chotto okiki shitai no desu ga ichigatsu nijûgonichi no ban heya wa aite imasu ka?
2. Sangatsu yokka

3. Shichigatsu yôka.
4. Hachigatsu jûsannichi.
5. Kugatsu futsuka.
6. Raishû no suiyôbi.
7. Raishû no doyôbi.
8. Saraishû no kin'yôbi

Answers to Exercise 6

1. Hitori desu.
2. Futari desu.
3. Sannin desu.
4. Yonin desu.
5. Watakushi to musuko desu.
6. Kanai to musume desu.

Answers to Exercise 7

1. Hitoban desu.
2. Futaban desu.
3. Yoban desu.
4. Goban desu.
5. Rokuban desu.
6. Isshûkan desu.
7. Nishûkan desu.
8. Ikkagetsu desu.
9. Rokkagetsu desu.
10. Shichikagetsu desu.

Answers to Exercise 8

1. Hitoban de nishoku tsuki de kyûsen gohyaku-en ni narimasu.
2. ichiman issen-en
3. ichiman yonsen-en
4. niman-en

Section B

Answers to Exercise 9

1. Watakushi ga yomanakatta hon.
2. Tegami o kakanakatta otoko no hito.
3. Kinô jimusho e konakatta otoko no hito.
4. Anata ga kawanakatta saifu.

Answers to Exercise 10

1. Nihongo o hanasanai otoko no hito desu.
2. Benkyô shinai kodomo desu.
3. Tabako o nomanai/suwanai otoko no kata desu.
4. Sashimi o tabenai Nihonjin desu.
5. Furusato e kaeranai tomodachi desu.

Answers to Exercise 11
1. Tôkyô e kaette kara denwa o kakemashita.
2. Kyôto e tsuite kara otomodachi ni aimashita.
3. Asoko ni kuruma o tomeba Fuji-san o miru koto ga dekiru deshô.
4. Ryokan ni rokuji mae ni todoku to ii desu.
5. Yûgohan no mae ni kuru to ii desu.

ANSWERS TO REVISION AND SELF-ASSESSMENT TESTS

CHAPTERS 1–5

Section 1
1. Kore wa watakushi no kaban ja arimasen.
2. Uchi ni ringo to (or ya) momo ga arimasu.
3. Nihon dewa kodomotachi wa hachiji ni gakkô e ikimasu.
4. Watakishi wa Yokohama e ikimashita.
5. Foster-san wa Kyôto de sashimi o tabemashita.
6. Yuki ga takusan furimasu.
7. Getsuyôbi kara kin'yôbi made jimusho e ikimasu.
8. Samuku wa arimasen.

Section 2
1. Yasashiku wa arimasen. Muzukashii desu.
2. Samuku wa arimasen. Atsui desu.
3. Chiisaku wa arimasen. Ôkii desu.
4. Waruku wa arimasen. Ii desu.
5. Yoku wa arimasen. Warui desu.

Section 3
jûichi.
nijûni.
sanjûsan.
yonjûroku.
yonjûshichi (or -nana)
gojûgo.
shichi- (or nana-) jûhachi
hachijûkyû
kyûjûyon
hyaku.

Section 4

    sen kyûhyaku rokujûgonen
    sen kyûhyaku hachijûnen

Section 5

    gozen (*or* asa) shichi- (*or* nana-) ji jûgofun.
    gogo hachiji yonjûgofun (*or* kuji jûgofun mae).
    yoji jippun mae.
    jûichiji sanjûgofun.
    kuji nijippun.

Section 6

naganegi.	goshujin
kudamono.	kugatsu
kuruma.	mokuyôbi
ame.	kyô
okusama.	mochiron.

Section 7

1. Iie, Rondon no haru wa mushiatsuku wa arimasen.
2. Igirisu dewa fuyu wa atsuku wa arimasen.
3. Nihonjin wa sakana ya gohan o tabemasu.
4. Nihongo wa gaikokujin ni muzukashii desu yo!
5. Nihon dewa kodomotachi wa futsû goji ni uchi e kaerimasu.

Section 8

1. It is large and red.
2. It is 6.30.
3. Black.
4. No, German.
5. Fish and rice (and other things!).
6. Saké or green tea.
7. No.
8. No.
9. In June.

CHAPTERS 6–10

Section 1

1. jûmai
2. futatsu
3. jippon
4. sambai
5. itsutsu

Section 2
1. Tegami o kaite imasu.
2. Kaimono o shite imasu.
3. Ebi o katte imasu.
4. Nihongo de hanashite imasu.
5. Tôkyô e kite imasu.

Section 3
1. Jimusho de hataraite tegami o kakimashita.
2. Tôkyô e itte kaimono o shimashita.
3. Uchi e kaette gohan o tabemashita.
4. Gohan o tabete shimbun o yomimashita.
5. Shimbun o yonde osake o nomimashita.

Section 4
1. Otera wa Kiyomizudera to iimasu.
2. Teeburu no ue ni nani ga arimasu ka?
3. Watakushi wa Nihonjin ni aimashita.
4. Kôcha ni shimashô.
5. Otera o mimashita.
6. Yûrakuchô kara Gotanda made eki ga muttsu arimasu.
7. Benri na hon deshô.
8. Ano hito wa Nihongo ga yoku wakarimasu.

Section 5
1. Massugu itte kudasai.
2. Hidari e magatte kudasai.
3. Mittsume no kado o migi e magatte kudasai.
4. Ano ôkina (or ôkii) tatemono no tokoro o hidari e magatte kudasai.

Section 6
1. Three.
2. 750 yen.
3. Germany.
4. 2500 yen.
5. A 10 000 note.
6. 7500 yen.
7. On the table over there; two.
8. October 13.
9. 2.25.

Section 7
1. Yûbinkyoku no yoko ni kusuriya ga arimasu.
2. Kudamonoya no mae ni denwa ga arimasu.

Section 8
Niman gosen-en.
samman rokusen-en.

sambyaku rokujû-en.
roppyaku yonjûgo-en.
sanzen nanahyaku-en.

Section 9

1. Yasumimashita.   *or* Hatarakimasen deshita.
2. Takai desu.   *or* Yasuku wa arimasen.
3. Tôi desu.   *or* Chikaku wa arimasen.
4. Karada ni ii desu.   *or* Karada ni waruku wa arimasen.
5. Nihongo wa yasashii desu. *or* Nihongo wa muzukashiku wa arimasen.

Section 10

1. As the rain is stopping how about a stroll?
2. How much is it? I don't know yet.
3. Let's come back again next Friday.
4. It's a little difficult but it is interesting.
5. After I came to Tôkyô I saw a Shintô shrine.

CHAPTERS 11–15

Section 1

1. Tomodachi wa byôki ni narimashita.
2. Otenki wa samuku narimashita.
3. Watakushi wa atama ga itai desu.
4. Kanai wa netsu ga demashita.
5. Watakushi wa kaze o hikimashita.

Section 2

Ichigatsu kokonoka.
sangatsu jûgonichi.
gogatsu muika.
kugatsu jûyokka
shichigatsu hatsuka.

Section 3

1. Watakushi wa osake ga dai kirai desu.
2. Watakushi wa mizu ga hoshii desu.
3. Watakushi wa Tôkyô ga suki desu.
4. Watakushi wa Furansu no kuruma ga arimasu.
5. Watakushi wa terebi o miru koto ga suki desu.

Section 4

1. Hatarakanakereba narimasen.
2. Mado o akenakereba narimasen.
3. Uchi e konakereba narimasen.

   4. Tomodachi ni awanakereba narimasen.

   5. Matanakereba narimasen.

Section 5
1. Sono ringo o tabenaide kudasai.
2. Sono mizu o nomanaide kudasai.
3. Matanaide kudasai.
4. Eigo o hanasanaide kudasai.
5. Ashita konaide kudasai.

Section 6
1. Itadakimasu.
2. Ohayô gozaimasu.
3. Gochisôsama deshita.
4. Dô shimashita ka?
5. Sore wa ikemasen ne.

Section 7
1. Nihiki.
2. Futari.
3. Nimai.
4. Nihon.
5. Futatsu.

Section 8
1. Benkyô sureba ojôzu ni narimasu.
2. Nihon e ikeba Fuji-san o miru koto ga dekimasu.
3. Kusuri o nomeba genki ni narimasu.
4. Jippun mateba ii desu yo.
5. Itô-san ni aeba issho ni ginkô e itte kudasai.

Section 9
1. I ate three cakes while watching television.
2. As I have a sore throat I don't want to eat.
3. I rarely eat prawns.
4. As the new book is too expensive I'm not going to buy it.
5. According to the doctor my wife can go out for a walk.

Section 10
1. Go and see a Japanese film.
2. Give explanations.
3. No, by taxi.
4. A thousand yen.
5. He had a stomach-ache.
6. He had no fever.
7. Next Friday.
8. No, the ninth.
9. Sixteen hours.
10. Visit Mr Jones's firm in England.

CHAPTERS 16–20

Section 1
1. Sumimasen ga otearai wa doko ni arimasu ka?
2. Keisatsusho wa doko ni arimasu ka?
3. Oisha san no ie . . .
4. Ryokan . . .
5. Ichiban chikai kôban . . .

Section 2
1. Eigo ga wakarimasu.
2. Yûmei na tokoro desu.
3. Tôkyô de umaremashita.
4. Oji ga kaita tegami o yomimashita.
5. Jirô to iu tomodachi wa shitte imasu ka?
6. Biiru ni shimasu.
7. Itsu tsuku to omoimasu ka?
8. Supaa no soba ni ginkô ga arimasu.
9. Takushii de kimashita.
10. Raishû kaeru ni kimatte imasu.
11. Kauntaa ni suwarimashô.

Section 3
1. Musume no tanjôbi wa shigatsu tsuitachi desu.
2. Musuko wa hassai desu.
3. Haha wa shichigatsu tôka ni kaerimasu.
4. Ani wa jimusho de hataraite imasu.
5. Imôto wa sen kyûhyaku gojûroku nen (Shôwa sanjûichinen) ni umaremashita.

Section 4
1. Akeru.
2. Shimeru.
3. Akarui.
4. Kurai.
5. Kyonen.
6. Kotoshi.
7. Ototoi.
8. Asatte.
9. Ureshii.
10. Sabishii.

Section 5
1. That's too bad.
2. It's a pity but there we are.
3. Take your time.
4. Take care.

5. Bill, please.
6. That's no good.
7. Congratulations.
8. Certainly, sir.

Section 6
1. Taberu koto ga suki desu. (*or*) Taberu no ga suki desu.
2. Eigakan e iku koto ga kirai desu.
3. Unten suru koto ga suki desu.
4. Hana o ikeru koto ga kirai desu.

Section 7
1. Oishasan e ikanakereba narimasen. (Kusuri o nomana-kereba narimasen.)
2. Yûbinkyoku e ikimasu. (Tabakoya e ikimasu.)
3. Ebi ya sakana ya nasu ya shiitake ya ika o taberu koto ga dekimasu.
4. Kusuriya (supaa) e ikanakereba narimasen.

Section 8
1. Ano/Sono kanji wa yomiyasui desu.
2. Ano/Sono hon wa yominikui desu.
3. Otenki wa kawariyasui desu.
4. Onamae wa kakiyasui desu.

Section 9
1. The man taking a photo lives over there.
2. The person wearing spectacles is a maths teacher.
3. The woman walking back here is my elder sister.
4. The man smoking a cigarette is a foreigner.

Section 10
1. I read a magazine while listening to some music.
2. As this dictionary is a good one your friend will find it useful.
3. Have you ever been to the theatre?
4. Don't feel at all embarrassed – go and have a bath before dinner.
5. The purse my wife didn't buy was a small red one.

Section 11
1. Yuki ga furu kamo shiremasen.
2. Hirugohan no mae ni tsuku kamo shiremasen.
3. Watakushi no kuruma o arawanakute mo ii desu.
4. Anata no pondo o en ni kaenakute mo ii desu.

Section 12
1. The aubergine and mushrooms Mrs Satô prepared are delicious.

2. I bought the book you wrote by going to that bookshop I didn't enter last week.
3. The room your friend chose was absolutely splendid.
4. Would you be so kind as to teach me the kanji I didn't know?

Section 13
1. Suwarimashô.
2. Kôza o hirakimashô.
3. Nobuo o tochû de hiraimashô.
4. Hairimashô.

Section 14
1. Go to the cinema.
2. This Friday.
3. His younger sister is coming from Yokohama.
4. Next Monday.
5. He'll pick his friend up by car.
6. The roads are crowded.
7. Underground.
8. In front of the station.
9. A new English film.
10. In the kitchen.
11. Two o'clock.
12. He has to meet a friend after lunch.
13. At seven thirty.
14. After seeing the film.
15. At a tempura restaurant.

NUMERALS

ichi	hitotsu	1
ni	futatsu	2
san	mittsu	3
shi *or* yon	yottsu	4
go	itsutsu	5
roku	muttsu	6
shichi *or* nana	nanatsu	7
hachi	yattsu	8
kyû	kokonotsu	9
jû	tô	10
jûichi		11
nijû		20
nijûichi		21
sanjû		30
yonjû		40
gojû		50
rokujû		60
shichijû *or* nanajû		70
hachijû		80
kyûjû		90
hyaku		100
nihyaku		200
sambyaku		300
yonhyaku		400
gohyaku		500
roppyaku		600
shichikyaku *or* nanahyaku		700
happyaku		800
kyûhyaku		900
sen		1000

nisen	2000	hachisen *or* hassen	8000
sanzen	3000	kyûsen	9000
yonsen	4000	ichiman	10 000
gosen	5000	ichiman issen	11 000
rokusen	6000	samman	30 000
shichisen *or* nanasen	7000	yomman	40 000
		hyakuman	1 000 000

TIME

ichiji	1.00
ichiji ippun	1.01
ichiji nifun	1.02
ichiji sampun	1.03
ichiji yompun	1.04
ichiji gofun	1.05
ichiji roppun	1.06
ichiji shichifun *or* nanafun	1.07
ichiji hachifun *or* happun	1.08
ichiji kyûfun	1.09
ichiji jippun	1.10
ichiji jûippun	1.11
ichiji jûgofun	1.15
ichiji nijippun	1.20
ichiji nijûgofun	1.25
ichiji sanjippun *or* han	1.30
ichiji sanjûgofun	1.35
ichiji yonjippun	1.40
niji jûgofun mae *or* ichiji yonjûgofun	1.45
niji jippun mae *or* ichiji gojippun	1.50
niji gofun mae *or* ichiji gojûgofun	1.55
niji	2.00
sanji	3.00
yoji	4.00
goji	5.00
rokuji	6.00
shichiji *or* nanaji	7.00
hachiji	8.00
kuji	9.00
jûji	10.00

jûichiji	11.00
jûniji	12.00
gogo sanji *or* jûgoji	3.00 p.m.
gozen sanji *or* asa sanji	3.00 a.m.
reiji	midnight

DAYS, DATES, MONTHS

getsuyôbi	Monday
kayôbi	Tuesday
suiyôbi	Wednesday
mokuyôbi	Thursday
kin'yôbi	Friday
doyôbi	Saturday
nichiyôbi	Sunday
tsuitachi	1st
futsuka	2nd
mikka	3rd
yokka	4th
itsuka	5th
muika	6th
nanoka	7th
yôka	8th
kokonoka	9th
tôka	10th
jûichinichi	11th
jûninichi	12th
jûsannichi	13th
jûyokka	14th
jûgonichi	15th
jûrokunichi	16th
jûshichinichi	17th
jûhachinichi	18th
jûkunichi	19th
hatsuka	20th
nijûichinichi	21st
nijûninichi	22nd

nijûsannichi	23rd
nijûyokka	24th
nijûgonichi	25th
nijûrokunichi	26th
nijûshichinichi	27th
nijûhachinichi	28th
nijûkunichi	29th
sanjûnichi	30th
sanjûichinichi	31st

ototoi	the day before yesterday
kinô	yesterday
kyô	today
ashita	tomorrow
asatte	the day after tomorrow

sensenshû	the week before last
senshû	last week
konshû	this week
raishû	next week
saraishû	the week after next

sensengetsu	the month before last
sengetsu	last month
kongetsu	this month
raigetsu	next month
saraigetsu	the month after next

ototoshi	the year before last
kyonen	last year
kotoshi	this year
rainen	next year
sarainen	the year after next

hitoban	one evening (night)
futaban	two evenings (nights)
miban	three evenings (nights)
yoban	four evenings (nights)
goban	five evenings (nights)
rokuban	six evenings (nights)
nanaban =	isshûkan = 1 week

ichigatsu *or* Shôgatsu	January
nigatsu	February
sangatsu	March
shigatsu	April
gogatsu	May
rokugatsu	June
shichigatsu *or* nanagatsu	July
hachigatsu	August
kugatsu	September
jûgatsu	October
jûichigatsu	November
jûnigatsu	December

The current era is Heisei. 1989 is *both* Shôwa 64 *and* Heisei Gannen. (Gan is used for the first year of a new era. Compare Ganjitsu, New Year's Day.) 1990 is Heisei Ninen, 1991 Heisei Sannen, 1992 Heisei Yonen, 1993 Heisei Gonen and so forth.

COUNTERS

Flat objects

ichimai	1 stamp, piece of paper, etc.
nimai	2
sammai	3
yommai *or* yomai	4
gomai	5
rokumai	6
shichimai *or* nanamai	7
hachimai	8
kyûmai	9
jûmai	10

People

hitori	1 person
futari	2 people
sannin	3
yonin	4
gonin	5
rokunin	6
shichinin *or* nananin	7
hachinin	8
kyûnin	9
jûnin	10
jûichinin	11
jûninin	12

Cylindrical objects

ippon	1 pen, umbrella, etc.
nihon	2
sambon	3

yonhon	4
gohon	5
roppon	6
shichihon *or* nanahon	7
happon	8
kyûhon	9
jippon	10

Animals

ippiki	1
nihiki	2
sambiki	3
yonhiki	4
gohiki	5
roppiki	6
shichihiki *or* nanahiki	7
happiki	8
kyûhiki	9
jippiki	10

Cupfuls

ippai	1
nihai	2
sambai	3
yonhai	4
gohai	5
roppai	6

Yen

ichien	1
nien	2
san'en	3
yoen	4
goen	5
rokuen	6
shichien (*or* nanaen)	7
hachien	8
kuen (*or* kyûen)	9
jûen	10

VERB TABLES

Weak verbs

taberu	to eat	infinitive
tabenai		negative infinitive
tabemasu		present
tabemasen		present negative
tabete		-te form
tabemashita		past
tabemasen deshita		past negative
tabeta		past plain form
tabenakatta		past negative plain form
tabetai		'want to'
tabereba		'if' form
tabenakereba		negative 'if' form

Strong verbs

yomu	to read	infinitive
yomanai		negative infinitive
yomimasu		present
yomimasen		present negative
yonde		-te form
yomimashita		past
yomimasen deshita		past negative
yonda		past plain form
yomanakatta		past negative plain form
yomitai		'want to'
yomeba		'if' form
yomanakereba		negative 'if' form

-te form and present tense of strong verbs

kaku	kaite	kakimasu	to write
hanasu	hanashite	hanashimasu	to speak
motsu	motte	mochimasu	to hold
aru	atte	arimasu	to be
kau	katte	kaimasu	to buy
isogu	isoide	isogimasu	to hurry
tobu	tonde	tobimasu	to fly
shinu	shinde	shinimasu	to die

Irregular verbs

suru to do	kuru to come	iku, to go
shinai	konai	ikanai
shimasu	kimasu	ikimasu
shite	kite	itte

SUPPLEMENTARY VOCABULARY

heavy	omoi
light	karui
long	nagai
short	mijikai
old (of people)	toshiyori no
old (not people)	furui
warm	attakai (*or* atatakai)
young	wakai
brown	chairo no (literally, tea-colour)
dark blue	kon no
green	midori no
grey	nezumiiro no (literally rat-colour)
purple	murasaki no

ear	mimi
face	kao
finger	yubi
hair	kami
leg, foot	ashi
mouth	kuchi
nose	hana
ring	yubiwa

glove	tebukuro
hat, cap	bôshi
shoe	kutsu
sock	kutsushita
trousers	zubon

bridge	hashi
crossroads	kôsaten
garden	niwa
park	kôen
south	minami
inside	no naka ni
underneath	no shita ni
ashtray	haizara
desk	tsukue
drinking-glass	koppu
mirror	kagami
plate	sara
room	heya
scissors	hasami
be in difficulty	komaru
break	kowareru (weak verb)
close	tojiru (weak verb)
compare	kuraberu (weak verb)
count	kazoeru (weak verb)
cut	kiru (strong verb)
enjoy oneself	asobu
get dirty	yogoreru (weak verb)
get tired	tsukareru (weak verb)
rejoice	yorokobu
run	hashiru (strong verb)
smile, laugh	warau
use	tsukau
itte mairimasu	said when leaving a house
itte irasshai	said to the person leaving
tadaima	said when returning home
o kaeri nasai	said to the one returning

GRAMMAR SUMMARY

LIST OF TOPICS

1. Types of verbs

(a) desu
(b) imasu/arimasu
(c) Weak verbs
(d) Strong verbs
(e) Irregular verbs

2. Nouns
3. Counters and Numbers
4. Tenses

(a) Present and present negative
(b) Past and past negative

5 Pronouns
6. Adjectives

(a) True adjectives
(b) Negative of true adjectives
(c) Other adjectives and their negatives
(d) Comparatives
(e) Superlatives
(f) Preference (. . . no hô ga ii)
(g) demonstratives (kono, sono, ano)

7. Adverbs
8. Particles

(a) ka, ne, nê, yo
(b) wa

14. **Plain form of adjectives**
15. **-te form of adjectives**
16. **Conjunctions**

GRAMMAR EXPLANATIONS

1. **Types of verbs**
(a) desu, the verb 'to be': the *present tense* – 'am', 'is', 'are'.
This verb *joins two words together*:

> watakushi wa Itô desu   I'm Itô
> kono hon wa akai desu   this book is red

After a noun, the *negative* of desu is ja arimasen:

> Hon ja arimasen.   It's not a book.

deshita: the *past tense* – 'was', 'were':

> Shôwa 42 wa 1967 deshita
> Shôwa 42 was 1967.

(b) imasu/arimasu
These verbs are also equivalents of the verb 'to be', but are used to express *position*. imasu is used with *people, animals, birds* and *means of transport*, whereas arimasu is used with *inanimate objects*:

> neko wa daidokoro ni   the cat is in the kitchen
> imasu
> kaban wa kuruma ni   the briefcase is in the car
> arimasu

(c) **Weak verbs**
All *weak* verbs end in -eru or -iru (although not all verbs that end in -eru or -iru are weak verbs).
(d) **Strong verbs**
Strong verbs end in -bu, -gu, -ku, -mu, -nu, -ru, -su, -tsu or -u. See p. 306 for the conjugation of these and of weak verbs – but be careful to *check each new verb* that ends in -eru or -iru you come across to ensure whether it is a weak verb or a strong one:

> En o pondo ni   I changed yen into
> kaemashita.   pounds.
> Tôkyô e kaerimashita.   I returned to Tokyo.

Kaeru, to change, is a *weak* verb; **kaeru**, to return, is a *strong* verb.

(e) Irregular verbs
There are only *three* in Japanese: suru, to do.
                                        kuru, to come.
                                        iku, to go.

Again see p.306.

2. Nouns
Hito is one of the very few nouns that has a *plural*, hitotachi or hitobito. Kodomo is another (plural Kodomotachi). Other Japanese nouns are either singular or plural *according to context*.

Kono hon o yonde kudasai	Please read this book
Kono hon o yonde kudasai	Please read these books

In the first case the speaker would be holding out one book, in the second more than one (but see also section **3** below):

Kippu o kaimashita	I bought a ticket *or* some tickets

3.   Counters and Numbers.
These are used to show the difference between *singular* and *plural*, and to specify *quantity*:

Kippu o ichimai kaimashita	I bought one ticket
Kippu o gomai kaimashita	I bought five tickets

In order to count one, two, three, etc. the system ichi, ni, san, etc. is used. But once *quantity* is involved, the *appropriate counter* must be used: ippon, nihon, sambon, etc. for *cylindrical* objects; ichimai, nimai, sammai, etc. for *flat* objects; hitori, futari, sannin, etc. for *people*; ippiki, nihiki, sambiki, etc. for *animals*; ippai, nihai, sambai, etc. for *cupfuls*. There is an 'all-purpose' system: hitotsu, futatsu, mittsu, etc. up to tô (thereafter use jûichi, jûichi, jûni, etc.) Lists of these counters are to be found on pp. 297 and 304.
Remember in each case the counter goes *immediately before the verb*:

Kasa o ippon kaimashita.	I bought one umbrella.

Sara ga rokumai arimasu.	There are six plates.
Nihonjin ni futari aimashita.	I met two Japanese.
Inu ga nihiki imasu.	There are two dogs.
Ocha o nihai nomimashita.	I drank two cups of Japanese tea.
Teeburu ga itsutsu arimasu.	There are five tables.
Isu ga jûichi arimasu.	There are eleven chairs.

4. Tenses

(a) *Weak* verbs form their present tense by cutting off the - ru and putting -masu. The *negative* ending is -masen:

taberu	to eat
miru	to see
tabemasu	I eat
tabemasen	I do not eat
mimasu	I see
mimasen	I do not see

(b) The *past* ending is -mashita and the *past negative* ending is -masen deshita:

tabemashita	I ate
mimashita	I saw
tabemasen deshita	I did not eat
mimasen deshita	I did not see

The endings are exactly the same both for *strong* verbs and for *irregular* verbs, but they form their tenses in a *different way*:

yomu	to read
yomimasu	I read (now)
yomimasen	I do not read
yomimashita	I read (yesterday)
yomimasen deshita	I did not read

A full list of the strong verb formations is given on pp. 306–7, also the irregular verbs.

5. Pronouns

These are mainly used to avoid ambiguity. Once it is clear *who* is doing the action, they can be omitted.

The *personal pronouns* are:

watakushi	I
anata (singular)	you
watakushitachi	we
anatagata (plural)	you

Ano hito *or* ano kata, meaning that person', can be used for 'he' or 'she', but if it is necessary to indicate the *gender* of the individual, you can use:

ano otoko (no hito)	that male person	for 'he'
ano onna (no hito)	that female person	for 'she'

kore means this object which is by me, or the one I am holding
sore means that object which is by you, or the one you are holding
are means that object which is by neither of us – i.e., over there
Kore wa watakushi no kaban desu This is my despatch-case.
Sore wa anata no keisu desu ka? Is that your case by you?
Are wa Itô-san no kuruma desu That over there is Mr Itô's car

6. Adjectives

(a) *True adjectives* end in -i, like chiisai, small, shiroi, white:

Kono keisu wa chiisai desu	This case is small
Ano neko wa shiroi desu	That cat is white

(b) They form their *negatives* by substituting -ku wa arimasen for -i:

Kuroku wa arimasen	It is not black
Ôkiku wa arimasen	It is not large

Other adjectives (momoiro pink, murasaki purple, kon dark blue) take no before the noun:

momoiro no kimono	a pink kimono

Still others take na:

benri na jibiki   a useful dictionary

(c) Adjectives that are *not true adjectives* form their negatives like nouns:

murasaki ja arimasen   it's not purple

(d) Comparatives

Kono zasshi wa ano zasshi yori omoshiroi desu.
This magazine is more interesting than that one.
Yokohama wa Matsumoto yori ôkii desu.
Yokohama is bigger than Matsumoto.

(e) Superlatives

Tôkyô wa ichiban ôkii   Tokyo is biggest.
desu.

(f) Preference
The construction no hô ga ii literally means 'This side is the good one – i.e., this course or system is preferable:

Chikatetsu no hô ga ii   The underground is better.
desu.
Kono hon no hô ga ii   This book is preferable.
desu.

(g) There are *three demonstrative adjectives*:

kono hon   this book (near me)
sono hon   that book (near you)
ano hon   that book (over there)

7. Adverbs
To form adverbs from *true adjectives*, you replace the -i with -ku:

hayai, fast   hayaku, quickly
Watakushi wa hayaku arukimashita   I walked quickly

The old form of ii was yoi, and today its adverbial form is still yoku:

> Ano hito wa yoku hatarakimashita ne.
> That chap did work well, didn't he?

8. Particles

(a) ka, ne, nê and yo

ka is a *verbal question mark*:

Itô-san desu ka?	Are you Mr Itô?

ne implies a measure of certainty:

Itô-san desu ne?	You're Mr Itô, aren't you?

nê abolishes all doubt:

Samui desu nê!	It *is* cold, isn't it!

yo lends emphasis:

Watakushi no kaban desu yo	It jolly well is my case

(b) wa

wa is an *attention-calling particle*:

kore wa hon desu	this is a book
watakushi wa Igirisujin desu	I'm English

It is sometimes tacked on to ni or de, again to *call attention*:

> Nihon dewa jimusho e hachiji ni ikimasu
> In Japan they go to the office at 8
> Fuyu niwa yuki ga furimasu ka?
> In winter does it snow?

(c) o

o shows the *object* of a *transitive verb*:

watakushi wa biiru o nomimashita	I drank beer
eiga o mimashita	I saw a film

There are cases when **wa** is preferred, once more for *emphasis*:

Nihonjin wa sashimi o tabemasu	The Japanese eat raw fish
Gohan o tabemasu ga sashimi wa tabemasen	They eat rice but not raw fish

(d) ga

ga usually stresses the *subject of a verb*:

Kore ga kaban desu	*This* is a despatch-case

(as opposed to **Kore wa kaban desu** This is *a despatch-case*) but as you saw in Chapter **12.3 (d)** this is one of the trickiest points in Japanese. There *are* several instances where **ga** is (almost!) essential:

1. To express 'There is/are':

   Isu no shita ni shimbun ga arimasu.
   There's a newspaper under the chair.

2. As the subject of a *relative clause*:

   Sensei ga kaita hon wa omoshiroi desu.
   The book the professor wrote is interesting.

3. With **wakaru**:

   Nihongo ga wakarimasu. I understand Japanese.

4. With **koto ga aru** and **koto ga dekiru**:

   Kyôto e itta koto ga arimasu ka?
   Have you ever been to Kyoto?
   Kono kanji o yomu koto ga dekimasu ka?
   Are you able to read these kanji?

5. With **suki, kirai, hoshii**:

Osake ga suki desu	I like saké
Ocha ga kirai desu	I hate green tea
Mizu ga hoshii desu	I want some water

(e) ni

1. Indicates *position or time*:

   Keisu wa kuruma ni
   arimasu.   The case is in the car.

   Shôgatsu ni Nihon e   I came to Japan in
   kimashita.   January.

2. Indicates the *dative*:

   Itô-san wa watakushi ni Nihongo o oshiemashita.
   Mr Itô taught me Japanese (= Japanese to me)

3. Is used with certain *verbs*:
   With au, to meet:

   Nobuo ni aimashita
   I met Nobuo

   With kimaru:

   Kuru ni kimatte imasu
   He's bound to come

   With suru:

   ocha ni shimasu
   I'll have green tea

(f) de
Unlike ni, de indicates *where* an action is taking place:

   Tomodachi wa Yokohama de hatarakimasu.
   My friend works in Yokohama.
   Yûbinkyoku de kitte o kaimashita.
   I bought stamps at the post-office.

(g) no
Best thought of as the equivalent of 's:

   Satô-san no hon   Mr Satô's book (the book
                                of Mr Satô)
   watakushi no kuruma   my car (I's car)
   Nihon no nomimono   a Japanese drink (a drink
                                of Japan)

(h) e
Means *towards*:

eki e ikimashita	he went to the station

(i) kara
Means *from*:

eki kara kimashita	he came from the station

(j) to, ya, ka, matawa

to
1. Means 'and' when linking *specific objects* or *persons*:

ane to imôto wa eki e ikimashita
My older sister and my younger sister went to the station
ebi to gohan ga arimasu
There are prawns and rice

2. Is used with certain *verbs*:

tomodachi ga iku to omoimasu	I think my friend will come
Yamada to iu hito	a person called Yamada
Satô-san to hanashitai desu	I'd like to speak to Mr. Satô

ya
Is used when *other objects not mentioned* are implied:

momo ya ringo ya nashi ga arimasu.
there are peaches and apples and Japanese pears (and other fruit)

ka
means 'or' *between two nouns or pronouns*:

kôhii ka kôcha ga arimasu	there is coffee or tea

matawa
means 'or else'

shichigatsu (matawa nanagatsu) shichigatsu (or nanagatsu)

(k) mo
Means 'too' or 'also':

> watakushi mo Igirisujin   I'm English too
> desu

(Do *not confuse* mo with mô, which means 'more': mô ippai one more cup.)

9. Expressing position

mae	in front
ushiro	behind
shita	beneath
ue	on top
naka	inside
yoko	beside
soba	near

> tsukue no ue ni hon ga   there's a book on the table
> arimasu
> ginkô no yoko ni hon'ya   there's a bookshop next to
> ga arimasu   the bank

10 Time
(a) hours and minutes
The suffix -ji is used for *hours* and -fun for *minutes* (see p. 299):

> ichiji jûgofun   1.15
> gozen jûji   10 a.m. (**asa**, morning, is
>   also used)
> gogo sanji   3 p.m.

When the *24-hour clock* is used, reiji (literally, zero hour!) can be used to express *midnight*.
The suffix -jikan expresses *extent of time*:

> nanjikan kakarimasu ka?   how long will it take?
> nijikan kakarimasu   it'll take two hours

(b) Days

> (see p. 301) kyô today
> kinô   yesterday

ashita	tomorrow
ototoi	the day before yesterday
asatte	the day after tomorrow

(c) Months
(see p. 303)

The suffix -gatsu is used to show a *specific month*.
The suffix -kagetsu is used to show the *number of months*.

sangatsu ni Nihon e kimashita
I came to Japan in March
sankagetsu tomarimashita   I stayed for three months

(d) Years
Although the A.D. system is official, the traditional way of reckoning years since the start of the *current Emperor's reign* is more common

sen kyûhyaku rokujû roku-nen wa Shôwa yonjûichi-nen deshita
1966 was Shôwa 41

ototoshi	the year before last
kyonen	last year
kotoshi	this year
rainen	next year
sarainen	the year after next

(d) Dates
(see p. 301)
The Japanese order is always *year, month, day*:

Shôwa rokujû-nen gogatsu nijûichinichi   1985, May 21

(f) Ages
The suffix -sai is used (see Chapter **16.3 (c)**).

11. Weather

ii otenki desu nê   lovely weather, isn't it!
warui otenki desu nê   foul weather, isn't it!

The verb furu is used with ame (rain) and yuki (snow):

| ame ga futte imasu | it is raining |
| kyonen yuki ga takusan furimashita | it snowed a great deal last year |

The verb kuru is used with taifû (typhoon).

kugatsu ni ôkina taifû ga kimashita
there was a big typhoon in September

12. Honorifics
The prefix o- is used traditionally with certain words:

otenki	weather
oisha	doctor
osake, osushi and osashimi	
ocha	green tea
o furo	bath

It is also used to distinguish the speaker from the person addressed:

tomodachi ni aimashita	I met my friend
otomodachi ni aimashita	I met your friend
ojôzu desu nê!	you *are* clever!
jôzu ja arimasen	I'm not good at it

(See Chapter 16.3 (a) for the family honorifics)
Certain words require the on or Chinese honorific prefix go:

gohan	rice
goshujin	your husband
gomen nasai (or kudasai)	pardon me

words associated with *money* usually take an honorific:

okane	money
otsuri (or okaeshi)	change
okanjô	bill

13. Verbs in use
(a) the -te form
(The -te form of weak and strong verbs is given on pp. 306–7.)

1. Giving instructions
Use kudasai (please) after the -te form:

koko e kite kudasai   please come here
kono hon o yonde   do read this book
kudasai

2. Continuous actions
Use imasu after the -te form:

ano hito wa Eigo de   he's speaking in English
hanashite imasu
neko wa sakana o tabete   the cat's eating the fish
imasu

3. Joining two sentences
To link *two sentences* together, put the *first verb* in the -te form:

Watakushi wa Yokohama e ikimashita. Tomodachi ni aima-
shita.
I went to Yokohama. I met a friend.
Watakushi wa Yokohama e itte tomodachi ni aimashita.
I went Yokohama and met a friend.

The tense of the *final verb* does not matter. The first verb is *always* in
the -te form:

Igirisu e itte Eigo o hanashimashô
I'll go to England and speak English
Hon'ya e itte zasshi o kaitai desu
I want to go to the bookshop and buy a magazine

4. Linked verbs
Sometimes *one* idea in English is expressed by *two* verbs in Japanese,
the first being in the -te form:

motte kuru   to bring
motte iku   to take away
sono shimbun o motte kite kudasai
please could you bring that newspaper?
kono haizara o motte itte kudasai
would you please take this ashtray away?

5. With kara

asagohan o tabete kara denwa o kakemasu
I'll phone after I've had breakfast
ginkô e itte kara okurimono o kaimasu
I'll buy the present after I've been to the bank

Be very careful not to confuse kara after the -te form, meaning
'after', with kara after *other forms of the verb* meaning 'because':

Igirisujin desu kara Eigo o hanasu koto ga dekimasu
Because he is English he can speak English

6. With arimasu
This is used to express a *state*:

namae ga kaite arimasu   the names are written
mado wa akete arimasu   the window is open

7. With shimau
This adds a note of *finality* or *completion*:

furusato e kaette shimaimashita
he ended up by going back to his home town
osake o nonde shimaimashita
all the saké has been drunk

8. With mite kudasai
An extension of 1 and 4, meaning 'to give something a try':

Nihongo o hanashite mite kudasai
have a go at speaking Japanese

(b) **Plain form** (given on p. 306)
The 'normal' verb-forms all have a *parallel plain form:*

mimasu   miru
mimasen   minai
mimashita   mita
mimasen deshita   minakatta

(See also Chapter **20 3 (g)**.)

326

These are used especially by *men in friendly or informal talk*:

> tomodachi ga kimasu   tomodachi ga kuru
> tabemasen deshita   tabenakatta

They are also used for *relative clauses* (see Section **(c)** below)

(c) Relative clauses

The plain form is used for the *verb in the relative clause*:

> sakana o taberu hito wa itsumo genki desu
> People who eat fish are always healthy
> osake o nomanai hito wa sabishii deshô
> People who don't drink saké are a cheerless lot
> kinô atta Nihonjin wa Amerika e ikimashita
> The Japanese I met yesterday has gone to America
> neko wa anata ga tabenakatta sakana o tabemashita
> The cat ate the fish you didn't eat

(See Section **8 (d)** on ga)

(d) Negative instructions

add-de kudasai to the *negative infinitive* (see pp. 306–7):

> tabenai not to eat, tabenaide kudasai   please don't eat
> yomanai not to read, yomanaide kudasai   please don't read
> konaide kudasai   please do not come

(e) -tai desu 'want to'
to *express a wish* cut off the -masu ending and put -tai desu:

> ikimasu   I go
> ikitai desu   I want to go
> benkyô shimasu   I study
> benkyô shitai desu   I want to study

(f) tsumori desu
Used after the infinitive to express *intention*:

> ashita ginkô e iku
> tsumori desu
> I intend going to the
> bank tomorrow

(g) Probable form

1. deshô is the *less definite form* of desu:

ano hito wa Amerikajin deshô	he's probably an American
Yamada-san wa konai deshô	Mr Yamada probably won't come
ashita kuru deshô	he'll probably come tomorrow
Tôkyô e itta deshô	he's probably gone to Tokyo

as such, it is used after nouns, pronouns or adjectives and verbs in the *plain form*.

2. -mashô

Using the ending -mashô instead of -masu implies *probability*:

yûbinkyoku e ikimasu	I'll go to the Post Office
yûbinkyoku e ikimashô	I'll probably go to the Post Office

This form is also used to express the idea 'Let's do something':

biiru o nomimashô	let's have a beer

(h) Must

Take the *negative infinitive* (shinai; ikanai; konai; tabenai), cut off the final -i and substitute -kereba narimasen:

benkyô shinakereba narimasen	I must study
gakkô e ikanakereba narimasen	I must go to school
mainichi koko e konakereba narimasen deshita	I had to come here every day
kodomotachi wa gohan o tabenakereba narimasen ne	children must eat rice, mustn't they?

(i) Need not
Take the *negative infinitive* (kaenai; nomanai), cut off the final -i
and substitute -kute mo ii desu:

en o pondo ni kaenakute mo ii desu	you don't need to change your yen into pounds
sono kusuri o noma-nakute mo ii desu	you needn't drink that medicine

(j) If

1. Take off the -u of the *infinitive* (miru, hanasu), and substitute
eba:

Ran to iu eiga o mireba	if you see a film called Ran
Nihongo o hanaseba	If you speak Japanese

2. to after the infinitive means 'when' or 'if':

Hakone e iku to Fuji-san o mimasu.
When/If you go to Hakone you'll see Mr Fuji.

3. (see (**h**) above)

benkyô shinakereba	if you do not study
Nihon e ikanakereba	If you don't go to Japan

(k) kamo shiremasen
After a noun or pronoun or the infinitive form of a verb, this means
'may':

Yamada-san kamo shiremasen	That may be Mr Yamada
Ame ga furu kamo shiremasen	It may rain

(l) naru

1. After a *true adjective*
Substitute -ku for the -i ending:

kodomo wa ôkii desu	he's a big boy
kodomo wa ôkiku narimashita	he's grown (become big)

| sora ga kuraku natte imasu | the sky's growing dark |

2.   After *other words*

Use ni:

| sensei ni narimashita | he's become a teacher |
| byôki ni narimashita | he's fallen ill |

14.   Plain form of adjectives

True adjectives are really *verbs*. akai means 'is red', and the desu is strictly speaking unnecessary. They have their *past plain form* – you substitute -katta for the final -i:

| (omoshiroi) omoshiro-katta (no desu) | it was interesting |
| (muzukashii) muzukashi-katta (no desu) | it was difficult |

Hence, you can see why the past plain form of the *negative verb* (see 13 (b) above) is formed that way – because minai is really an *adjective*.

15   -te form of adjectives

Substitute -kute for the final -i. You can now *link adjectives* the way you linked sentences (in 13 (a) above):

| akai desu. chiisai desu. | It is red. It is small |
| akakute chiisai desu | It's red and small |

Hence, you can see why the 'need not' form in 13 (i) above is formed that way.

16   Conjunctions

(a)   ga and keredomo:

watakushi wa Nihonjin desu ga kanai wa Furansujin desu
I am Japanese but my wife is French
Kippu o kaitai desu keredomo taihen takai desu
I want to buy a ticket but it's very expensive

keredomo is perhaps marginally stronger, equivalent to 'however'.

(b)   kara

See 13 (a) above.

HIRAGANA

あ	a	い	i	う	u	え	e	お	o
か	ka	き	ki	く	ku	け	ke	こ	ko
さ	sa	し	shi	す	su	せ	se	そ	so
た	ta	ち	chi	つ	tsu	て	te	と	to
な	na	に	ni	ぬ	nu	ね	ne	の	no
は	ha	ひ	hi	ふ	fu	へ	he	ほ	ho
ま	ma	み	mi	む	mu	め	me	も	mo
や	ya			ゆ	yu			よ	yo
ら	ra	り	ri	る	ru	れ	re	ろ	ro
わ	wa							を	o*
ん	final n or m								

*Used only for object particle.

が	ga	ぎ	gi	ぐ	gu	げ	ge	ご	go
ざ	za	じ	ji	ず	zu	ぜ	ze	ぞ	zo
だ	da	ぢ	ji	づ	zu	で	de	ど	do
ば	ba	び	bi	ぶ	bu	べ	be	ぼ	bo
ぱ	pa	ぴ	pi	ぷ	pu	ぺ	pe	ぽ	po
きゃ	kya			きゅ	kyu			きよ	kyo
ぎゃ	gya			ぎゅ	gyu			ぎよ	gyo
しゃ	sha			しゅ	shu			しよ	sho
じゃ	ja			じゅ	ju			じよ	jo

ちゃ	cha	ちゅ	chu	ちょ	cho
にゃ	nya	にゅ	nyu	にょ	nyo
ひゃ	hya	ひゅ	hyu	ひょ	hyo
びゃ	bya	びゅ	byu	びょ	byo
ぴゃ	pya	ぴゅ	pyu	ぴょ	pyo
みゃ	mya	みゅ	myu	みょ	myo
りゃ	rya	りゅ	ryu	りょ	ryo

KATAKANA

ア	a	イ	i	ウ	u	エ	e	オ	o
カ	ka	キ	ki	ク	ku	ケ	ke	コ	ko
サ	sa	シ	shi	ス	su	セ	se	ソ	so
タ	ta	チ	chi	ツ	tsu	テ	te	ト	to
ナ	na	ニ	ni	ヌ	nu	ネ	ne	ノ	no
ハ	ha	ヒ	hi	フ	fu	ヘ	he	ホ	ho
マ	ma	ミ	mi	ム	mu	メ	me	モ	mo
ヤ	ya			ユ	yu			ヨ	yo
ラ	ra	リ	ri	ル	ru	レ	re	ロ	ro
ワ	wa	ン	final n or m						

ガ	ga	ギ	gi	グ	gu	ゲ	ge	ゴ	go
ザ	za	ジ	ji	ズ	zu	ゼ	ze	ゾ	zo
ダ	da					デ	de	ド	do
バ	ba	ビ	bi	ブ	bu	ベ	be	ボ	bo
パ	pa	ピ	pi	プ	pu	ペ	pe	ポ	po

キャ kya			キュ kyu			キョ kyo
シャ sha			シュ shu	シェ she		ショ sho
チャ cha			チュ chu	チェ che		チョ cho
ニャ nya			ニュ nyu			ニョ nyo
ヒャ hya			ヒュ hyu			ヒョ hyo
ミャ mya			ミュ myu			ミョ myo
リャ rya			リュ ryu			リョ ryo
ギャ gya			ギュ gyu			ギョ gyo
ジャ ja			ジュ ju	ジェ je		ジョ jo
ビャ bya			ビュ byu			ビョ byo
ピャ pya			ピュ pyu			ピョ pyo
		ウィ wi			ウェ we	ウォ wo
クァ kwa						
ツァ tsa					ツェ tse	ツォ tso
		ティ ti				
ファ fa		フィ fi			フェ fe	フォ fo
		ディ di	デュ du			
(ヴァ va		ヴィ vi	ヴ vu		ヴェ ve	ヴォ vo)

COMMON KANJI

一	ichi	1
二	ni	2
三	san	3
四	shi	4
五	go	5
六	roku	6
七	shichi	7
八	hachi	8
九	kyû	9
十	jû	10
百	hyaku	100
千	sen	1,000
万	man	10,000
円	yen	
日	nichi	Sunday
月	getsu	Monday
火	ka	Tuesday
水	sui	Wednesday
木	moku	Thursday
金	kin	Friday
土	do	Saturday

日	本	Nihon	Japan
銀	行	ginkô	bank
電	話	denwa	telephone
交	番	kôban	police-box
会	社	kaisha	office
郵	便局	yûbinkyoku	post office
地	下鉄	chikatetsu	Underground
病	院	byôin	hospital
医	者	isha	doctor
薬	屋	kusuriya	chemist's
危	険	kiken	Danger
開		a (keru)	open
閉		shi (meru)	shut
入	口	iriguchi	entrance
出	口	deguchi	exit
駅		eki	station
男	子	danshi	GENTLEMEN
女	子	joshi	LADIES

WORDS FREQUENTLY
SEEN IN KANA

アイスクリーム	aisukuriimu	ice cream
アパート	apaato	apartment, flat
バス	basu	bus
ビール	biiru	beer
デパート	depaato	department store
フィルム	firumu	film (for camera)
ガソリン	gasorin	petrol
イギリス	Igirisu	England
カメラ	kamera	camera
キロ	kiro	kilogramme
コーヒー	koohii	coffee
クレジットカード	kurejitto-kaado	credit-card
パン	pan	bread
ラジオ	rajio	radio
レストラン	resutoran	restaurant
リットル	rittoru	litre
サンド	sando	sandwich
スーパー	suupaa	supermarket
タクシー	takushii	taxi
テープ	teepu	tape
テレビ	terebi	television

さしみ	sashimi	
すきやき	sukiyaki	
すし	sushi	
たばこ	tabako	cigarettes
てんぷら	tempura	

USEFUL BOOKS
AND
ADDRESSES

DICTIONARIES

Kenkyusha's New Japanese–English Dictionary (Tokyo: Kenkyusha).
The Modern Reader's Japanese–English Character Dictionary (Tokyo: Tuttle).
The Oxford Duden, Pictorial English–Japanese Dictionary (Oxford: OUP).
Pocket English–Japanese Dictionary (Tokyo: Kenkyusha).
New Collegiate English–Japanese Dictionary (Tokyo: Kenkyusha).
Takahashi's Romanized English–Japanese Dictionary (Tokyo: Taiseido).

REFERENCE BOOKS

P.G. O'Neill, *Japanese Names*, (New York and Tokyo: Weatherhill).
Malcolm D. Kennedy *A History of Japan* (London: Weidenfeld and Nicolson).
E. Papino, *Historical & Geographical Dictionary of Japan* (Tokyo: Tuttle).
Charles J. Dunn, *Everyday Life in Traditional Japan* (Tokyo: Tuttle).
Sokyo Ono, *Shintô* (Tokyo: Tuttle).
Suzuki, *Zen and Japanese Buddhism* (Tokyo: Japan Travel Bureau).
Keene (ed.) *Anthology of Japanese Literature* (Tokyo: Tuttle). 2 vols.
P.G.O'Neill, *A Guide to Nô* (Tokyo: Hinoki Shoten).
A. Waley, (trans) *The Nô Plays of Japan* (Tokyo: Tuttle).
A.S. & G.N. Halford, *The Kabuki Handbook* (Tokyo: Tuttle).
Donald Richie, *Japanese Cinema* (New York: Anchor).
Peter Swann, *Art of China, Korea and Japan* (London: Thames & Hudson).
Akiyama Terukazu, *Japanese Painting* (London: Macmillan).

Bradley Smith, *Japan, A History in Art* (Tokyo: Gemini Smith).
Masterworks of Ukiyo-e (Tokyo: Kodansha) 10 vols.
Kenneth Roxroth, *100 Poems from the Japanese* (New York: New Directions).
Henderson, *An Introduction to Haiku* (New York: Anchor).
Nobuyuki Yuasa (trans.) *Bashô* (London: Penguin).
Harry and Lynn Guest and Kajima Shôzô, *Post-War Japanese Poetry* (London: Penguin).
Rafael Steinberg *The Cooking of Japan* (New York: Time-Life).

ADDRESSES

Japanese Embassy	46, Grosvenor Street W1 (visas 01-493 2475)
Japan Association	43, King William Street EC4 (01-623 5324)
Japan Centre	66, Brewer Street W1 (01-437 6445)
Japan Foundation	35, Dover Street W1 (01-499 4726)
Japan Travel Bureau	Canberra House, Maltravers Street WC2 (01-379 6244)